The Malevolent Eye

American University Studies

Series XI
Anthropology and Sociology

Vol. 64

PETER LANG
New York • Washington, D.C./Baltimore • San Francisco
Bern • Frankfurt am Main • Berlin • Vienna • Paris

Pierre Bettez Gravel

The Malevolent Eye

An Essay on the Evil Eye, Fertility and the Concept of Mana

PETER LANG
New York • Washington, D.C./Baltimore • San Francisco
Bern • Frankfurt am Main • Berlin • Vienna • Paris

Library of Congress Cataloging-in-Publication Data

Gravel, Pierre Bettez.
The malevolent eye: an essay on the evil eye, fertility and the concept of mana/ Pierre Bettez Gravel.
p. cm. — (American university studies. Series XI: Anthropology and sociology; vol. 64)
Includes bibliographical references.
1. Evil eye. 2. Mana. 3. Fertility cults. I. Title. II. Series: American university studies. Series XI, Anthropology/sociology; vol. 64.
GN475. 6. G73 133.4' 25—dc20 94-37744
ISBN 0-8204-2275-4
ISSN

Die Deutsche Bibliothek-CIP Einheitsaufnahme

Gravel, Pierre Bettez:
The malevolent eye: an essay on the evil eye, fertility and the concept of mana/Pierre Bettez Gravel - New York; Washington, D.C.; Baltimore; San Francisco; Bern; Frankfurt am Main; Berlin; Vienna; Paris: Lang, 1995
(American university studies: Series. 11, Anthropology and sociology; Vol. 64)
ISBN 0-8204-2275-4
NE: American university studies/11

Cover design by James F. Brisson.

© 1995 Peter Lang Publishing, Inc., New York

All rights reserved.
Reprint or reproduction, even partially, in all forms such as microfilm, xerography, microfiche, microcard, and offset strictly prohibited.

Thou art Woman.
To Thee
I dedicate this book.
As long as thy spirit
and thy body endure,
Life will go on.

Pierre Bettez Gravel

Acknowledgements

Immediately and materially, I had the help of many people in preparing the manuscript. Sarah Bowen and James M. Hoffman read a preliminary outline of the manuscript and made comments that got the project on its way. I am beholden particularly to my friend and colleague, Professor Ralph Bowen who, as only a good friend would, undertook a painstaking reading of the first draft and provided me with a critique which was most helpful in bringing the manuscript to its final form. John Roberts helped me with the Indian material. Robert Ridinger helped me in the the library. I am grateful to all those on whom I have tested my ideas in seminars and otherwise, and who have responded with enthusiastic discussions: friends, *confrères* and graduate students. I am much obliged to those who have given me permission to reproduce photographs and more particularly so to Dr. Michel Odent who has graciously given me his authorization to use a photograph that is a key element in my illustrations. I owe thanks to Karen Blaser and Dolores Henry of the Word Processing department in the College of Liberal Arts and Sciences, and our Art-Photo Department for taking on the task of the publisher in getting the manuscript photo-ready for publication. I must thank the Chairman of the NIU Department of Anthropology, Fred Smith, for graciously offering some of the Department's resources to defray some of the costs of doing all this. Kathy Truman and Susanne Dewey, I have to thank for their patience and understanding over the years it took me to research and write this book. I would like to single out Hilkka Tellervo Itkonen for her sensitive line drawings. I thank my colleagues in the Department of Anthropology at Northern Illinois University for their accommodation, both moral and physical, and their encouragement. I thank my children, Anne, Eric and Marc for their loving support, and for providing me with the pride necessary for a book—after all—on fertility.

Table of Contents

PART I: The Evil Eye. Introduction

PART II: A New Look at the Evil Eye

ILLUSTRATIONS

Line drawings by Hilkka Tellervo Itkonen
except where indicated

Figure
Number

1.0 These "life signs" are remarkably like the Parturient Woman symbol (See below under that title).

1.1 Life sign on a field "kelli" (*κελλιον*, a cell), on the island of Kythnos, Greece, 1971. A kelli is a one-room structure built to accommodate harvesters. Compare this sign to some of the "parturient Woman" symbols below as well as to fig. 1.3.

1.2 Rose design on Kythnos street pavement. The rose may have been chosen because it is "pretty," but the rose is nevertheless a fertility symbol.

1.3 Street geometric design, Kythnos. This is the most frequent design in the village and it is similar to the "life sign" in fig.1.1. Photo by author.

2.0

2.1 Protective fish emblem above the entrance to a house. Kythnos.

2.2 Protective fish emblem, entrance to a house in Varanasi, India. (Photo: John B. Roberts)

2.3 Protective horseshoe—Vermont, U.S.A.

8.0

8.1 Bas-relief from a Roman wall, site of Leptis Magna (Lybia). Line drawing from a photograph in Johns. The phallos has a phallos and a phallic tail; the lion's paw is a phallic symbol. They all point to the eye, which is a kteis.

8.2 Bas-relief from a Roman wall in Leptis Magna (modern Labdah, Lybia). Line drawing from a photograph in Johns. Again here, the phallic symbols, centaur, scorpion, bird and snake, all point to the kteis, which is represented by an eye.

8.3 The Woburn Marbles, also known as the Bedford Marbles because they were in the care of the Duke of Bedford, were first used as illustration by Otto Jahn, who interpreted the scene as being that of a man defecating on "the ever-suffering eye." Every student of the Evil Eye has since adopted Jahn's interpretation and his phrase. In terms of what we know of the Evil Eye symbolism, however, it is more likely to be a woman in the birthing position of the times: squatting. All the symbols surrounding the eye were Roman phallic symbols: the lion, the lion's paws, the snake, the scorpion, the birds, the man and Jove's bolt which he holds in his left hand, and the trident. Line drawing by author.

8.4 Phallic Bird from Rome. The "bird" is perched on four ktenes symbolizing the four stages in the developing maturity of women. From Knight and Wright.

8.5 Polyphallic tintinnabulum from the ruins of Herculaneum. Between 100 B.C. and 100 A.D. This one is a generic model drawn by the author principally from Knight and Wright, but modified on the basis of various photographs of actual tintinnabula.

8.6 Plates showing emblems with a multitude of phallic symbols around a kteic symbol, which itself is almost always an eye. Illustrations from Elworthy, pp. 129, 130, 131. Notice the recurrent Jove's bolt.

12.0

12.1 "Eye of God" from England. From a photograph in the Readers' Digest's *Folklore Myths and Legends of Britain*. Second edition. Pleasantville, NY: Readers' Digest Association Inc., 1977. This "eye" is looking out from the belfry of the church. The local inhabitants claim that there is a legend that says the "eye" was placed there to protect the parishioners against witches. To us it looks like a kteis and, as such, it protected people against "the Evil Eye" and assured them of prosperity, a tradition probably inherited from ancient times.

12.2 "Eye of God" above the altar in a small chapel on the Aegean island of Kythnos. It is also the blue swirl "eye" emblem that protects against the Evil Eye in Greece. Consistent with Evil Eye apotropaics, this eye is painted blue. Photo by author.

12.3 "Eye of Horus." Drawn by the author from an amulet found in Tutankhamen's tomb.

13.0

13.1 Stone effigy of the vulva at *the instant just before* crowning. From the site of Lepenski Vir, Yugoslavia. House No. 51, level Ic. From an illustration in Srejovic.

13.2 Stone effigy of the vulva *at the moment of* crowning. From the site of Lepenski Vir, Yugoslavia. House No. 45, level Ic. ca. 5,600 B.C. The author of the site report identifies this as a fish. See next illustration. From an illustration in Srejovic.

14.0

14.1 The stoup in the Romanesque church of Saint-Barthélémy-de-Farges, in Farges-lès-Mâcon (Saône-et-Loire) in France. Photo from Gantner and Pobé, fig. 8. The caption says that the figure "displays a mask formed by lines which correspond to the lines of the geometrical, plant-like ornament next to it." However, if one disregards the mouth added to make a "face," the "decorations" are not "plant-like" but rather clearly show the conditions of the vulva as it develops from pre-crowning on the right, continuing around and to the left, on to the crowning point, shown in the "eyes" of the grotesque "face." The grimace of which may be the representation of the effort and pain of giving birth, as it is in so many other fertility figures.

14.2 Detail, in line-drawing, of 14.1.

14.4 Line drawing from a photograph of a Gypsum Eye goddess from Tell Amar. Late XVIIth century B.C. New York Metropolitan Museum of Art.

14.5 Red-tinted egg baked at Easter in bread dough in the shape of the vulva at the Moment of Crowning. Island of Kythnos (Greece), 1972. Photograph by the author.

15.0

15.1 Female initiate's belt representing the vulva as a truncated oval. East Africa. Line drawing by author after a photo in Dames, whose caption reads: "Cowrie shells on the loincloth of a Chagga (Tanzania) woman repeat the shape of the genital organ and also resemble eyes. . . ." Compare the truncated oval to figures 15.2 and 20.3.

15.2 Line drawing of a Tsonga fertility statue from Malawi, South-East Africa. Detail from a photograph in Delange. The original item is part of the collections of the British Museum. Note the truncated oval.

16.0

16.1 Sheela-na-gig from Oaksey. The vulva is hypertrophied and in the shape of the Moment of Crowning. The Oaksey sheela is unusual, as sheela, in that it has large breasts. But as such, with its equally large vulva, it exhibits the female triad. Compare the hanging vulva to that of the African figure # 20.3.

16.2 The Montpazier "Venus" (Dordogne, France), probably of the Gravettian period, ca. 27,000 B.C. Drawn after a photograph in Gomez-Tabera. The vulva is hypertrophied as in the Oaksey sheela.

16.3 Corbel from the Romanesque church of Villanueva de Cangas in the town of Cangas de Onis, Asturias, Spain. Photograph by Carmen Fernandez y Cordogan.

17.0

17.1 The Gorgon from Etruria. Photograph of a bronze plate meant to decorate the front of a chariot. It is presently in the Pinakothek in Munich.

17.3 Sheela-na-gig from the church in Kilpeck, England. The Kilpeck Sheela is probably the best known of the Sheelas. Drawn from a photograph in Weir.

17.4 Carving from Kathmandu, Nepal, in a "Sheela" position. Line drawing after a photograph in Jorgen Andersen's *The Witch on the Wall.*

17.5 50 cm. "sheela" from Capdenac-le-haut, Lot, France, ca. 4,000 B.C. Line drawing from a photograph in Clottes et Carrière. Gimbutas interprets this as a "bird goddess."

17.6 Carving from Lepenski Vir (Yugoslavia), having all the characteristics of a sheela, ca. 4,950 B.C.

17.7 Sheela from Cavan. Now at the Museum in Dublin. Photo courtesy of the Dublin Museum.

17.8 Birthing grimace. Photograph by Lennart Nilsson in *A Child is Born*, Dell Publishing Group. Childbirth is stressful and painful. This is the photograph of the face of a woman at the instant of birth. This instant of stress and pain is what is manifested in the grimaces of sheelas, of gorgones and in the Lepenski-Vir effigy. It symbolizes that instant, and therefore, the grimace itself becomes a symbol of life and fertility. This birthing grimace is remarkably constant. Compare the photographs of the same moment by Wayne Miller in *The Family of Man*, and by Michel Odent in *Birth Reborn*.

18.0

18.1 Double tailed mermaid from the romanesque cathedral in Saint-Dié, department of Vosges, France. Line drawing after a photograph in Gischia and Mazenod.

18.2 Carving from a temple in Nepal. Line drawing after a photograph in Devereux.

18.3 Painting in the shape of a Parturient Woman symbol on the interior of a prehistoric sarcophagus of Chibusan tomb, west of Yamaga city, Japan. Interpreted as "shaman" by Kidder. Line drawing after a photograph in Kidder.

18.4 One of many "Anchor" amulet pendant from the site of Servia, Macedonia (Greece). ca. 2,600 B.C. Hoddnot calls them "horns." They have the shape of the Parturient Woman.

18.5 The anchor is a Christian symbol of Hope. It is derived from the Parturient Woman symbol. Drawing by author.

19.0

19.1 Cave wall drawing from Val Camonica, Southern Alps, Italy. Re-drawn from Anati and Graziozi.

19.2 Sign for good fortune drawn with vermillion paste on a libation jar. Modified from Mookerjee, *The Tantric Way*.

19.3 From Australia. Contemporary. Line drawing after a photograph in Pericot-Garcia.

19.4 Sepik (New Guinea) protective figure from the front of a house. Redrawn from Forge.

19.5 Pangolin effigy from Africa. Line drawing after a photograph in Laude.

19.6 The Parturient Woman design on a Zanzibar door panel. Line drawing after a photo in F. R. Barton, *Man*, 1924.

19.7 Parturient Woman symbols re-drawn after Graziosi, 1973, p. 186. Graziosi's caption reads, in translation, "Human figures schematized as W's and incised on the wall of the hypogeum." The figures are from a series of underground chambers at Moseddu, near Cheremule (Sassari, Sardinia.) The broken lines are presumed reconstructions.

19.8 Parturient Woman design above the window of a private dwelling on the island of Kythnos in Greece.

20.0

20.1 Parturient Woman design. Engraving on pottery from the site of Kalesovice (Bohemia), ca. end of 6th Millennium B.C. Line drawing after the *Deutscher Historiker Gesselschaft*. Also in Gimbutas who calls it a birth-giving goddess in the shape of a toad. (Her fig. 131).

21.0

21.1 Pentagram. A symbol for the Parturient Woman. Graphics by author.

21.2 Plane tree leaf (*platanus*). A fertility symbol among the ancient Romans. The photograph here is actually of a North American Sweetgum (*liquidambar styraciflua*). However, that which is called *platanus occidentalis* in the United States, is a "false" plane tree, or sycamore, and not a plane tree as it is known in Europe. The European plane tree's leaf is similar in shape to that of the North American Sweetgum.

22.0 N.B. The three following illustrations are "bucrania," or the skulls of bulls as symbol. The bucranium is a double fertility symbol inasmuch as the horns are male, but the image of the skull turned upside down becomes the Omega of the Parturient Woman.

22.1 Buffalo head from West Africa, where it explicitly represents both male and female elements of fertility. Line drawing from a photograph in Leuzinger.

22.2 Bucranium design on Halaf Ware from the site of Arpachiyah (Iraq), ca. 5,000 B.C. Re-drawn from Beatrice Goff.

22.3 Bull head from the site of Billcze Zlote in NW Bulgaria. Late Cucuteni culture, 4th Millennium B.C. Drawing from a photograph in Gimbutas.

23.0

23.1 Early Menorah. That the menorah as a symbol might have originated in the Parturient Woman symbol is re-enforced by the fact that it is accompanied by "cult objects" called *lubab* and *ethrog* (to the left) and *shofar* (to the right). At least two of these are fertility symbols: the ethrog is a citron, and like the fig it is a female fertility symbol. The shofar is a horn and therefore a male symbol. It might also be meaningful that these ritual objects are used during the harvest festival (Succot). (Consultant: Dr. Arnold Fox.) Drawing after Sukenik.

23.2 Design on a peasant's house mud wall in Rajastan, Northern India, to invoke fertility and abundance. It is drawn with rice paste. Drawing after a photograph in Mookerjee: *Rituals of India*. Mookerjee calls it an "invocation of the goddess of fertility and abundance."

23.3 Parturient Woman symbol on a wood door panel. Pindi: Africa. Contemporary, after a photograph in Biebuck. The original is in Hamburg.

23.4 Protective Parturient Woman symbol above a barn door in Finland, interpreted as a "hawk" for good luck. Line drawing by author, after a photograph in Vuorela.

24.0

24.1 This photograph of the moment when the fetus' crown appears in the open vulva, illustrates the inspiration for
1-The Parturient Woman posture, 2-The grimace caused by the stress and pain of childbirth, and, 3-The perfect oval shape of the vulva. Reprinted with permission from *Birth Reborn* by Dr. Michel Odent.

25.0

25.1 The Celtic Cross at Kilkieran, Cty. Kilkenney. It is deemed to have been carved in the Mid-8th Century. But, it is clearly phallic and was probably carved out of a prehistoric menhir. Compare to the menhir at St Duzec in Britanny which is

"Christian" only because the menhir has been encumbered with a cross on its top.

27.0

27.1 The Buddhist Circle of Life. Graphics by author.

27.2 The Shield of David, Star of David, or Seal of Solomon. Graphics by author.

27.3 The Ankh, the Mirror of Venus and the Orb. The latter two are variations of the Ankh. According to Budge, the oldest amuletic sign used by the dynastic Egyptians was the ankh (p. 134). "The meaning of the word ankh is 'life,' 'living,' in fact 'everlasting life'" (p. 135). "There is no good reason for doubting that it is a conventional representation of one of the principal organs of the human body used in the process of generation or coition" (p. 340). Graphics by author.

28.0

28.1 The ideogram for woman in the pre-cuneiform writing of ancient Sumer.

29.0

29.1 Calla Lily. A symbol of fertility for obvious reasons. Ironically, the Church has made it the symbol of the "purity" of the Virgin Mary. Photograph by author.

29.2 Arum Lily (Diffenbachia). In Africa, for instance, among the Pangwe, aroid lilies (Zantedeschia aethiopica) like this one are fertility symbols, (see Talbot, 1957, p. 54). Photograph by author.

30.0

30.1 Egyptian sistrum drawn by author. The systrum was the ceremonial representation of the virgin uterus.

31.0

31.1 Line drawing of a statuette from the site of Cernavoda, Romania, ca. 5,000 B.C. Dames says: "combines the two modes of the deity," but see text, pp. 65-66.

31.2 "Venus of Savignano," Savignano sul Pangro, prov. of Modena, Northern Italy, ca. 22,000 B.C., drawn from photographs in many sources.

31.3 Necklace bead, from the site of Dolni Vestonice, Czechoslovakia, ca. 27,000 B.C., from photographs in Marshack and others. Drawn after several sources.

31.4 "Female figurine" from the site of Arpachiya, (Iraq), Halaf Period, ca. 5,000 B.C., identified as a "goddess" on the grounds that the geographical area and the time are pervaded with busts of "long-necked" goddesses, and so they are. But, in spite of Goff's identification, there is no denying that this figurine looks more like a phallos than a female. There can be little doubt that it represents both male and female fertility. Re-drawn after a drawing in Goff (fig. 103).

31.5 Figurine from the site of Tepe Sarab in Turkey, ca. 6,000 B.C., after a photograph in Redman, Charles. This statuette is remarkable. It is clearly female, yet it is as clearly impossible to escape the phallic aspect of the "neck" and "breasts."

31.6 Line drawing from a photograph in Gimbutas' *Goddesses and Gods*, fig. 83. This is from the Sesklo Culture and is in the Archaeological Museum of Volos (Greece). Gimbutas identifies this as a "Bird-headed Goddess" with a long neck and large breasts, from the site of Agia Anna in Thessaly, c. 6,000 B.C.

Again, "beak" notwithstanding, the neck and breasts manifest the male dimension of fertility in that they portray a phallos.

32.0

32.1 East Gravettian "stick" effigy from the site of Dolni Vestonice, Czechoslovakia, ca. 27,000 B C. The figure is clearly phallic as well as clearly female.

32.2 One of the numerous and typical statuettes from the Aegean Islands (Greece), ca. 2 or 3000 B C., drawn after photographs in various sources.

32.3 A "baton" made of reindeer antler, from the site of Le Placard (France), ca. 15,000 years. Line drawing after a photograph in Marshack.

32.4 Phallic female figurine found at Mezhirich, Siberia (USSR), ca. 15th Millennium B.P., after Gladkih, Kormietz and Soffer, 1984 (p. 175).

32.5 Well-publicized "female" figurine found at the site of Dolni Vestonice (Czechoslovakia), ca. 27,000 B.C., after photographs in Marshack and many others. The figure has no face and the head and breasts are phallic. Yet, Marshack thinks that the vertical lines represent a nose, and Gimbutas thinks of them as "a stream flowing down the body of the deity," which, because it begins at what she interprets as "eyes," make the eyes "a source of divine liquid." (p 51).

32.6 Savignano, (same as 31.2).

32.7 Line drawing from several sources. Petersfels. Marshack's caption for Petersfels: Fig. 156, p. 284, reads: "Sculpted, highly polished coal pendant from Petersfels, south Germany, depicting a stylized, abstracted female form whose primary features are the large buttocks and slightly bent knees. Upper Magdalenian." It may be indeed a "stylized, abstracted female form," but the buttocks in conjunction with the "legs" are a "stylized and abstracted form" representing, even more obviously, a penis and scrotum, which, in turn, as phallos, is the representation of the male dimension of fertility. Petersfels, therefore, is a perfect double representation. It is not unique and can easily be compared in style, for instance, to the Gravettian statuette from the central cave at Weinsberg and others.

33.0

33.1 "Violin" shaped female figurine from the Cyclades (Greece), "Pelos Group" in the Goulandris Collection, ca. between 3,300 and 2,800 B.C. The "Pelos Group" includes Melos, Siphnos, Despotikos, Antiparos, Paros and Naxos. Drawn after a photograph in *L'Art des Cyclades* (see Bibliography under Goulandris). Item No. 338 in the collection itself.

33.2 Same as fig. 32.2.

33.3 From the site of Mal'ta in Siberia, identified as a "flying bird," whereas it obviously is not. Line drawing after many sources.

33.4 Female figurine from the Island of Naxos (Greece). Between 2,300 and 3,000 B.C., after a photograph in Zervos.

33.5 Female figurine from the Island of Syphnos (Greece). Between 2,300 and 3,000 B.C., after a photograph in Zervos.

33.6 Female figurine from the Island of Despotikos (Greece). Between 2,300 and 3,000 B.C., after a photograph in Zervos.

34.0

34.1 Figurine from the Cyclades (Greece), Bronze age, Paphos district, ca. 3,000-2,300 B.C. Although this one is itself too large to be worn at the neck, it illustrates at least one use of these statuettes. Photograph from a photograph in *The Greek*

Museums (see bibliography under Ministère de la Culture (France), or Andronicos, Manolis). In *Art and Culture of the Cyclades*, p. 418, fig. 185: steatite figure with amulet from Cyprus. Archaeological Museum, Nikosia. 3,000-2,500 B.C. Height 15.3 cm.

35.0

35.1 Figurine from Priene (Turkey), ca. 5th Century B.C. Original in Müseum für Völkerkunde, Berlin.

35.2 Figurine from the site of Ghelaesti (Romania), ca. 5th millennium B.C. Cucuteni A-B Culture. Line drawing from photograph in Dumitrescu.

36.0

36.1 Medieval paper watermarks, after C. M. Briquet. The watermarks are invariably based on fertility symbols, and the papermakers were Albigenses (Cathars), a manichean religious sect.

36.2 Negative image of a graffito photographed by Brassaï at the turn of the century in Paris. It is remarkable for the spontaneous (?) re-creation of a phallic heart symbol combined with a kteic one. Note that the kteic heart is slit and that there is an another phallic shape, besides the phallic heart, directed toward it. This being a graffito from the streets of Paris it is highly improbable that the artist's immediate goal was to represent fertility, yet, he used what turns out to be traditional conventions in his design.

37.0

37.1 Long poles topped by cow genitals stretched on a frame, placed at crossroads leading to the entrance of a village. Arussi Province, Ethiopia. Photograph taken by the author, ca. 1953.

38.0

38.1 VIIIth Century copper plate from the Eglise des Pèlerins at Narbonne, France. After Gischia, plate #57. (Also in Salvini and in others). Note that the Alpha has the definite shape of a phallos and that the upper-case Omega (Ω) is the symbol for the uterus, whereas the lower-case Omega (ω) is a symbol for the Parturient Woman, which is that shown here.

39.0

39.1 Mosaic floor at the entrance of a Roman house in Roman Lybia, at the site of Susa, Tunisia (Sousse in French). This is a symbol to protect the household against the Evil Eye. Note that the phallos is flanked by two ktenes and directly connected to one of them by an ejaculation. Black and White in Marcadé (fig. 104B). The caption reads: "Phallus and vulvae (prophylactic mosaic), Museum of Sousse."

39.2 Mosaic floor at the entrance of a Roman house in Moknine, Tunisia. It is almost identical to the Sousa mosaic, except that the kteis is represented by an eye, making the identification of eye and kteis inevitable. This device of an eye toward which a phalos or symbols of phalloi are directed was a common apotropaic in Rome. From an illustration in Jean Marcadé's *Roma Amor*. The caption reads: "Fish phallus, eye and snakes (prophylactic mosaic,) *Moknine*."

40.0

40.1 A contemporary mantle bauble. To whomever designed it, it probably meant only a pretty decoration. To the author of this monograph, after looking at thousands of fertility symbols from across the ages, and from across the planet, it seems to be as old as mankind. In that sense, it could be simply an occasional Rorschack Test. Or could it be explained through Carl Jung's archetypes? Or can we invoque Bachhoffen's "Unity of the human mind" perpetually and sub-consciously re-inventing the same symbols over and over and again as, for instance, in Brassaï's photograph of a graffiti from a factory wall (fig. 36.2), or McLean's photograph of a magisterial "venus" from military barracks in France.

Preface

Siegfried Giedion, in his magisterial work, *The Eternal Present: A Contribution on Constancy and Change*, argues that there are certain human manifestations that endure "with a remarkable constancy" in spite of distortions brought about by changing cultural perspectives. Symbols fall in this category. He concludes therefore that "[t]he present revival of interest in the symbol and its meaning leads us back to its origins in prehistory." Certainly the Evil Eye considered as a symbol rather than as a cult object reflects and supports this proposition.[1] In that sense the Evil Eye is a neglected topic. Not because the literature is lacking—on the contrary it is abundant—but rather because it consists almost exclusively of descriptions of latter-day "folk" wisdom which generally perceives the Evil Eye as some kind of natural (but enigmatic) substance emanating from the body of others and having a life of its own. Moreover, analytical works by scholars, follow upon this "folk" perception. Yet, for those of us who stand outside of the tradition, there are no completely satisfactory explanations for the existence of such a belief, nor of its origins, nor of its ecumenical distribution both in time and across the world, nor of the anatomy of what can appear to be a complex and mysterious organism. This book is an attempt to scrutinize these questions by going back in time in order to see if indeed we can trace the origins and therefore the primordial meaning of the Eye as symbol rather than the Eye as tangible emanation. I have confined myself to the evidence from the Old World. The similarities between the New World and the Old, however, exposes one to the temptation to include the New World material, but the information from the Old World is already so abundant that I have had to be greatly selective. My problem, then, has been how to limit myself rather than to expound on the subject. The New World will have to wait, for somebody else perhaps, but wait it must.

I am well aware, and the reader should be aware, that I shall not always follow conventional academic paths. I do want to question consecrated interpretations, or else there would be no point in writing this book. That is the way of scholarship and research; we do have to seek new horizons, explore new possibilities, try out new ideas. In the social sciences especially, we are at a disadvantage in that in the process of questioning, we often disturb things considered as sacred, whether they be convictions of a religious, political, academic, economic or cultural order. Each and every one of us is programmed by a particular culture and a personal upbringing that somehow filters our view of the universe we observe. Stagnant explications are characteristic of, but not peculiar to the social sciences: in the eighteenth century, the father of modern chemistry, Lavoisier, was castigated for suggesting that the accepted scientific practice of explaining combustion through the "phlogiston" theory might need to be replaced. The contempt for such truly revolutionary ideas was ironically evident in the words of the judge who sent him to the guillotine during the French Revolution: "The Republic does not need scholars." So much for the exact sciences, and I hope nobody sends me to the gallows.[2]

The book started out as an essay on the Evil Eye and it still is that, but my original working hypothesis has led me to cope with the fact that there exist obvious links between the Evil Eye, the symbolism of fertility rituals and the concept of *mana*, so that now, the book explores all three topics. By the same token, it quickly became apparent that the uncanny persistence of the beliefs in the Evil Eye, was directly related to the equally uncanny perseverance of fertility rituals. Hence, I had to examine and try to explain the incredible staying power of the symbolism involved.

This given and after a brief introduction to a description of what the Evil Eye is today, I have proceeded to place the structure of its beliefs back into the setting of the type of society in which the Evil Eye originated. Because this context includes the concept of *mana* which is critically essential in understanding the power that symbols have for the people concerned, I try to evoke the ambiance of a world replete with *mana*. The concept of *mana* is the driving force behind the concepts of fertility and of the Evil Eye. The symbolism of the Evil Eye has so much in common with the symbolism of fertility, that one cannot disregard the relationship. A look at fertility rituals and fertility symbols through history and prehistory will reveal why fertility is so important.

Finally, I will show that the Eye itself is a fertility symbol which refers to prosperity, affluence, happiness and luck and that the odious aspect (the "evil") of the Eye refers to the fear of unproductivity and misfortune. I will conclude that the Evil Eye, although the idiom has changed its intrinsic meaning over time, remains today a struggle by people to protect themselves against infertility, adversity and illness, and, once protected, to enhance prosperity, affluence, happiness, health, and Good Fortune in general, although they may not always articulate it that way.

I will be dealing with regularities; granted that in a complex procedural system like the Evil Eye, found in different environments, it is sometimes difficult to distinguish between significant and non-significant variables.

A few words about what I am *not* trying to do:

1-I am not trying to decipher the particular role of the Evil Eye in a particular society, contemporary or otherwise. My interest is in the nature of the Evil Eye original system of beliefs rather than in the role it plays now in a particular society.

2-By the same token, I am *not* trying to find out what individual perceptions might be created by the presence of an Evil Eye "organism" in a particular environment, but rather, I want to know what the broad underlying causes are that gave a cultural survival value to the Evil Eye.

THE EVIL EYE

PART ONE

INTRODUCTION

Chapter I

The Evil Eye

Introduction

The Evil Eye is perhaps the most wide-spread complex system of beliefs in the world and in history, yet, to anybody who is not part of an Evil Eye culture, the Evil Eye is an enigma. Its persistence is phenomenal. Yet the most remarkable thing about it is the fact that its study has been largely neglected by scholars. Among the many introductory manuals in anthropology, in which one would expect particular attention paid to the topic, there is scarcely a text that mentions the Evil Eye except for some vague passing references.[3] Yet, given its importance in controlling the behavior of people, it is obvious that a substantive code of beliefs like that of the Evil Eye should be understood in the context of the type of social organization and of social sanctions in which it originated. The particulars of its occurrence seem to tell us, among other things, that, in a world of intimate relationships in which people produce that which they subsist upon, and who depend only marginally, if at all, on the existence of a market, one cannot disregard the fact that the view of "kinship" is organizational, anymore than one can ignore the worldview of people living in such societies. The cultural ambiance under which the Evil Eye came into being is not that which exists now in the world of modern industry and world-wide money markets. The values and the beliefs, especially the collective perception of ourselves as product of a special creation meant to master and dominate the rest of nature, make it difficult for us to empathize with the feelings, and even more difficult to understand the vision of peoples who have a radically different view of the Universe, peoples who do *not* separate themselves from the rest of nature, who think of themselves as an integral part of Nature. My goal in the following chapters, is going to be to place the Evil Eye back in the cultural context in which it originated and still thrives in order to find out how it could possibly have come about. But first, what *is* the Evil Eye?

Contemporary Folk Perception.

It is characteristic of the species (and therefore also of scholars) that we should feel secure and comfortable only in traditional ideas. Weston La Barre says it best in the introduction to his book *Muelos*:

> The scientist pioneers in the most modish thinking in the small area of his expertise, but only at the price of impiety to sacred culture; while he, in most other matters like the rest of us citizens, rests, comfortably or uncomfortably, in an old stone age of the mind whose momentum and inertia are incalculable. In the governance of human lives, there are not only neuroses and psychoses from individual childhoods, but also group *archoses:* nonsense and misinformation so ancient and pervasive as to be seemingly inextricable from our thinking, a sacred ghost dance entrenched in the forgotten. (p. 10)

The contemporary folk perception of the Evil Eye is an "archosis." If this is true, then it poses obvious problems if we are going to try to go through this "nonsense and misinformation so ancient and pervasive as to be inextricable from our thinking." How, then, are we going to define the Evil Eye if it was not perceived then as it is perceived now? Evidence for a belief in the Evil Eye appears in the first decipherable written documents from ancient Mesopotamia, 5000 years ago, and, even then, it seems to have been already a well-established belief. Not only is it highly unlikely that the cultural milieu was the same then as that which came to prevail in latter-day cultures but we should take it as a matter of procedure that it was fundamentally different. The cognitive value of "Evil Eye" for the people living in the culture that developed it, had to have been different also. Five thousand years is a long time. It is obvious that the Evil Eye evolved from a cultural configuration now so distorted by time and by a changing environment, that it is probably best to begin by formulating a working definition of the Evil Eye on the basis of what we do know about it, that is, the "archosis" of contemporary folk belief. We can then perhaps work our way back through time and, from this "stone age of the mind," dig out the concept in an approximation of its original cognitive value.

Present-Day Folk Perception

As it exists now, no matter where the concept of the Evil Eye surfaces, we find a number of practices and expectations common to all instances. The first and best-known of these is the belief that somehow, there are individuals who, wittingly or unwittingly, exude an aura of bad luck and ill health, and who seem to have a special faculty of bringing disaster upon others. These individuals are referred to as having the Evil Eye. Whether they are identified or not, their influence is to be counteracted, generally or particularly, by a number of preventive measures whose common attributes are: the same talismans, amulets, gestures, the cures, the prophylactics, all of which have a sexual character, plus the single eye, the glance and envy.

The Single Eye

It is significant, as we shall see later, that in all languages, the Evil Eye is always singular, never plural. In European speech, only German generally (not always) refers to a "glance" (*böse Blick*) rather than to an "eye." Even then, the glance is singular, and the language has an alternative which is the universal "Evil Eye" (*böse Auge*). This "eye" is said to cast a sinister glance. The most vulnerable to this glance are children and pregnant women, closely followed by domestic animals, fruit trees and field crops. This aspect has remained, to this day, the central concern. However, it is to be noted that as productive activities increase and become more diversified and complex, the concern tends to spread to things other than the direct products of nature. All objects that make "us" prosperous must be protected. That is, anything, any business, any device, any being, any life, any means, including money, that is part of the production and reproduction process, including interest on investments must be protected from the evil of sterility and scarcity.[4]

The Glance

Scholars have generally accepted this explicit contemporary folk perception and have concentrated their attention on that part of the belief which is predicated, not on the symbolic, but on the literal interpretation of the term "eye," which presumes the existence of the power of a glance in order to explain the existence and persistence of the system. K. F. Smith, for instance, presumes that the Evil Eye is "derived . . . from the primeval explanation, whatever it was, of vision" (p. 294). This presupposes that people "naturally" adhere to a kind of archaic Aristotelian theory of sight: namely that there is some substance or some power that emanates from the eye that settles on the object seen. This substance, or power, when projected by some people, is believed to cause harm. This glance or gaze explanation postulates that all counter-charms are designed to divert the noxious glance. Hence their sexual configurations which, according to this theory, is designed to attract the attention of the Evil Eye and deflect its impact. Margaret Hasluck, for instance, says: "The amulets, in short, are a species of lightning conductor, just as the power of overlooking is thought popularly to be a kind of electricity which resides in the eye."[5]

In fact, the most remarkable mode of the Evil Eye complex system of belief is one that probably has far greater significance than is given to it: *virtually all amulets, all gestures, all imprecations that protect against the Evil Eye are sexual in character.* One might note at this point that even in our contemporary "sophisticated" world ignorant of the Evil Eye, many gestures and imprecations designed to be defensive (and offensive) have retained their lewd character without being related consciously to the Evil Eye. In pursuing the problem of origins, conjectures have been based on the fear of envy and on the literal concept of "eye" and "vision." But focusing on this gazing behavior tends to obscure the fact that *the Eye is a symbol and not a conscious entity, and that, therefore, one ought to focus on what the symbol represents*, and not on the folk presumption of material effects allegedly produced by the organ of sight of some people who have no voluntary control over its power.

The Evil Eye without the Eye.

However, if the Evil Eye is only a symbol, then the term, Evil Eye, is just an idiom. The same system of beliefs ought to be found elsewhere, functioning with a different terminology and different symbols. As a matter of fact, many of the constituent beliefs of "the Evil Eye" *do* exist without the idiom of the Evil Eye. Even among the people who use a word meaning "glance," "look" or "gaze," the harm attributed to the "Evil Eye" is thought to be dependent upon the conviction that some individuals radiate a vague, not necessarily visual but intuitively recognizable emanation which, when it settles on others, brings misfortune in one form or another. In the absence of an "Evil Eye" vocabulary, one could say, for instance, that the possessor of such an unfortunate disposition is a *jinx*, that is, "a person, thing or influence supposed to bring bad luck, . . ., something that unaccountably foredooms to failure or misfortune."[6] The same can be said of being a witch in certain parts of Africa. In either case, most of those who are thought to possess these characteristics would not be conscious of having them and, if confronted with the accusation of being a witch or a jinx, would sincerely refuse to accept such a judgment passed upon them, whether it is called "having the Evil Eye," or being a witch or a jinx. In that sense, one has the Evil Eye, or is a witch or a jinx, only if others believe one has, or is, any of these aberrations. Given this logic, it follows that if one believes that there can be something harmful emanating from certain individuals, then, one can also believe that some injurious matter issues from the glance of dispossessed or alienated individuals or, by extension, from a peculiar gaze, or from the active envy of others.

Envy

Among those things that can be damaging is the envy of others. The idea of envy is such an integral part of the belief system of the Evil Eye that in some places, such as North Africa, and many of the Muslim countries, the Evil Eye takes on the name of the Eye of Envy.[7] As a matter of fact, the concept of envy has become so much a part of the Evil Eye system of beliefs that Richard and Eva Blum use the terms "Evil Eye" and "envy" as if the two concepts were analytically interchangeable. In their book on *The Dangerous Hour*, they quote Heliodorus, who is speaking of envy, as if he were speaking of the Evil Eye. Chances are that he was, but it cannot be taken as *evidence* that he was speaking of the Evil Eye. Even in the contemporary folk perception (see below), one can speak of the Evil Eye without speaking of envy explicitly or implicitly. This fact notwithstanding, it is generally true that from a practical point of view, people have a tendency, and perhaps it is safe, to identify one concept with the other. Elworthy also, who is an authority on the Evil Eye, equates the concept of Evil Eye with the concept of envy. He says of the Evil Eye:

> Its supposed manifestations have given rise to many divergent ramifications, finding their expression in more or less descriptive definitions; and these in their turn have further branched out and acquired conventional meanings, which at first sight seem to have no connection with the original idea of the "evil eye." Such, for example, is our English word "envy," meaning *malignant* or *hostile feeling* that may be said to arise from natural jealousy—as in 1 S 18, where Saul "eyed David." It is obvious how close is the connection here between the definition and the fact denoted. The classic *invideo* describes most accurately what we mean to-day by "over-look"—"to gaze with evil intent" (see Trench, Syn. of NT, 1876, pp. 83-106). The Latin *invidia* not only denotes the feelings connected in our minds with "envy," but is today an alternative word for the modern Italian *malocchio*.[8]

Elworthy further paraphrases Bacon's essay "On Envy": "there is a belief in a power of working evil which is ejaculated upon any object it beholds, that has existed in all times and in all countries." To which Elworthy adds: "Notwithstanding modern science and education, this belief is as strong as ever it was."[9] Elworthy also quotes the Roman aphorism (p. 611) "Laudet qui invidet," which he translates as "He who envies, praises," but which, given Latin syntax, certainly means also "He who praises, envies." People believe that the exudations which, in their minds, characterize the Evil Eye, are emitted by those who tend to be envious of the good fortune of others. That is why one must not brag about one's resources, lest it become a cause for envy. Anything that may be taken as a manifestation of covetousness must be avoided. Hence, the reluctance to accept praise graciously. To this day, in the Mediterranean area, it is bad form to praise a child ("oh what a beautiful baby!"), and counter-measures must be taken immediately, lest the baby be harmed by the envy (*invidia*) implicit in the compliment. The same is true for crops or any form of production: one must not mention these because discussion and comments might elicit the envy of neighbors.

Ever since Marcel Maus wrote his *Essai sur le Don*, we have become aware of the fact that in simple societies where goods, services and relationships in general are governed by the principles of reciprocity and cooperation, the rule for people to get along with each other has been: wealth is not to be accumulated for keeping, but is to be redistributed.[10] The very act of giving to others, puts the others under the customary and cultural obligation of reciprocating under the same circumstances, thus assuring one's own survival. If, instead, one accumulates wealth for one's own profit, one not only disrupts the system, but is considered greedy and attracts the resentment of the community, who will then isolate one, and one cannot survive in isolation. This collective disapprobation keeps people in line, but by the same token, it can be and is interpreted as envy in any individuals, but especially in those who have peculiarities considered odd.[11] In short, the Evil Eye was born in a pre-feudal egalitarian world in which cooperation was crucial, where competition was counter-productive, and where, therefore, it was a matter of critical importance for one's survival to share with others. In that light, greed, which is a characteristic of human beings, must be controlled. Envy was considered the ultimate vice because its relation to production and reproduction was considered as harmful to the harmony of reciprocity.

Finally, the literature also shows that any adult, male or female, can be a caster of the Evil Eye, but only women relay the folklore associated with it and transmit it from one generation to the next. Women are also the curers of the ills brought about by the Evil Eye.

Chapter II

Distribution

In most parts of the world a belief in the Evil Eye is still alive. It is so common that F. T. Elworthy was induced to say that it "must be set down as one of the hereditary and instinctive convictions of mankind," which is an overstatement of course, but it is, by the same token, a testimony to the fact that this authority on the Evil Eye was impressed by the frequency of its occurrence.[12] All over the Mediterranean and in Asia, peasant life is often governed by the atmosphere of suspicion and acrimony created by a belief that there are individuals who possess "the ability to cast an evil glance." Belief in the Evil Eye has been transplanted to the New World by migration. It is, in fact, as widespread as the belief in a High God, and has lasted a longer time.[13] Elworthy says that "The origin of the belief is lost in the obscurity of prehistoric ages" (p. 3) and indeed we can trace it back historically to the very beginnings of writing. According to E. A. Wallis Budge, "The oldest mentions of the Evil Eye are found in the texts which the Sumerians, Babylonians and Assyrians wrote in cuneiform upon clay tablets; the Sumerian texts date from the third millennium before Christ, and they form the basis of later Babylonian and Assyrian magical literature" (p. 358). However, if we are to believe James Mellaart, a belief in the Evil Eye may be as much as 3000 years older. In describing the site of Çatal Hüyük which he discovered, he says: "There are also stylized hands, probably charms against the Evil Eye, such as are used to this day."[14] I am not at all sure that this is a "proof" that the Evil Eye idiom existed in the sixth millennium B.C., but it can be taken as ancillary evidence that the hand (a sexual symbol) was used as protection against infertility then as it is used now in that area of the world.

The descriptive reports on the Evil Eye from all parts of the world are so numerous and the similarities so great that describing each case would be redundant, and the repetitions, tedious. In the sketches below, I am going to describe particular cases, trying not to repeat too often the wearisome details. Whatever I say for the one set of beliefs and rituals will be essentially true also of the beliefs and rituals in other parts of the world, notably Greece, Italy, Spain, Turkey, Scotland, Ireland, Finland, Germany, Poland, the Muslim world in general. The similarities are striking and the differences superficial. Only India shows greater differences but again, these are not fundamental.

The Evil Eye in Greece

Greece, like the rest of the Mediterranean, has a long oral and documented history of Evil Eye lore. The language has a very special word for the phenomenon: βασκανια (vaskania) from which Latin derived the term *fascinatio*, parent-name of fascination. The tradition, however, is older than the Greeks. The major and oldest protective device (φυλακτον, philacton) is the head of the Gorgon. Harrison, who speaks of the protective figures—the technical generic term for these is: *apotropaic*—placed in the homes and the workplaces in need of protection against the Evil Eye, says: "Of such βασκᾴνια, the Gorgon mask was one and perhaps the most common shape" (p. 191).[15] The image of the Gorgon was inherited by the Greeks from the Etruscan, who had pictured her in the posture of the Parturient Woman (see that chapter, and see illustration no. 17.1). The Greeks in the course of time reduced her to a head and a mask (gorgoneion).

My own active professional interest in the Evil Eye dates from 1970, when I went to Greece, to do field research on the power structure of a small isolated island community. My research program at the time had nothing to do with the Evil Eye, but I did find myself surrounded with gracious and pleasant people whose courtesy and undeniable hospitality seemed to be mixed with guarded caution. I also found out that there were certain topics more difficult to broach than others. It was difficult to speak of field and tree crops, of the health of children, of domestic animals, or of the beauty of a young woman, without some elaborate precautions. At first, I surmised that the informants were suspicious of outsiders who might, after all represent a central government, which, to them, always acts surreptitiously and mysteriously, customarily takes away their resources and drafts their young men. I discovered later that this was not actually the reason for their reluctance. It was that praise implies envy, and the strong emotions that issue from envy are part of the syndrome that people call the Evil Eye. My observations thereafter took account of this important cultural determinant.

People on the island seemed to sense the presence of the Evil Eye everywhere. Misfortunes, failures, illnesses were attributed to the Evil Eye of someone who must be identified. The villagers were on the alert and on the defensive. They surrounded themselves with protective rituals and protective symbols. They were steeped in an atmosphere of suspicion and fear against which they felt they must protect themselves. They seemed to believe that the Evil Eye lurked everywhere to prey at any moment on the unwary. One could feel secure only if well protected by traditional talismans.

The most frequent of the amulets against the Evil Eye in Greece is an oval blue swirl having the appearance of an eye (fig. 12.2). The cross, which they also wear frequently, is worn as a protection against the Evil Eye rather than as a badge of Christian identity. The horn is used in various ways as a talisman, sometimes represented by claws or anything that has a phallic shape. The monks of Mount Athos, according to Hasluck, are said to carve crosses out of the horn of a single-horned animal. This charm is called a *monokeros*, from *μονοκερο*, unicorn.[16] It is used against the Evil Eye. The houses are painted white with blue trimmings (the colors of Mary),[17] children are made to wear garlic on their persons, and cloves (the spice) are regularly used in curing rituals. The kellies (one room shelters, used in the fields during planting and harvest) are decorated with designs symbolizing "life" (fig. 1.1), and the designs whitewashed on the narrow streets of the villages are remarkably similar to these "life" symbols (fig. 1.3). Sometimes the street geometric decoration may be interrupted by the drawing of a rose (see fig. 1.2). A fish often appears as a protective symbol above the entrance to a house or a shop (see figs. 2.1 and 2.2). These designs (the life symbols, the rose, the fish) happen to be ancient fertility symbols. All this feverish activity is contrived for protection against the Evil Eye. Women are the ones who are called upon for cures. Gubbins, however, reports that a woman must transmit her knowledge to another woman through the agency of a man. If Gubbins is correct, it is unusual that a man should interfere, but even Gubbins acknowledges that the *practitioners* are women.[18] One exception is the male priest who confines himself to the formal incantations prescribed by the Church. The Greek clergy generally act in an institutionalized and prescribed manner, and the rituals there come close to being a kind of exorcism. Generally speaking, if a child, is sick it is immediately presumed to have been "overlooked" and it is brought to a healer. Each woman has her own recipe for treatment, but all recipes fall within the traditional mode of the Evil Eye everywhere. The use of cloves, olive oil, fire and water is frequent. Various magical formulae are invariably used. These formulae often include invocations to various saints, particularly Mary (the Panagiya), but they are an obvious concession to the encroaching power of the Church. Saint Cosmos and Saint Damien are frequently mentioned.

One must not brag about crops, nor praise children or livestock. Great efforts are made to identify those who cast an Evil Eye. Traditional and superficial identifying characteristics are used, such as blue eyes, dark eyes, or eyebrows joined above the nose. A person living alone is a witch of course, but all witches are considered to have the Evil Eye. My field notes record the case of an elderly widow, who was born and brought up on another island in the Aegean but had married a local man. After her husband's death she remained in her husband's village where she had spent most of her adult life. She survived comfortably, which was suspect from the villagers point of view, for she had no blood relatives in town. She was considered to have the Evil Eye. She was greatly feared, as a consequence of which people helped her, a fact which contributed to her comfort.

As is true everywhere else in the Mediterranean, gestures are used. In Greece, the gesture which is the equivalent of the *mano cornuta* in Italy, or the *mano fica* in Spain (see figs. 3.1 & 3.2), consists of throwing both hands up, fingers widespread, palms towards the object of scorn and "making a face." Also, as in Italy, the open palm, fingers together, will be extended out in the direction of the object of scorn or fear. I saw a Greek friend spit at a newly acquired pet bird for "good luck," that is, to protect it against the Evil Eye. Spitting at someone in Greece, and among us, is a gesture of contempt as well as a gesture of protection in the same sense that "giving the finger" to someone expresses both contempt and protection.[19]

The Evil Eye in Italy

Probably for historical reasons, Italy has been singled out by travelers and amateurs of folklore as the prototype for the countries where the Evil Eye prevails. The result is that there are many descriptions of "mal'occhio." The belief in Italy is so pervasive that the protective symbols have almost become a badge of ethnic identity among Italians abroad. In Chicago, where there is an important contingent of people of Italian ancestry, wearing a "corno" almost identifies one as

Italian. Although the primary meaning of the word "corno" is "horn," it has come to refer to all apotropaic amulets against the Evil Eye, horn or not. Elworthy points out that "In modern Italy any glass bead or stone having a marking at all like an eye is carefully preserved as an amulet (p. 612, op. cit.)."

In Italy, women have a special role in the Evil Eye beliefs, as is the case wherever the beliefs occur. They are the transmitters of the folklore, and they are the curers. In his book, *Mal Occhio, The Underside of Vision*, Distasi, who is male and who is of Italian parentage, says that the Evil Eye in his family was the "unmentionable of unmentionables," while at the same time it was taken for granted: it was part of their life. He tries to explain the "nondiscussability" of the topic, but it was probably not discussed with him, because he is male.[20] Neil Rocco Meccia, wrote an unpublished paper on the Evil Eye among ethnic Italians in Chicago. As in Greece, Italian women are the repository of the knowledge about the Evil Eye. Meccia began by interviewing his older male relatives, every one of whom said something to the effect: "Oh, I don't know anything about the Evil Eye. Go see your grandmother or your old aunt." When he finally got to the older females, the most important information he received from them was that the secret lore had to be transmitted preferably to one other woman, sometimes two, and then only at certain times of the year (Christmas and Easter).[21] Meccia did obtain some spells from an informant who was willing to bend the rules, but not to the point of giving him the information for the asking: she insisted that it be done at Easter (p. 28). Buonanno in an article on the Evil Eye among Italian-Americans, reports that his informant told him that she could not reveal the healing incantations because: "To reveal it without the proper intent is to ruin its efficacity. It may be revealed to only two people during her lifetime, and this only at midnight on Christmas Eve" (p. 243). As in Distasi's family, Meccia's family had had an "expert" who was his grandmother, but she had died recently. In any case, he would probably have obtained few details from her, since he is male. Those involved strongly believe that, were they to violate the taboo, not only would their ability to cure disappear, but it might even be that harm would come to them from this imponderable and undefinable force that governs the Evil Eye. Distasi says that his aunt Carmela, who had no hope of ever getting married, was considered to have the Evil Eye. On the other hand, she was also a curer. Indeed, just as it is their special province to transmit the folklore of the Evil Eye, women are also the healers. Much of the lore transmitted by them consists of recipes for cures. Not all women are endowed with this *gift*; moreover, there are rare exceptions to this sexual distribution of labor. A recent case in point is the Rev. Germano Ventura, pastor of the parish of Santa Maria Causa Nostra Letitzia (Holy Mary Cause of Our Joy) in Italy, who, his followers believe, "possesses the power to heal as well as antidotes to combat the evil eye."[22] However, Father Ventura's actions, as opposed to those of the Greek priests, seem to be personal.

The Turks, the Middle East and Islam in general

The prophet Mohammed himself believed firmly in the Evil Eye. The sacred book of the Muslims, the Koran, attests to this. The particular verses (sura) that mention the Evil Eye are included in small scrolls rolled up and enclosed in a leather covering hung from the neck as protection against the Evil Eye.[23]

Among the Muslim Turks the belief in the Evil Eye is so intense that it is carried into exile. Sachs, for instance, made a study of how migrants in Sweden frustrated the efforts of physicians to cure their Turkish patients because of their Evil Eye convictions. One, the mother of a sick child, went so far as to make a special and costly trip back home to Turkey to consult an Evil Eye curer who would understand her convictions better than the physicians in the free clinic in Sweden.[24]

According to Eda Lindquist, the Persians (read Iranians) still made use of the rue as protection against the Evil Eye, particularly in marriage ceremonies.[25] The rue was used in antiquity all over the Mediterranean world (ancient Egypt, Rome, Greece) to ward off the Evil Eye, and it was still widespread during the Middle Ages in Europe, not only to encourage fertility in people, fields and domestic animals, but also to encourage the multiplication of gains in money investments.

In Islam, the open hand, palm forward is another favored symbol for protection against the Evil Eye. It is found elsewhere, of course, but it is preferred by the Muslim who call it "the Hand of Fatima." It is often represented with an eye in the palm; as a jewelry amulet it appears in the stylized form of a triangle from which hang five small strings of beads, worn either as earrings or as a pendant on a necklace.

Westermarck reports that: "The gesture with the five outstretched fingers is used against the evil eye in Algeria, Tunis, Syria and Palestine, among the Sennaarese and the Kababish in the Anglo-Egyptian Sudan, and in modern Greece."[26] This gesture is used aggressively and is considered as vulgar, as opposed to the Hand of Fatima which is used sedately, almost religiously.

Otherwise, the Evil Eye beliefs in Islam, and the Middle East in general, is congruent with the format elsewhere. A recent dissertation from the Department of Folklore, Indiana University, purports to show that the popular Islamic beliefs of the Sudan have remained unchanged since the Fung era (1505-1821), and this includes a belief in the powers of the much feared Evil Eye.[27]

The Evil Eye Among the Jews

It is called "en Ha-ra" by Ludwig Blau; "Ayin Hara-ah" by Friedenwald; "Eyin-ho-re" by Lillienthal; "einehore" by Kirshenblatt-Gimblett; "en-rah" by Brav. The Hebrew word is ע י ן ה ר ע . Besides the references to the Evil Eye in the Old Testament, the richest sources are from Jewish folklore and rabbinical tradition. All the descriptive accounts of the Evil Eye among the Jews show the remarkable congruence of their Evil Eye beliefs with those of Catholic Italy, Muslim Turkey, Orthodox Greek or Hindu India. The Evil Eye syndrome of beliefs cuts across religions, even those professing to believe in a unique High God. To wit: as Ludwig Blau writes in the Jewish Encyclopedia Vol. V, p. 280):

> Children are especially susceptible to the influence of the evil eye. On account of their beauty they arouse the envy of the mothers of other children, who cast upon them their evil glances; but "wise women understand how to counteract the influence which such glances may exert." . . . "Whoever is on the point of entering a city and is afraid of the evil Eye, should stick his right thumb in his left hand and his left thumb in his right hand; . . . the gesture rests on the heathenish notion that obscene gestures protect against the evil eye."

Blau tells us that red is a protective color, although his explanation of the origin is doubtful. A student of Blau, Raphael Patai, points to the importance of the color blue.[28]

The Evil Eye in Northern and Central Europe

There is tendency to identify the Evil Eye with the Mediterranean and the Middle East, and of course it is indeed rather obvious there, whereas it is more discreet in northern countries. The literature on the British Isles certainly leaves one with the impression that the Evil Eye was prevalent in Scotland, but, in fact, it may have been as widespread in the rest of the Islands. It is probably still extant in England and certainly was so at the end of the nineteenth century. Elworthy, who was from Somerset in Southwestern England, tells us in the preface to his book on the Evil Eye (p. vii):

> Long ago while noting the peculiarities of my native dialect I became fully aware that the belief in a personal evil influence was not only prevalent but almost universal. Familiarity with the modes of thought of country-folk convinced me that every obscure ailment and every unaccountable misfortune was habitually considered to be a "wisht thing." At the same time I have known, since I can remember, one or more persons whose business it was to discover the witch, or, in other words, the possessor of the evil eye.

A case is cited by Ruth St. Leger-Gordon whose uncle, a parson, had "the gift" of curing warts, adderbites and ringworms. His talent was related to the Evil Eye. The author discusses it in a chapter under that title, and in keeping with other Evil Eye healers, "he refused to discuss the subject. In his own words, he felt that should he do so 'the virtue would leave him'" (St. Leger-Gordon, p. 154). The case is interesting, not only because it is comparable to Buonanno's quotation cited earlier, but also because he is a male healer and, as in the Greek case, a minister of the faith. By far, the most interesting fetishes against the Evil Eye in the British Isles, particularly in Ireland, are the sheela-na-gigs discussed in a later chapter.

A belief in the Evil Eye occurs also in continental Europe. Mircea Eliade, quoting Rantasalo, says that "in Finland and Estonia, they used sometimes to sow at night, naked, saying softly: 'Lord, I am naked! Bless my flax!' The object certainly to make the crop thrive, but also to protect it against the evil eye or the depradation of rabbits."[29]

These naked activities against the Evil Eye are also characteristic of Germany and India. Vuorela reports that Finn peasants paint what he interprets as a "hawk" figure above their barn doors for protection against the Evil Eye (fig. 23.4). The figure is easily recognizable as a Parturient Woman symbol (see the Chapter by that title).[30] The hex signs of the Pennsylvania Dutch served the same purpose.

The Evil Eye in Spain

One of the names of the Evil Eye in Spanish is a contraction: *aojo*, whose etymology seems to include the meaning of "eye-shaped." It is interesting to note that Luciano Castañon's report on the "mal de ojo" (another name for the Evil Eye) includes a rare but true observation, namely that the Evil Eye is always singular: "se cree que el mal de ojo, productor del aojamiento, esta solamente en un ojo, y no en los dos." (It is believed that the Evil Eye, the cause of fascination, resides in one eye only, never in both. [My translation].)[31]

Although the Evil Eye, as a cultural form, certainly existed before the Islamic occupation of Spain, the Evil Eye beliefs were influenced by the Muslim occupation. This is manifested mostly in the talismans which often feature a crescent with its points down, that is to say an Omega shape called by Hildburgh "lunar crescents." He says:

> The simplest form of lunar crescent in these compound fig-hands of jet is perhaps that shown in Pl.D, 12, which is little more than a sketchy face cut in the edge of the palm. The amulet which embodies it is, however, of considerable interest to us, in that its "wrist" portion is constituted of four small open-hands, because the open hand (the European-styled "Hand of Fatima") was in Moslem Spain a device having just such prophylactic virtues as were attributed by Christian Spain to the fig-hand, both long previously and subsequently, as in Roman Spain and in Italy itself.[32]

Nevertheless, the most frequent amulet (and therefore the one considered as the most effective) in Spain is a hand in the "fig" display carved in jet. As elsewhere the symbols are piled up on the amulet, as if there could never be enough of them: not only is black the color considered effective against the Evil Eye, as it is in India, but jet itself is apotropaic. As it exists now, the Evil Eye in Spain, as in other Christian countries, has adapted to its religious environment, especially by including God and the saints in the various curing invocations.

The Evil Eye in Africa

Although they exist in Africa South of the Sahara, the cluster of beliefs and practices associated with the Evil Eye is not always called "the Evil Eye" by the indigenous populations. In Ethiopia, for instance, among the Amhara and the Galla, it is called "buda." Buda does not properly mean evil eye, it refers to people who have the Evil Eye, although the buda syndrome has all the characteristics of the Evil Eye. The concept of buda, one might say, is a cross between the concept of the Evil Eye and the concept of witch. It merits an analysis of its own. Figure 37.1 is a photograph taken in the Province of Arussi in Ethiopia, where the Arussi Galla protect themselves by displaying the pudenda of ritually sacrificed cows stretched on a frame and planted on top of long poles at crossroads. The fact is recorded also by Waterman among the "arabs" of North Africa, where it is said to protect against the Evil Eye.[33]

Among the Nyakyusa, those beliefs associated with "The Breath of Men" are also those of the Evil Eye.[34] There are strong indications that the Evil Eye belief system is present among the Nyansongo of Kenya. Robert and Barbara LeVine report that those susceptible to the Evil Eye are children, light-skinned adults and animals, and trees with red flowers. (Light-skinned adults are likely to be women and "light-skinned" animals are likely to be domestic.)[35] Although the Reverend D. S. Oyler reports on the Evil Eye among the Shilluk of the Sudan, the syndrome as described by him seems to have more in common with witchcraft. Oyler himself speaks of "the Evil Eye," and well he should since the concept of witchcraft and of Evil Eye are related, but there is no indication in his article as to whether the Shilluk themselves use the symbolism of "eye" in dealing with this "power." The Evil Eye is reported by Burton among the Wamrima and the Swahili, although in both cases it may have been a custom imported by the Arabs, as it may have been in all the areas of Africa where the syndrome exists and the symbolism of the eye is used.[36]

The Evil Eye in India

William Crooke (1968) says that "few natives care to speak about it except in a furtive way" (p. 1). This may be true under certain circumstances, but it may not be the general rule. People in the ruling castes, like people in the upper classes everywhere, are secretive and jealous of their prerogatives. They are notoriously difficult to interview. They may be the ones about whom William Crooke is speaking. According to John B. Roberts, the people he contacted, particularly among the lower castes, were quite willing to speak of the relationship between the Evil Eye and productivity. Belief in the Evil Eye in India is part of everyday life among the common people in the cities as well as in the countryside. He reports from the field: "Varanasi is oozing with layer upon layer of fertility symbols. The Indians recognize these symbols as fertility symbols and readily admit so. They also freely admit that these symbols are for good luck, and to protect against the eye."[37] He informs us that in the city of Varanasi people adorn their persons and their buildings with a great number and variety of protective amulets, some of which are illustrated in figures 2 & 4. As in the European Middle Ages (and less conspicuously later), Indian merchants have a great concern to protect their profits from the Evil Eye. Whereas the European merchants put a sprig of rue in their money boxes, or craftsmen stamped a fertility symbol (such as a cross, an ox-head, a heart, an oval, a double-tailed mermaid, a fish, etc.,) on the product of their craft, so do the Varanasi merchants frame the entrances to their shops with garlands of peppers-with-lime and protective mango leaves. Women, who here as elsewhere are the primary repositories of Evil Eye lore, decorate their own eyes and their children's with black eye-liner, not as cosmetics, but to protect themselves against either receiving or unwittingly casting the curse of the Evil Eye (see fig. 5.1). The pundits (religious practitioners), however, have taken over the ritual healing process from the women to an extent greater than have the priests in Greece. Like the priests, they perform ceremonies that are solemn, complicated and tantamount to exorcism.[38] Entire temples specialize in the curing of afflictions attributed to the Evil Eye. John B. Roberts reports that for several months, he lived next door to such a temple. The local practitioners run what is comparable to a health-care program which includes not only the ritual curing of their patients, but the prevention of malignant attacks that they believe are caused by the Evil Eye. The rituals by the pundits are combined with the fertility symbolism of lingam and yoni representing the fertility aspect of god and goddess respectively. The sexual imagery is clear and abundant. Mulk Raj Anand says of the philosophical basis of Hindu erotic sculptures: "The union of male and female became the symbol from the earliest times, for the union of all forces, and the pleasure of the body in mating became, under accepted religious and social forms, linked with the sanctity of procreation and an end in itself."[39]

The lingam (the symbol for the male component of fertility) and yoni (the symbol for the female component of fertility) together represent life and prosperity and are the heart of the sanctuary in Hindu temples. They are usually carved in stone and they come in various forms, sometimes stylized, but often quite realistic. The linguam is inside the yoni. There are continual ablutions of the altar piece. Even when no one is tending it, a container drops a liquid on the lingam-yoni sacred object (fig. 6.1). The symbolism is much more frankly erotic than anywhere else. The "third eye" (tilak) of the god Siva is very likely to have originated in the same yoni imagery as that of the Evil Eye, as is suggested by the fact that in the myths Siva agreed to "marry" a certain goddess in return for the gift of her "third eye." It is useful to remember also that in Hindu theology all gods and goddesses are merely different manifestations of the single deity who, in the final analysis, represents the exaltation of life and fertility (see *Hinduism and Fertility*—Chapter XIII).

Peacock feathers are often used in the ritual cures against the Evil Eye. When they are used for that purpose, they are gathered together in a phallic bunch and are topped by the kteic "eye" characteristic of the peacock feather (fig. 7.1). A great abundance of bells appear in temples and at the entrance of houses. They are, as they were in ancient Rome, fertility symbols and as such they are apotropaic.

But again, ritual exorcism is still principally in the hands of the women, particularly outside the cities. As in Greece therefore, one will find life symbols, such as that of the Parturient Woman, on house walls or libation vases (fig. 23.2 and 19.2). These are placed there by women fulfilling their traditional role of warding off the Evil Eye. William Crooke says in speaking of India (p. 2): "walking about villages, you will constantly see special marks on houses, and symbols and devices of various kinds, which are certainly intended to counteract it [the Evil Eye]." At weddings, "obscene" dances may be performed (Crooke, p. 8), or there are "prostitutes" hired to accommodate the males of the bride's family. All this is done in the name of insuring fecundity and prosperity in the new union.

Chapter III

The Evil Eye in Literature and Scholarship

The earliest known reference to the Evil Eye, dates from the 3rd millennium B.C. in Sumer.[40] E. A. Wallis Budge says that the Sumerian texts "form the base of later Babylonian and Assyrian Literature." In spite of the efforts of some scholars to find allusions to the Evil Eye in the Old Testament, the references to "an evil eye," although they are there, are sporadic. Budge refers us to quotations in the Bible:

> The Hebrews were well acquainted with the Evil Eye and its dire effects, but it is clearly referred to in such passages as Deut. xv. 9, and Ps. cxli. 4. On the other hand we have: "eat not the bread of him that is evil of eye (*r'a 'ayin*), neither crave thou his dainty meats" (Prov. xxiii. 6). Still more direct allusions to the Evil Eye are found in the *Wisdom of Solomon*, "for the bewitching of naughtiness doth obscure things that are honest" (iv. 12), and in Ecclesiasticus xiv. 8, where the Greek has πονηρὸς ὁ Βασκανίων ὀΦθαλμῶ.[41]

Jewish folk tradition and rabbinical literature, on the other hand, are very rich in references to the Evil Eye, in tales about it, and in discussions of statements of belief in the Evil Eye. The Midrashic documents even have a reference, found nowhere else, to a Good Eye as a counterpart to an Evil Eye.[42] The ancient worlds of Egypt, Greece and Rome carried on the tradition quite strongly and explicitly. The advent of Christianity did not weaken the strong feelings attached to it, although the constant efforts of the Church to eradicate the belief may eventually have obscured the basic rationale behind it.

It is impossible to review here the entire body of literature concerning the Evil Eye and I shall not attempt to do so, but for a quick overview of the literature, refer to Dundes who devotes several pages to listing and commenting on the pertinent authors.[43] I shall single out only a few works as being either basic, or more recent efforts at unravelling some of the problems raised by the Evil Eye. The first of my choice is a treatise published by Johann Christian Frommann in 1675. It is an enormous compilation of 1067 numbered pages, plus a two-page epilogue, a 43-page index and 3 pages of errata, written in medieval Latin by a monk bent upon destroying the "sinful" vulgarities which were part of folk belief. It was part of the Church's attempts to extirpate once and for all what was left of fertility rituals such as the Feast of Fools (or of the Asses), the "mummers," the cults of phallic and kteic saints, or the remnants of the cult of Diana as a "fertility goddess" still in existence among the peasants of Renaissance Europe, and still in evidence today in the language of the Swiss Romands.[44] The book is important as much for its intentions as for its contents.

Among other later works of substance we might mention Otto Jahn (1855), whose treatise was, according to Dundes, the first by a scholar whose motivation was intellectual curiosity. He was a proponent of the gaze theory. He held that a glance from the eye was to be treated in the same manner as other "emanations" such as bodily odor, breath, speech and presence.[45]

Frederick Elworthy (1895) is notable for his erudition and for his insights. He certainly sensed the breadth and depth of meaning of the Evil Eye and remains one of the most interesting authority on the subject. Siegfried Seligman (1910) has a great abundance of data.[46] It is perplexing that these many authors noted the fact that the rituals, the ritual language and the prophylactics against the Evil Eye (apotropaics) were "obscene" in character without, for all that, coming to the conclusion that the Evil Eye is associated with fertility. They skirt the issue. For instance, Elworthy and Inman, two Victorians who wrote on the Evil Eye and on ancient symbolism respectively, tiptoe gingerly through a forest of what they seem to have considered prurient vulgarities.[47] Elworthy, after warning us that there are things about the Evil Eye that he cannot report in detail if his book is to be read by all members of the family, says in a footnote on p. 16: "Frommannd [sic] also gives an account of the fescinnine songs (fescennini versus) which were most unchaste and lascivious, and were sung at weddings in the belief that they would avert the evil eye. It was usual to interpolate the most disgraceful and obscene expressions, thinking that the more abominable these were, the more certain in effect. Nemesis, Cunina, and Priapus were all invoked in these licentious songs."

More recently, Jean Marcadé, writing from the point of view of art history, has a very comprehensive view of the symbolism used by the ancient Romans and the ancient Greeks. He says: "Obscenity—crude, outright obscenity that made one laugh and look away—was a powerful defense against the evil eye: anything concerning sex and copulation, anything representing the male or female sexual organs." (Marcadé, 1961, p. 26). He states that these symbolic defenses were present in the fields, in the workplaces, and on the battlefield as well as at home where they protected house, food, properties and bed chamber. Marcadé attributes the symbolism to the obsession of the Romans with magic, the Evil Eye being part of that "magic." He thinks, therefore, that the symbols protected against magic in general and more particularly against the magic induced by the envy of others. But, he says, "It is less clear why sexual imagery should have been considered the most effective protection against magic" (1961, p. 33). Marcadé, in spite of his remarkable perspicacity, is left with the same theoretical interpretation, and therefore, with the same questions, as most other student of the Evil Eye.

In the end, these authors offer no encompassing theory to account for the existence of the Evil Eye complex of beliefs as a cultural phenomenon. They confine themselves to descriptions of what they seem to have considered odd customs, or at best they speculate on the effects of envy for its own sake, or express the opinion that those who believe in the Evil Eye also believe in the power of a hostile gaze.

Two recent books by anthropologists attempting to explain the Evil Eye are collections of essays, one edited by Clarence Maloney (1976),[48] the other by Alan Dundes (1981).[49] Brian Spooner, in "Concluding Essay I," in the former book, recognizes that the authors of the collection are only (in the words of Hocart) adding "instances to instances." In the latter book, Dundes recognizes the abundance of the literature on the subject, but, he says quite accurately: "By far the majority of discussions of the Evil Eye represents anecdotal reporting of the phenomenon in a single cultural context, often without reference to the occurrence of the same or similar phenomena elsewhere."

Spooner goes over the various attempts at theoretical explanation and classifies them roughly as diffusionist, functional and psychological. He concludes that none is entirely satisfactory. He ends his presentation with one short question which states the real problem left if one is to use these approaches: "Why the Evil Eye?," meaning, fundamentally, why an *eye*? A second "Concluding Essay II" in Maloney, written by Garrison and Arensberg, deals strictly with psychological universals, leaving us no further advanced than before because a psychological explanation accounts only for the occurrence of the phenomenon in individuals now, but it does not explain why it has lasted, culturally, for 5,000 years over such a wide area. Some who favor psychological approaches will say that culture consists of psychological universals. I disagree, for many reasons, but if only for the fact that we cannot presume that what we identify as psychological universals today are applicable to pre-history. To give an extreme example, Michael Carroll, a Kleinian theorist, has suggested that the obsession with the eye depended upon the child's obsession with the female nipple during the period of breast-feeding. This implies, of course, first, that the nipple looks like an eye to the theorist who then transfers his own impressions to "the child;" in my opinion, it is frivolous to suggest that the psychology of one contemporary individual is generally applicable, 5,000 years ago; not that it is impossible, but it is, to say the least, unprovable.[50] But more to the point, there are no instances in the ethnographic literature of nipples being assimilated to eyes. An inference therefore is unjustifiable. Dundes, on the other hand, calls his concluding essay a psycho-cultural explanation, which in the end, although it is very erudite and insightful, turns out to be based on a combination of freudian psychology and Levi-Straussian binary opposition theory, which, again, for all its interest, does not explain all of the numerous dimensions of the Evil Eye system of belief, nor does it explain origins. Neither Spooner nor Dundes claim to have the definitive solution. They have made contributions to the theories of envy or gazing, and perhaps more. But the fact remains that their interpretations explain only some narrow aspects of the Evil Eye lore.

Michael Herzfeld (1981), who wrote after Malone's publication but before Dundes,' has made a real contribution in suggesting a semiotic approach, that is a theory of signs and symbols. The Evil Eye after all *is* a symbol and its meaning needs to be scrutinized. What Herzfeld makes of it is another matter, which I need not discuss here since he addresses the personal local perceptions of destiny and character and suggests how these need not have an Evil Eye etiology in spite of the fact that an Evil Eye vocabulary is used. The semiotic question in this book is different. My question addresses the broad cultural origins of such a widespread symbol as that of the *eye* (why an eye?) and what has made the use of such a symbol persist for such a long time and over such a wide area. I am concerned with the function it fulfills in a particular community only in so far as this sheds light on the ultimate problem.

Anthony Galt (1982), like Herzfeld, seems also to have published before he read Dundes (1981). His greatest contribution is an excellent critical analysis of the contributions made by Roberts, Spooner, Arensberg & Garrison (in Malone 1976), and Herzfeld. His own attempt to understand the Evil Eye is based on a model proposed by Rodney Needham called *synthetic models*. He denies that synthetic models are another name for Jung's *archetypes*, but it is difficult not to make the comparison. He would rather compare the synthetic models (and hence, the Evil Eye) to a general theme in jazz music, upon which individual variations are played. The result is, as he says, that while "such [synthetic] images probably cannot be ascribed universal meaning, functions, or causal explanations, they do serve as symbolic frames, or boxes, which can be filled with local and even individual meanings" (p. 664). But again, Galt's question regarding the material is not our question, so that whether he answers his own question or not, he certainly does not answer ours.

A recent book (1983) by Toby Siebers, *The Mirror of Medusa*, is based, like all others, on the contemporary literal interpretation of the folk belief of gaze and glance. That is, the premise is that people believe in a literal "emanation" (his word) from the eye. Siebers chooses to present the case from "the perspective of the individual accused of the evil eye or narcissism." He sees the caster as victim. Furthermore, it is a freudian psycho-analysis with overtones of Jung's archetypes, although Jung is never mentioned in the text. He may or may not be right in saying that anthropologists' observations are biased, but Siebers' work remains an analysis of the Evil Eye as a personal reaction, albeit in a social context, but a personal phenomenon nevertheless.[51] Among other things, he equates the Evil Eye with narcissism, with the head of the Medusa and with superstition as a personal belief. Siebers, like so many others, takes the symbolism of "the Eye" literally: to wit, his sub-title: *The Underside of Vision*. The "vision" aspect, as would be expected, is also stressed by most professional ophthalmologists who have taken an interest in the "power of vision." A. Potts, who wrote *The World's Eye* is an example.

Finally, there is another work which, for purposes of this book, needs to be singled out. It is not on the Evil Eye proper, but it must be mentioned because it bears upon the interpretation offered here. That is,

Richard Payne Knight's *A Discourse on the Worship of Priapus and its Connection with the Mystic Theology of the Ancients*. Knight, born in 1750, was a member of the British Parliament and a scholar of many talents and interests. Among his preoccupations, as with many members of his class at that time, were the literature and mythologies of the Ancients. He was particularly interested in their fertility rituals and how they had persisted into the modern era. With the intellectual curiosity of a good scholar, and with the idea of scrutinizing the religions of our predecessors, Knight published his book in 1786, in which he analyzes in detail the beliefs and rituals pertaining to his subject. The book included graphic descriptions of sexual symbols and their meaning. Although published in a limited edition, it created a scandal. Knight immediately withdrew the book from circulation by recalling all the copies he could find, not out of prudery but rather because as a politician he was sensitive to public opinion. Significantly, the initial edition was prefaced with "*An Account of the Remains of the Worship of Priapus, lately Existing at Isernia in the Kingdom of Naples: in Two Letters.*" The first letter, dated 1781, written by Sir William Hamilton and addressed to Sir Joseph Banks, suggests that there may be a link between the numerous amulets against the Evil Eye and the cult of Priapus.

> I had long ago discovered, that the women and children of the lower class, at Naples, and in its neighbourhood frequently wore, as an ornament of dress, a sort of Amulets, (which they imagine to be a preservative for the *mal ochii*, *evil eyes*, or enchantment) exactly similar to those which were worn by the ancient Inhabitants of the country for the very same purpose, as likewise for their supposed invigorating influence; and all of which have evidently a relation to the cult of Priapus. . . . The modern Amulet most in vogue represents a hand clinched, with the point of the thumb thrust betwixt the index and the middle finger; . . . . We have a proof of the hand above described having a connection with Priapus, in a most elegant small idol of bronze of that Divinity, now in the Museum of Portici, and which was found in the ruins of Herculaneum: it has an enormous phallus, and, with an arch look and gesture, stretches out its right hand in the form above mentioned; and which probably was an emblem of consummation: and as a further proof of it, the Amulet which occur most frequently amongst those of the Ancients (next to that which represents the simple Priapus), is such a hand united with the Phallus.[52]

The second letter is by "a person residing at Isernia" describing the cult of the two curing phallic saints, Cosmos and Damien, to whose sanctuary in Isernia, those afflicted with sterility brought ex votos of waxen *phalloi* (and probably of *ktenes* also, although these are not mentioned in

Knight). To replace the phallos, the Christian clerics had devised the idea of having their faithfuls refer to Saint Cosmos' "Big Toe." But by 1780, although the pilgrimages still occurred, and perhaps because the faithful were still treating the euphemic "big toe" for what it was, the letter suggests that the priests were trying to suppress the rituals and the ex voto. Elworthy adds in a footnote on page 306 that "the sale of the objectionable *membri* was prohibited by the Government in 1780."

Knight's work was not published again until 1865, when it was issued by the publisher John Camden Hotten who, in collaboration with Thomas Wright, added an essay by the latter: *On the Worship of the Generative Powers During the Middle Ages of Western Europe*.[53] By then, however, the well-informed world, had become aware of the obsession of the ancients with reproduction and its "worship," through new archaeological discoveries and scholarship in general. Jacques Antoine Dulaure, for instance, had published his *Des Divinités Génératrices, ou Du Culte du Phallus Chez les Anciens et les Modernes*, in 1805.[54] This book, and its 1825 edition, had been read by Wright. It seems probable that Wright had discovered Knight through reading Dulaure. In 1934, when Dulaure's book was published in the United States by Panurge Press, under the title of *The Gods of Generation*, the prudery of the time was still such that the translator and editor, Adolf Frederick Niemoeller, identified himself only by his initials: A.F.N., and the edition was limited to 2,000 copies destined to collectors of erotica.[55] Although still controversial, the publication of such material had become more acceptable.

A predecessor of Knight, the great classical scholar and archaeologist, Johann Joachim Winckelmann (1717-1768), had dug at Pompeii. Being of his time, he had thought that the phalloi at the entrance of houses, were hallmarks for houses of prostitution. This error was perpetuated through the 19th Century and beginning of the 20th. As late as 1926, for instance, Paul Hans Brandt (alias Hans Licht) describes the houses as bordellos.[56] Marcadé in 1961 still feels the need to "correct" the impression that Pompeii was full of brothels. The new scholarship, however, had already revealed that the Pompeiian phalloi were really protective symbols which, for ages, had been customarily set out at the entrances of Roman homes to protect the inhabitants against the Evil Eye.

Other Works on Generation and Fertility.

As for the literature on fertility cults, given the timidity of scholars and the prevailing prudery of the churches, the great number of works on that and related topics, is surprising. Following Knight's ill-received publication, and with the development of an evolutionary perspective during the 19th century, there arose among scholars an interest in the origins of everything involving human beings. A spate of books were written speculating on the "stages" of progress in the development of religion which, it was deemed, included a period of "primitive sex worship." The efforts of great scholars in the development of religion are well-known and only their name need be mentioned: Weber, Durkheim, Lange, Müller, Westermark, Fraser, Tylor, Schmidt, Marett, Forlong, not to mention the indirect contributions by Freud and Lévy-Bruhl and others. Their works brought the attention of the reading public to the frequency of fertility rituals in the ethnography of the world and their similarity with those of classic antiquity. Clerics who for centuries had ignored the grotesques sexual carvings in Romanesque churches in Europe, suddenly took notice of them; they were scandalized but had a difficult time trying to uproot the underlying cult of these statues. Accounts of the fertility rituals of India, Nepal and South-East Asia, and descriptions of the ancient monumental carvings portraying explicit sexual encounters were discreetly published during and because of the occupation of these areas by the British and the French.

Folklore and "popular tradition" journals collected descriptions of "odd" fertility rituals not only in the non-European world, but often in Europe outside of the big cities, particularly as they were seen as remnants of very ancient customs. Some journals were even created as source books for the convenience of "the curious": such was the French publication, *L'intermédiaire des chercheurs et curieux*. All this produced, at the end of the 19th century, a flood of books, anthologies, articles and chapters on "phallicism," "nature worship," "mother goddesses," "temple prostitution," "ritual coitus," "sex worship," some published anonymously or hiding their identity under a pseudonym. An example of this is Abisha S. Hudson who published first anonymously under the title of *Ancient Sex Worship* and then with the pseudonym of Sha Rocco under the title of *The Masculine Cross and Ancient Sex Worship*.

Books were plagiarized: Sanger Brown's from Richard Payne Knight and Robert Allan Campbell's from Antoine Dulaure. Some were purely descriptive (Bourke, John Gregory. *Scatologic Rites of all Nations*,

1891.) There were authors whose thesis was that sex and love is the basis of life and of the development of religion. (Gamble, Eliza Burt: *The God-Idea of the Ancients or Sex in Religion*, 1897. Wall, Otto Augustus: *Sex and Sex-Worship*, London, 1904. Westropp, Hodder M.: *Primitive Symbolism as Illustrated in Phallic Worship or The Reproductive Principle*, 1885.) There were others, and the interest in sex as religious ritual continued into the 20th century. This latter-day "Renaissance" provided a flood of information which still needs to be synthesized. It also did produce a hodge-podge of interpretations which has to be sorted out, and the whole related to other fundamental human beliefs.

THE EVIL EYE

PART TWO

A NEW LOOK AT THE EVIL EYE

Chapter IV

Introduction to Part II

The attempts that have been made to formulate a theory of the Evil Eye have explained some aspects of the belief system, but not all; some have explained nothing, and none has given a comprehensive explanation. Yet, because of the regularity and the frequency with which the same customs, the same rituals, the same gestures, the same symbols, the same associations, the same beliefs occur together in the Evil Eye complex, wherever the syndrome exists, one is strongly tempted to look for a bond between them. When we consider these similarities and regularities, we find that, *independently of present-day folk perceptions*, there are certain ideas and concerns that characterize the Evil Eye: sexuality, fertility, productivity, prosperity and luck.

It seems reasonable to suppose that there must be a structural reason which has caused so many highly diverse peoples to retain the customs and the symbols of the Evil Eye for such a long time. It is also reasonable to suppose that, through the centuries, the original meaning of the symbols has been weakened or distorted, as is suggested by LaBarre's term, "archoses,"[57] so that only a certain feeling of "luck" or "protection" has been retained, as is suggested by Hocart. In other words, the Evil Eye is a cultural configuration that, over the millennia, has lingered in the "collective unconscious" of peoples who, because of evolving cultural perceptions, have come to distort the original meaning of the configuration, but without being able to rid themselves of the absurdities that they may have collectively created in the process of change. A. M. Hocart said of it: "The evil eye is known to us mainly, if not solely, as a survival; in other words, the theory has disappeared and only emotional associations remain to give it vitality."[58] To paraphrase Hocart: there may have been a time when the primordial objectives of the Evil Eye were clear in everybody's minds, but with time and changes, the original meaning faded away, and only the strong feelings associated with the initial symbolism have remained without anyone being able to account for them except through *post facto* rationalization. More specifically, the symbolism of the eye has been lost and *only a literal interpretation of the word "eye" remains*. I shall suggest that the original eye-symbol had a powerful and universal referent with a highly-charged emotional content. That referent is *fertility*, that is: *there is strong evidence that the customs related to a belief in the Evil Eye have their roots in pervasive prehistoric and protohistoric fertility rituals concerned with production and reproduction. The sexual symbolism is derived from this source.*

Indeed, a concern with fertility was the dominant feature of the belief-system of small-scale societies, as we can easily appreciate when we think that in early societies sheer survival depended on it. People in simple subsistence societies have an exquisite consciousness of the intimate relationship that exists between all things and all beings.[59] They stand in awe of the mysterious natural forces of which they are a part. They have a vivid consciousness of the fact that *no force of nature is greater than the forces of production and reproduction, and of the fact that human beings partake of that force*. Production and reproduction are viewed as two inseparable aspects of the same thing. Reproduction is the life-force that guarantees production. Production and reproduction are the beginning and the end of everything. To be sure, Nature is awesome and there are so many unpredictables that it causes people to agonize over the uncertain fertility of the environment. The capacity of the forest, of the sea, of the lakes and rivers, of the fields, of animals (including humans) to produce and reproduce is impressive and people try to control it. Survival is directly dependent on production and reproduction. And since people in simple subsistence societies can no more conceive of the "ownership" of land than we can conceive of the "ownership" of the air we breathe, they value life and fertility above anything that might be called "property." Fertility is the nexus that links people to nature and to each other. That is, to those who have a holistic view of reality, fecundity, fruitfulness means survival. If the plants, the forest, the animals (including humans), are to subsist and survive, they have to reproduce. We, in the modern world of industrial state societies, are so far removed from Nature that we cannot always grasp the depths of the natural beliefs of peoples who live at the subsistence level. It is difficult to empathize with the profound intensity of the feelings that they have towards the critical need for fecundity, which is identified by them with production and survival. This makes reproduction not only desirable but imperative. It is encouraged, sacralized; it is considered the core of life, and becomes an obsession. Prosperity, abundance, welfare and the continuation of life itself are directly related to fertility. To convey this paramount concern, a deliberate effort has been made in this book to explore the worldview of people living in simple subsistence-oriented societies. This does not mean that only people in pre-industrial societies believe in the Evil Eye, but it does mean that if we are to understand the persistence of such a system of beliefs, it behooves us to grasp first the cognitive context within which this remarkable phenomenon came to develop. That context includes the concept of *mana*, which will be the subject of our next chapters.

Chapter V

Worldview:

The World of Mana and the Evil Eye

Background for The Evil Eye

A great deal of work has been done by anthropologists since the turn of the century among people who live under conditions remote from modern science and from the belief system of industrial society (see Appendix I). It is into this mass of ethnographic data that we have to dip in order to be able to interpret the concrete information gathered by archaeologists. Our knowledge of prehistory is inevitably based upon inference from ethnography. Some will question this but, in fact, anything else leaves us with nothing but purely speculative and imaginary reconstruction. Not that interpretations based on inference need no imagination, they do, but at least inference provides a footing in empirical reality, as it does in geology for instance. If our ethnographic explications change, so then will our interpretations of prehistory. This point is rather important for what is going to follow because my interpretation of prehistory is going to be dependent upon the fact that I shall also re-interpret some ethnographic material.

Mana as Part of the Natural World

If we try, for a moment, to mentally situate ourselves in the place of foragers or incipient agriculturalists roaming the forests and valleys of Central Europe some 10,000 or 20,000 years ago, or for that matter, if we try to empathize with peoples living in a natural environment today, using a rudimentary technology, we have to think of communities made up of only a few people who are related to each other by personal ties. The character of the links they have to each other is governed by feelings of personal obligation, and has nothing to do with the fact that individuals may, or may not, be related biologically. There is no impersonal law to interfere from outside the group, since the group is perceived to be the entire society. Everyone's survival depends upon the willingness of each individual to share the available resources with the other members of the group. These resources are perceived as part of the natural world. In such a world, people think of themselves as an integral part of nature and do not think of themselves as different in essence from the plants that they gather or the animals they hunt. The idea that humans are part of a special creation and that the rest of nature was "given" and subordinated to them is inconceivable. They view the forces of Nature as inevitable and indivisible.

To them, one of the characteristics of nature is that it is permeated with *mana* (see Appendix II). The word is from a Melanesian language, but it is used generically by anthropologists who have found that the concept, or one like it, is widespread in small-scale subsistence and quasi-subsistence societies. When the concept was discovered by western European scholars in the 19th century, it was considered an alien view of the world. It was widely debated, not with full understanding, but with enough insights so that an idea of what mana is can actually be formed from reading the reports. In the 19th century, Max Müller, the author of *Lectures on the Origin and Growth of Religion*, for example, wrote a lengthy essay on mana in a chapter on what he calls "fetishism." In it, he quotes from his correspondence with R. H. Codrington, a British missionary who was the first to introduce the concept to western scholarship who says that among Melanesians: "There is a belief in a force altogether distinct from physical power, which acts in all kinds of ways for good and evil, and which it is of the greatest advantage to possess or control. This is Mana" (Codrington, quoted in Max Muller, p. 51). By now, anthropologists have come to some agreement on the definition of mana. In the following description of mana, however, I am going to expand the definition a bit, so that it be more comprehensive. It has been customary to translate it as "power," but the notion is closer to the concept of energy in physics. Mana resides in everything: people, animals, plants, inanimate objects, natural events such as a storm, the sea or the forest, activities such as the act of procreation, the seeding of the fields, a position in a social structure, and the social structure itself; mana is also present in all human emotions love, anger, joy, fright, anticipation, envy, all partake of mana. The idea of mana is impersonal and existential; that is, like the rest of the Universe, it is just there and is not a reflection of anything else. No question is asked about its origin.

It is simply part of reality. The amount or the degree of power possessed depends upon circumstances, the many permutations of which result in differences in power. Individuals have their own mana, but so has the family in general. A particular tree in the forest has mana and so has the forest as a whole.

Mary Douglas has written an essay called "Heathen Darkness" in which she argues that, contrary to common understanding, so called primitives are not obsessed with the supernatural. Their perception of the "natural" extends to all the forces contained in the notion of mana. Murray and Rosalie Wax, speaking of magic, which, after all, is an aspect of mana, have said:

> We Westerners tend to see Power as referring to something awesome and wonderful, like a miracle, involving a force superior or contrary to the "laws of Nature." Viewed by a person in the Magical World, Power is awesome and wonderful, but at the same time, it is an intrinsic feature of the natural order. . . . Thus, any activity of note or worth can only occur because of it. A bountiful harvest, a successful hunt, a healthy birth—these and countless other activities and accomplishments of living are predicated on the possession of Power. Conversely, those individuals or peoples who fail in their activities and suffer misfortunes, lack Power.[60]

However, because the concept is not part of what Mary Douglas calls "our traditional set of distinctions,"[61] we interpret other people's idea of the *forces of nature* in terms of our own worldview, which includes hierarchies, gods, kings, souls, private entrepreneurs and a sense of the "personal" that is peculiar to us. As a result we think that these "primitive" peoples are speaking of "the *spirit* of the forest" or "the *goddess* of fertility," or "household *gods*," whereas we would be closer to their conceptualization if we spoke of the "mana of the forest," the "mana of fertility" or the "mana of the family." The mana of gestures, the mana of language, the mana of events, the mana of personalities and circumstances, the mana of witchcraft and of life and death are all of the same nature. Those things interpreted by scholars as "ancestor worship," the "High God," "witchcraft," "fertility cults," etc., are simply various manifestations of interacting "mana."

Viewed in this way, the manner of thought or people living in small scale societies becomes accessible to our intellect. If anything partakes of mana, the Evil Eye does, and its study must be placed in the context of a study of mana. Like mana, surely the Evil Eye is power, a tyrannical and mysterious power perhaps, but power nevertheless. It is because of the widespread belief in the existence of some impersonal and imponderable force influencing the fate of people, in other words, a belief in mana, that it is possible to explain the link between the concept of mana, the concept of envy and the Evil Eye. The concept of envy is an integral part of the system of beliefs of the Evil Eye.

The Mana of Words, Thoughts and Actions

The same principle of mana or power applies to witchcraft, to divination, to the "breath of men."[62] The last, like the others, is a particular manifestation of mana. It was described among the Nyakyusa by the Wilsons, but the concept is similar in Rwanda and elsewhere although it appears under other names. The term used here is only the literal translation by the Wilsons of the Nyakyusa phrase: *embeyo sya bandu*. One does not speak evil of others because the mana of words will hurt the person spoken of and—by the same token—hurt the person uttering the evil. The reverse is true also. One who speaks well of others will be blessed. Feelings of envy hurt. Some people are conscious of their own feelings, but others are not. The latter are all the more threatening in that they lack the awareness necessary to control their feelings.[63] They "eat" their relatives, the persons closest to them. They are witches.[64] These witches may be considered as such by most of the community but would be shocked at the thought of being considered witches. It is in that sense that individuals believed to have the Evil Eye are believed to be witches. The mana they emit is negative and general. It is also in that sense that this destructive mana—one may as well call it the Evil Eye—exuded by people who are envious, is detrimental to the prevalent well-being of the community and to the particular productive and reproductive activities of individuals. By the same token, some people have special powers such as that which controls illnesses, or the ability to interpret dreams, or that which cures by the laying of hands. These people have a great deal of mana in that they are believed to be able to cast illness as well as cure. An old woman whom I knew in Rwanda had the largest goat herd in the community because of her ability to interpret dreams. Her neighbors would come to consult her, and each gave her a goat as a sort of *ex voto*. I am sure she thought of herself as possessing a special form of mana, but, from my cultural vantage point, she was a woman of unusual perspicacity, with a great deal of experience and knowledge of the people of the community. But for her own people, she exuded real mana on a personal level.

In sum, "the breath of men" is mana also. By whatever name, it is a powerful form of social control characteristic of small-scale societies. That is, it is not much different from what we say of gossip: gossip hurts the person who is slandered, but by the same token, it hurts the person who slanders. Whatever difference there is "the Breath of Men" is a broader concept, and the belief in it is sufficient in a small scale society to keep people from disrupting cooperative relationships which must be maintained if the group is to survive. What it says in the end is that envy must be avoided at all cost. The *envy* syndrome is the same as that attached to the Evil Eye lore. It can occur with or without the symbolism of the Evil Eye.

If one does not want to be hurt by the "breath of men" or the Evil Eye the recipe is "get along with your neighbors" by avoiding negative words, thoughts or actions that might be engendered by envy. Envy among the Nyakyusa, when it occurs, is directed at precisely these things that are *produced* by the Nyakyusa, beginning with cattle and children, followed by produce from the fields and forest. And of course, the Nyakyusa have their "magic" to protect themselves, and although they are not specifically the same items as in the Evil Eye system, they are generic equivalents.

Although I shall be concentrating on simple subsistence societies, I do not mean to say that the concept of mana is absent from our own culture. It is not. We do not call it mana, but we do think in terms of good and bad luck.[65] Religion notwithstanding, we believe, by and large, that chance and hazard are part of the imponderable forces that play a role in our lives. We do try to control events by putting the onus of fortune and misfortune on the individual: "Heaven helps him who helps himself." There is a perpetual search for formulae with a quasi-magic quality, e.g.: "The Power of Positive Thinking"; "The Power of Prayer"; "How to Win Friends and Influence People." Those formulae have become institutionalized. In French, and perhaps in other Romance languages, the term *génie* (*genius* in Latin and *genio* in Italian and Spanish) has a semantic component of mana in that it refers to forms of imponderable power difficult to define otherwise: *le génie de la langue*, *le génie du travail*, *le génie de la famille*. At the risk of oversimplifying, we could say that living with the concept of mana is like living with the vague, undefinable power of "luck" only, which, being neither good nor bad in itself, must be controlled so that it will manifest only its good aspect, and not its bad side. In pre-industrial societies, the particulars may be different, but the essentials are the same, and that fact helps to account for the perpetuation of such belief-systems as the Evil Eye.

Chapter VI

Looking for mana: applications

Understanding mana and what it means is critical to an understanding of the idioms of the Evil Eye and of fertility. This cannot be overstressed. J. D. Unwin was unwittingly speaking about the Kamba concept of mana when he said that the meanings of various native concepts are not only unclear to us, but that the Kamba themselves seem to "confuse" one concept with another, whereas they may be simply be referring to different manifestations of the same mana. "That is to say, there was little difference in the Kamba mind between the conceptions which we denote by (a) the power in the universe, (b) 'the spirits of the dead.' Thus any attempt to separate them is absurd and misleading."[66] What Unwin should be saying is that those distinctions we make between the power of the Universe, ancestor worship, and fertility, are not made by people living in such cultures as that of the Kamba, or, I might add, by people in state societies living in isolated communities, as is often the case for the peasants of the Mediterranean. Unwin's "spirit of the dead" is the translation of the Kamba word "muzimu," although, more recently it has been interpreted as "nature spirits" by Nurse and Spears, who were also puzzled by its cognitive value among the Swahili.[67] When I went to Rwanda to do field work, I had accepted Elizabeth Colson's definition of the word.[68] She thought of muzimu as the spirit of the departed ancestors. When I questioned an informant one day about the whereabouts of the muzimu of the deceased head of his family, he responded that it was in the household of his brother who had inherited the headship. When, however, I tried to make a distinction between the muzimu of the deceased and his personality by asking my informant to disregard the muzimu, and to tell me where the individual was that this man had been, the answer was a simple "I don't know. He is dead." Still having "spirits" in mind, I pushed the question further. His response then, was the most revealing statement I have heard in the field: "He who has been eaten by death, has never returned to tell us what there was in her stomach." I don't know if this was his own colorful way of expressing himself, or if his response was a local conventional aphorism, but in any case, my neighbor was obviously not much concerned with life after death, and it left me with the question of what the muzimu is if it is not the "spirit of the dead"? In the end, the muzimu, like the Evil Eye, is still another manifestation of mana. In the case of this muzimu, it was the mana of an individual who had occupied during his lifetime a position of power in the social network and whose mana lingered after his death.

The concept of mana is so pervasive that we can consider the idea of a "High God," in the same light. In Rwanda, the word translated by missionaries as God, is simply the generalized verbalization of "the power," "the force" that pervades everything. In other words, it is the concept of mana in an abstract, absolute way, independent of any specific application. Missionaries, by virtue of their status and their training, believe that all humanity is descended from two particular individuals, Adam and Eve and that after they fell from grace, only a Chosen People among their descendants retained a "knowledge of God." It is the missionaries' duty, then, to look for evidence of this forgotten "knowledge of God" among those who are not heir to the traditions of the Chosen People; they look for words that, in their view, will describe the attributes of the Divinity. The words they usually find are those that answer to the above definition of "mana." Mana, indeed, in its abstract sense, is *omnipotent* since it does refer to the power that is inherent to everything. It is *infinite* and *ubiquitous*, since it is, in an abstract way, everywhere. It is *eternal*, since it has been and will be there always. If one is looking for the concept of "God," it is easy to conclude that these are the impersonal attributes of the Judeo-Christian divinity, and that if the natives do not agree that the concept in question represents a supernatural being who possesses very personal virtues of goodness, justice and compassion, it is because they are presumed to have "forgotten" the personal dimension of the High God. Max Müller, the 19th century philologist, recognized from his correspondence with the missionary, R. H. Codrington, that "the notion of a Supreme Being is altogether foreign to them."[69]

The concept of a High God, or of a Supreme Being, is not universal. Anne L. Barstow in "The Prehistoric Goddess," says, rightly:

> Our problem lies, at least in part, in the word dominance, for it is, in fact, foolish to judge this material by our common definition of power. When we

> apply the usual Western concept of centralized power or of "power over" to tribal or early urban societies, we may well be led to ask the wrong questions. Power can be seen as power with rather than power over, and it can be used for competence and cooperation, rather than dominance and control. In reflecting on the dependence on nature that prehistorical people had to contend with, it occurred to me that a cooperative use of power may have been necessary, indeed crucial, for them.[70]

She further says, in speaking of the neolithic people of Çatal Hüyük in Turkey: "In the public sphere, the usual public leadership roles appear not yet to have existed: there is no evidence of central political organization, . . ." (p. 9). If this is so, then the people had no idea of a central deity, male or female, and there were no priests and she is right in coming to the conclusion that the symbols, the rituals, were not indicative of worship of gods or goddesses: "It is rather," she says in a beautiful phrase, "a celebration of fecundity and rebirth" (p. 13). The case for a belief in, and the desire for control of, and the necessity for respecting this impersonal potency of nature is re-enforced by Joan Oates' analysis of "Religion and Ritual in Sixth-Millennium B.C. Mesopotamia." She comes to the conclusion that:

> Although some of the figurines, especially among those from Arpachiyah, may have been "charms" or purveyors of sympathetic magic in pregnancy, there is no reason to associate the vast majority of Mesopotamian figurines with any form of fertility cults, or even with child birth. We must conclude that despite some very interesting, at times even spectacular, evidence for what are certainly ritual practices, we know nothing of the "religion" behind them.[71]

That is, in view of what we know of the universal belief in the mana of nature, the figurines are simply emblematic amulets, used to manipulate what is perceived as the natural forces of nature, as they are in association with the Evil Eye. There is no belief in goddesses or gods, therefore, in that sense, there is no "cult." There is no creed in a supernatural world, only the world of nature is there and humans are part of it. As a celebration of fecundity, the reference is to the mana of fertility, which, in the context of the scale of values in a simple society, is a blessing. It is regarded as good, and ensuring survival. This brings us back to the Evil Eye, in which the "evil" is infertility. Anne Barstow's point must be stressed because fertility was certainly a concept more accessible to the minds of the early agricultural people of Çatal Hüyük and Arpachiyah than the concept of a goddess or a god, so that the portrayal of a male or a female in statuette form is not the image of a god or a goddess, but rather a representation of fertility itself. The people of Çatal Hüyük, who, like all populations of prehistory, depended directly on nature to survive, were as obsessed with their symbols of fertility as were peoples of a later time with the Eye, precisely because the eye became a symbol of fertility. Fertility—or the lack of it—was the fundamental fact of life.

The fact that "all peoples" have a cosmogony to explain their origins does not mean that they believe in a supernatural world superseding the real world. While it may be true that there are "myths of origins" everywhere, it is *our* worldview that makes them part of a theology. That is, because we have made the myths of our origins an integral part of our religious belief, we jump to the conclusion that the existence of myths of origin necessarily indicates the presence of a religion. Among peoples of stateless societies, the meddling into their lives of characters (culture heroes) from their traditional cosmogony is an unacceptable thought, because these beings have, for them, only a conceptual and etiological existence. Because of our way of thinking, our Indo-European languages usually have the concept of time built into verb conjugations. Benjamin Whorf showed how the Hopi verbs expressed a "reality" dimension versus a "non-reality," rather than a temporal dimension. Myths, therefore, in the Hopi language were referred to in the "non-reality" mode, as were those events that we would call "future." To the Hopi, the future has no reality as an event. No matter how predictable an event may be, it still has no verifiable reality because it has not occurred. In the same way, the culture heroes are part of a world that does not exist in a verifiable reality.

Chapter VII

Family, Marriage and Fertility

It would be difficult to omit a discussion of the concept of marriage and family in an essay involving human reproduction, production and fertility. When people are directly dependent on the natural environment to produce food on which to subsist, fertility is everything. It is a question of survival. That is why the control of the mana of fertility is so important. "To control mana" is the key phrase. People want to be able to control production by controlling reproduction. Institutions devised precisely for this purpose are of the type that we call the family and marriage. These two words, however, have a meaning that is culturally defined and that definition can be misleading. All human institutions, are complex and varied. It would take several volumes to address the complexities and the details. Therefore, what follows is a greatly simplified synthesis which deliberately ignores particularities. The picture drawn is meant to convey the functional dimension that is taken for granted in alien societies.

For most of the world, even today, the alien words we translate as "family" usually do not have a biological criterion in their definition. The "family" is designed to organize and regulate social, political and economic relationships. However defined, the fundamental units of organization are based upon the personal obligations people have to each other. This pragmatic way of thinking of personal ties provides the group with a flexibility that would be impossible if the groups were defined in biological terms. In that sense, there is nothing fictive about anthropologists' "fictive kinship." Individuals validate their rights through the group to which they belong.

The groups in turn are responsible for the individuals that make them up. A child does not only have a "mother" and "father" responsible for him: he has many "fathers" and many "mothers," the words being defined in terms of the obligations they have towards him or her. The "Fathers" and the "Mothers" could happen to be biologically related to the child but even then, that fact is not what defines the relationship. No matter what the circumstances, the child will be provided with affection and sustenance, not by surrogates but by people who stand in exactly the same relationship to him as the persons who may have happened to have produced him biologically, a circumstance which remains organizationally and socially fortuitous. The result is that each individual, not only has a strong feeling of belonging to his small tightly-knit group, but he also knows he can always rely upon those persons who are closest to him and who can express their own affiliations in personal terms. He never relies on any distant and impersonal relationships such as we have in a society in which the relationships are governed by law, which, by definition, is impersonal.

In turn, the small, intimate corporate group to which one belongs tries to enhance its stock of mana by making alliances with other like groups. This alliance is defined through a set of mutual obligations, one of which is usually, but not necessarily, the obligation to provide the other groups with spouses. In other words, the "marriage" consists in the bonding of two groups and not in the mating and setting up of a new household by a couple. This latter is only one result of the alliance (see Appendix III). The groups' solidarity ensures the rights and the ability of the constituent groups to control production and reproduction. The alliance has mana.

The mana of mating is kept distinct from the mana of alliances, but they both partake of the mana of fertility. In that sense, marriage is a cultural institution meant to regulate the relationships between groups and between individuals. It organizes group life. Marriage is not essential for reproduction, whereas mating is. Mating is limited by the biology and the physiology of beings, whereas marriage takes on many forms, depending on the society where it occurs. No matter that it has become amongst us a personal affair, in the pre-industrial world, it was and is an institution that exists for creating alliances. Its societal job is to control mana in general and the mana of fertility only incidentally. Fertility is a problem in and of itself.

Primitive Paternity

So many ancient symbols of fertility are dependent upon the coupling of the male and the female generative organs that it is unrealistic to argue that "primitives" are ignorant of the role of the male in conception. Yet that is what was believed and still is believed by many anthropologists.

The mistake arose during the last century. The Victorian epoch, especially in England, was a period of intense cultural conceit. To Edwin Sydney Hartland for instance, the world had gone through a development that could be compared to an individual's infancy, childhood, adolescence and maturity, and, of course, Victorian England was eminently mature. He completely overlooked (as did the Social Darwinists) the fact that an individual's development in one thing, and the development of a species is another. On the basis of such a premise, he wrote a book called *Primitive Paternity*, in which he has a chapter entitled "Physiological Ignorance on the Subject of Conception." In it, he argues that "primitives" could not possibly know or understand the relationship between copulation and birth, on the grounds that too long a time elapses between the instant a man deposits the "seed" that causes menstruation to stop and the moment in which the woman gives birth. This argument is strictly an intellectual exercise based on the premise that "primitives" are in an "infancy" stage of development and that therefore individuals in such societies think like children. Ironically, Hartland comes to this conclusion after going out of his way to explain at great length how natives, being close to Nature, have uncanny powers of observation, saying how exquisite the sensitivity is that makes them observe the slightest variations in their environment, put the clues together and come to conclusions that are practical and allow them to survive. He follows this accurate description by saying that "primitives" who are so responsive to the processes of nature could not possibly be so perceptive as to note all the changes that occur in the process of reproduction of plants, animals and their own kind. Hartland did not take into account, either, the fact that "primitives'" sense of family is organizational. Any biological relationship, whether it is there or not (and most often it is) would be irrelevant and immaterial because their concern is the organizational dimension of "family" and not the biological. Without going into further details, let it be said that *people* in general, although they may not understand the laws of modern genetics, know very well that it takes a contribution from both a male and a female for a child to be born. Often, the explication is that it is the mixture of male discharge and female effluences that produce the offspring. In agricultural societies, and perhaps in all gathering societies, the analogy is almost inevitably that the man "sows his seed" in the woman, who, then, like the Earth, provides the necessary environment (including her own effluences) for the seed to develop. In Latin, the word "semen" means seed, and the word "sperm" comes from the ancient Greek word "sperma" for seed, and in both languages, the respective words have also the cognitive value of "a man's sexual discharge." The belief is not scientifically correct, but this does not invalidate the argument that people living in pre-scientific societies understand the necessity for coupling a male and a female in order to have offsprings, and that a man's discharge is his contribution to the process.[72]

Chapter VIII

Symbols

The Nature of Symbols

The Evil Eye is a symbol, and symbols have mana. We seldom really stop to think of what it means to use symbols. We are surrounded by them, and yet, like the air we breathe, we have only a vague awareness that they are there. We take them for granted. Symbols are objects, graphic signs, gestures, sounds or beings, that conventionally stand for something else, usually a complex abstraction, and sometimes their meanings are lost in the history of times unremembered.

By their very nature, symbols need not be exact images of what they represent. In any given culture, once convention has assigned a meaning to a graph, an object, a sound or a gesture, that graph, object, sound or gesture symbolically *becomes* the thing that it epitomizes. There is therefore no need for the symbol to picture literally what it represents, so long as it can be identified because of the convention. But even in the case of representative images, if primitive man wants to draw an animal, why should he try to make it as "realistic" as possible, if it is not to emulate the real animal? Yet, a drawing, in fact (independently of what the artist thinks), can never be a "real" animal. That is where the value of the symbol comes in: the representation, as symbol, comes to have, for the artist, the same value (the same mana, if you will) as the thing it represents. Giedion says of palaeolithic art: "In every instance, actuality has been translated into symbolism, however realistic it may appear" (p. 79).

Symbols have their own mana. It is difficult for us to grasp the kind of power or mana that pre-literate peoples attribute to symbols. Not because we have no powerful symbols (think of Catholics for whom the host is not "just" unleavened bread), but rather because we are unfamiliar with other peoples' symbols, and therefore cannot attribute any "power" to them. For the initiate, symbols convey meaning at a distance and across time. That is a manifestation of real mana, the mana of symbols.

Symbols need not be representational

Writing is the very essence of what Leslie White calls "the ability to symbol." That is why it is awesome: little squiggles on a flat surface can cause someone at a distance, at another time, to know the thoughts of another person. The graphic symbols of writing are not an image of the sounds they represent. They represent sounds only in a very conventional manner. That is why "Linear A" writing from ancient Crete remains undeciphered. Without a clue, we cannot possibly know what sounds the signs of "Linear A" represented, let alone what words they are or what they mean. It becomes a little easier to guess at the meaning when the symbols *are* images, or when they are recognizably derived from images. Like writing, however, symbols in general do not have to be representational. That is why, from the very beginning of graphic endeavors, geometric designs came to have a quasi-writing character, with all the mystery and the mana of writing. But whether writing, art or symbol, we can never be absolutely sure of the meaning of those deliberately produced signs and artifacts that we find as remnants of ancient worlds. We can only infer from what we know, or as an alternative we can work our way back if there are enough records to show continuity. That is seldom possible in the case of palaeolithic material. There may even be things which had a great and profound significance to these ancient folk, but mean absolutely nothing to us because we have no referent with which to assign a meaning, as vague as it may be.

The Symbols of Fertility

Pre-literate peoples feel that their survival depends on the inherent power of symbols to control nature. Because of the mana of symbols, symbols of fertility have the kind of particular power that people will consider as influencing the course of events. They become pivotal in the belief systems of people who rely intimately on the ability of nature to reproduce itself. Fertility is everything. It is life itself because life depends on production and reproduction. People in subsistence societies venerate it. The verb "to venerate" comes from the Latin *venerare*, which itself is derived from "Venus," as is "venereal." This obsession with the mana of fertility is expressed in symbols and in the fact that many fertility symbols are multidimensional; that is, they express fertility in more than one way, and they can represent more things than just fertility. There seems to be, moreover, a tendency to pile up the symbols, as if there existed a feeling that there can never be enough of them. Lee Alexander Stone, in his *Story of Phallicism* says p. 116: "Because of the superstitious awe in which this symbol [of the phallos] was held, and because of its supposed ability to keep off the evil eye, it is evident that man might, by intention, combine more than one symbol representative of the phallus, believing that the more he showed, the greater would be his protection from such malign influence." Elworthy, speaking of an ancient amulet having four of the same protective symbol, says: ". . . the fact of finding four hands combined shows that already in those days, 500 to 1000 B.C., there was a tendency to pile up amulets by way of adding to their power" (*The Evil Eye*, p. 242). This collective *angst* expressed through the use of symbols is one of the features which appears over and over and again, and seems odd to us. One example of this, among many others, could be the numerous Roman *tintinnabula* representing a winged phallos having a phallos of its own and a phallic tail. This assemblage, often surmounts several vulvae, or is hung with bells, which are symbols of the vulva, as are the wings (see fig. 40.3). Many of the artifacts collected at the site of Ancient Pompeii are of this design (see Illus. Nos. 8 & 8.4, 8.5, 8.6. See also Knight and Wright, plates XXV, XXVI, XXVII.)

The most obvious symbol of fertility is the act of procreation. This has caused many observers of the past, particularly of the 19th Century, to refer to "Sex Worship." It must be pointed out, however, that if anything is "worshipped," it is fertility and not sex.[73] Most people in small-scale societies venerate the mana of reproduction and are driven by it. They may concentrate their attention on a symbol in the form of a woman giving birth, but that does not mean that they "worship a goddess" any more than we worship Liberty in the form of a woman holding a torch. That is, their reverence for fertility may equal ours for liberty, but no more and no less (cf. section on "the Parturient Woman"). Yet, scholars and missionaries (with some exceptions), in their eagerness to find a "High God," or a High Goddess, have obscured the significance of fertility rituals by not mentioning them or by treating them as if they were oddities or perversions. Michel Eyquem de Montaigne (1533-1592) perceived this paradox when he said: "It is our duty to hide ourselves and blush while we are creating life; but it is the fountainhead of many virtues and a glory to know how to destroy what we have created. What monstrous animal is this whose delights are a torment, and who dotes on unhappiness!"[74]

Kteis and Phallos

Fertility, then, in the broadest sense possible, is what has to be encouraged. Fertility is what is venerated. That, in human terms, fertility results from sexual activity is a corollary. I am not saying that people in prehistory and antiquity did not enjoy sex—there is no reason to believe that they enjoyed it any less than we do—I am only saying that it is fertility that is sacralized and not the sex act. As a matter of fact, however, it is likely that their vision of life and survival allowed them to satisfy the natural appetites with greater abandon. Edwin Smith, quoted by Parrinder, says of the Ba-Ila:

> to write of the Ba-Ila and omit all reference to sex would be like writing of the sky and leaving out the sun; for sex is the most pervasive element in their life. It is the atmosphere into which the children are brought. Their early years are largely a preparation for the sexual function; during the years of maturity it is their most ardent pursuit, and old age is spent in vain and disappointing endeavours to continue it. . . . To them, the union of the sexes is on the same plane as eating and drinking, to be indulged in without stint on every possible occasion.[75]

A German Catholic missionary, J. Winthuis, who, according to Giedion (p. 224), had spent more than seven years among aborigines in New Britain in the southwest Pacific, without hesitation, deemed that the basis of all thought and philosophy among primitives was based solely upon sexuality and the need for fertility. Giedion quotes Winthuis:

> To the primitive all straight lines signify *membrum virile*, the phallus; whatever is circular or sickle-shaped is the *membrum muliebre*, the vagina. However unlikely this statement may appear, it is our only way of gaining insights into primitive thought; indeed, into the basic meaning of the whole spiritual culture, their legends, songs, cults, arts, and magic.[76]

The most obvious and most universal symbol of fertility is still the fact of reproduction, whether manifested in coitus or parturition (childbirth). In turn, the most obvious symbols of coitus are the sexual organs: the *phallos* (male) and the *kteis* (female). Given the fact that people living close to nature understand the double nature of fecundity, the two symbols generally appear together, because if one is to have "life," one has to have both components of fertility: male and female. This sacralization of, and collective obsession with fertility has made it so that *anything and everything that in the most remote way can be said to be perceived morphologically as phallos, kteis or intercourse, has been understood at one place and one time or another as a symbol of fertility.* An enumeration would be lengthy and pointless, but we can illustrate the extent to which this is true by mentioning buttonholes as apotropaics in Southern England.[77] It is as if, after personifying human society, we were to subject it to a vast Rorschach Test, it would definitely come out diagnosed as being obsessed with its own reproduction, with more than just the delights of coitus. Furthermore, one will note that an extraordinarily large number of fertility symbols are of a double nature. That is, they represent both aspects of fertility, male and female.

Because fertility was identified with abundance, which was identified with affluence, which was identified with good fortune, and because of the evolution of our perceptions, fertility, over time, has come to mean almost exclusively "good luck" to us, without our realizing that most of these representations, sometimes considered as "idiomatic," really originated in fertility symbols. The abundance and the variations of fertility symbols is such that it can easily lead to over-interpretation, an analytic sin committed by, for instance, Leroi-Gourhan who was refuted by many (Bourdier, Ucko & Rosenfeld, Bordes, etc.) and supported perhaps only to a point, by Giedion. But the abundance of fertility symbols known in an uncontestable ritual context is so great that one does not need to dispute the controversial cases. It must also be said that many symbolic representations have been under-interpreted. Such is the case for the fertility statuettes discussed below.

The Greek word *kteis* (*ktenes* in the plural) actually means comb (*κτενιον*) and may share a common origin with the name of the scallop (*κτενι*). Both comb and scallop are symbols of the vulva.[78] The vulva is the external *entrance* to the female genital organism. It is not the genitalia proper but it symbolizes it, and is therefore to be taken as such. The term "kteis" has been in use as a complement to the term "phallos" and is found in that sense, in works on symbolism and in folklore and art history.[79] Because *kteis* is a Greek word, for the sake of consistency, I have adopted the Greek spelling of the word referring to the male counterpart of kteis, which is *phallos* (*phalloi* in the plural), rather than the Latin *phallus* (*phalli*), except, of course, in quotations.

It is interesting to note the origin of the word *kteis*. We have already noted that the basic word, in Greek, means *comb*. It was in antiquity, and still is, the common term used to refer to the vulva. By extension, kteis also refers to the scallop shell, Venus's symbol. There is evidence that the symbolism of the comb-as-kteis was already extant in the fifth millennium B.C. in Central Europe. Marija Gimbutas published line-drawings of three combs from that period of time, all of which represent a spread-legged female, with the tines of the comb as pubis.[80] The symbolism may well have been still extant in medieval Europe and later. There is a great number of folk songs referring to women, or girls, using or losing their combs. In the Arthurian Romance of Christian de Troyes's *Le Chevalier de la Charette*, there is an episode qualified by Gérard Brault as "curious."[81] Queen Guenevere has been abducted by Meleagant. Lancelot goes to the rescue. In his search he passes by a fountain and finds a comb. It is Guenevere's comb. Lancelot then loses his composure. He kisses the comb, he raves over it, he is fascinated and even swoons. Brault tells us that the episode is ignored by scholars because it is thought to be incomprehensible and therefore insignificant. He goes as far as to say that "our initial impression, of course, is that it (the comb) is a kind of extension of her body," but after considerations that should have led him to conclude otherwise, he gives the episode a religious and moralistic meaning. However, Medieval Europe had retained some of the ancient concrete significance of the symbols (Brault himself testifies to this); I would suggest, then, that if indeed the tale is based on an ancient fertility myth, Lancelot—as the male dimension of fertility—was not merely gazing at a comb, but, symbolically, he was looking at the very essence of female fertility, represented by the vulva of Guenevere. Brault re-enforces this interpretation unwittingly by saying that: "The anatomy of love in Chrétien de Troyes centers to an astonishing degree on the eye and the heart." As we shall see, both the eye and the heart are symbols for the vulva, the eye, of course, being critical to the thesis of this essay. To paraphrase Brault, then, he might perhaps have said that "the anatomy of love in Chrétien de Troyes center to an astonishing degree on symbols of the vulva."

To complement this, we may quote Thomas Wright:

> The figure of the female organ, as well as the male appears to have been employed during the middle ages of Western Europe far more generally than we might suppose, placed upon buildings as a talisman against evil influences, and especially against witchcraft and the evil eye, and it was used for the purpose in many other parts of the world. It was the universal practice among the Arabs of Northern Africa to stick up over the door of the house or tent, or put up nailed on a board in some other way, the generative organ of a cow,

> mare, or female camel, as a talisman to avert the influence of the evil eye. (Essay on the Worship of the Generative Powers, p. 138)[82] (See also fig. 37.1.)

The Morphology of it all

Wright, after the quotation above, goes on to deplore the fact that we do not always recognize the symbolism of the female member as easily as we do the male. Faced with the unknown, we tend to guess at the significance of a symbol on the basis of what it looks like to us. That is probably why Catherine Johns says that the vulva, being amorphous (her word) is seldom represented "artistically" in comparison to the male genitals, which are obvious. "All in all," she says, "from the technical point of view alone, there is a strong case for representing the female genitals symbolically rather than realistically" (Johns, p. 72). It may be true that the kteis is often represented symbolically, illustrated for instance by the triangle on its point, but the phallos can be represented as frequently by abstract forms such as the triangle on its base. What Johns may be saying is that from an "art" point of view, as opposed to a ritual point of view, it is easier to recognize a *realistic* representation of the triadic male organ than it is to recognize the visible parts of a woman's genitals, if either is to be represented *sans* body. However, in the context of symbolic significance, her argument is immaterial because the genitals as symbols, do not have to be realistic representations of the *primary* sexual organs to be significant. "Primary" means: ovaries, Fallopian tubes, uterus and vagina, all of which are completely hidden from sight, well inside the body. In both females and males, a representation of *that which is readily visible* is enough. Therefore, for women, it is sufficient to symbolize the vulva, or that other part of the body which is readily identifiable as "female": the breasts. Female breasts are prominent, and therefore noticeable, while the vulva is, to use Johns's term, "amorphous" and somewhat concealed. That is why there is a female symbolic triad made up of the vulva and the two breasts, i.e. the greater part of the body. This constitutes a counterpart to the male triad of penis and the two testicles. These triads are not often recognized, yet they often complement each other by the melding of the representations of breasts and testicles, as we shall see below.

Then again, it is probably not exactly true to say that the female genitals are "seldom represented artistically" because "artistically" means something very different to us from what it could have meant to the people who might have wanted to epitomize the kteis by drawing an almond shape (i.e. an eye), or a triangle on its point, a fig shape, an apricot, a comb, a lotus petal, the leaves of certain trees, a grain of wheat, rice or rye, a cowrie or a scallop shell, all of which symbolize the female genitals because of their perfunctory resemblance to the vulva. It may be that female symbolism, in fact, occurs *more* frequently (not less) than male precisely because of the "amorphous" nature of the female external genitals. Anything that resembles the soft curves of the *mons veneris* becomes a kteis, whereas a phallos is a phallos and is generally depicted as such because it is more easily identifiable. The question of "art" is moot because "art" is a convention just as writing is a convention. In a sense, one could refer to writing as an art, if art is meant to convey a message.

Both male and female genitals are represented "artistically" in Malta and Sicily, where the literal conjunction of phallos and kteis forms the focus of fertility rituals that prevailed on the islands in the 4th Millennium B.C. The conjunction was placed conspicuously at the entrance of temples. The phallos coupled with the kteis, in figure 10.1 from Sicily, is obvious. In figure 10.2, the same type of carving located on both sides of the entrance to the largest temple in Malta at the site of Hal Tarxien, the phallos is certainly as abstract as the kteis and yet the figures from the two sites are unquestionably related. Incidentally, the same graphic and abstract theme is found in Romanesque churches of the eighth century in France.

Change

The entire ideological system and the intense feelings associated with fertility and the Evil Eye have been carried along in the historical development of society and have persisted in spite of the changes that have occurred since the world was oriented to an agricultural or a gathering economy. As home industries and crafts began to appear, they came to be treated like all other productive activities, and therefore were treated in the idiom of the mana of fertility. Symbols of fertility, including those involved in the Evil Eye folklore, then acquired the much more comprehensive functions of insuring prosperity and protecting against adversity. Fertility symbolism appears everywhere, and not only in situations directly affected by fecundity. Soldiers in armies and knights in battle used the symbols to protect their lives. The shields of ancient Greek soldiers were covered with protective symbols of the same nature as the apotropaics against the Evil Eye. Keeping in mind that coats-of-arms developed from shield markings in the European Middle Ages, it is possible to say of these images, whether they are from Greek antiquity or from medieval Western Europe, what Philip Waterman says of heraldic signs: "The entire 'science' of heraldry, which concerned itself with the devices worn by knights in the Middle Ages, included few, and perhaps no, symbols that cannot be shown to be developments of either the male or female symbols."[83]

With the development of trade and crafts, the ideas of production and reproduction were transferred to profits and the output or products of artisans. Merchants in the Middle Ages in Europe used to place a sprig of rue in their money boxes to protect from the Evil Eye and increase the profits from their ventures. Artisans stamped apotropaic hallmarks on their products. Until very recently, the production of iron in East Africa was pervaded with sexual terminology meant to maintain and increase production.[84] Merchants in India now place apotropaics all over the entrance to their shops and perform elaborate rituals to protect their business against the Evil Eye.

Even today, amongst us and in Western Europe, there are many apotropaics now referred to only as "good luck pieces" or "portofortuna" or "porte-bonheur." Invariably these can be traced back to fertility symbols, or prophylactics against the Evil Eye. The idea of fertility came to be identified with luck, good fortune and happiness. It was, and it seems that it had been for a long time, much more than just the reproduction of domestic animals, of the grain in the fields, or of people. The famous aphorism from Pompeii, "Hic habitat felicitas," accompanying an apotropaic phallos, has been translated: "Here lives happiness." But in fact, in terms of the Latin root-meaning of *felix*, it means much more. According to Andrews' *Copious and Critical Latin-English Lexicon*, *felix*, *felicis* (adj.) comes from the generative root *feo, fevo*: to bear, to produce, whence we get *fetus*, *fecundus*, *femina* (and its diminutive *femella*), *fenus*, all of which contain the idea of bearing fruit, fruitful, fertile.[85] By extension, Andrews says, it means: That which brings good luck; of good omen; auspicious; favorable; propitious; lucky, happy, fortunate. The term *fenus* in particular had come to mean in ancient Rome, that which was gained from investment of capital (Andrews, p. 606). The Pompeiian apotropaic phallos, a fertility symbol, then was meant to bless the household with prosperity in general, and not only the "natural" increase of grain, domestic animals or people. It was also meant to protect the household from the lack of these benefices, and, by extension, from any form of harm. That is, it protected against the Evil Eye.

Chapter IX

The Principle of Duality in Life Symbols

Introduction

Not only has the universality, in time and space, of fertility symbolism been underestimated, but its nature has been misunderstood. It seems to have become difficult for some of us to think of fertility symbols as having a double nature: male and female. It should be easy to look for, and find, the *complementarily* in a symbol; after all, from the point of view of the species, and aside from personal preferences, it is the complementarily that is appealing. We are individuals, but part of each our individuality is that each one of us is either male or female, and that duality is what allows the species to perpetuate itself. Yet for some reason, we seem to have alienated ourselves so much from nature that when we look at the symbolism of yesteryear, we fail to understand how critically important the duality of fertility was to our predecessors. In this chapter, I want to make the point that ancient fertility symbols are almost always dual representations, that is, they symbolize both the male and the female principles. Even when one only is emphasized, the other is usually implied. Already in prehistory, whenever a uniquely female symbol was displayed, it was accompanied by a uniquely male one. Not only is the duality itself critical, but so is the fact that, for thousands of years, people have found it essential to express this duality in their fertility symbols. This fact is fundamental to an understanding of the Evil Eye, because it will explain that the constant preoccupation of people with production and reproduction is the same as their constant preoccupation with the Evil Eye. The sheer abundance of double symbols is overwhelming, but they must be understood for what they are: the union of the male and female principles, which in reproducing also produce the means whereby people survive. It will explain also the abysmal anxiety of people faced with non-production. Non-production means death and starvation. Hence the collective obsession with symbols of fertility. The Eye as the representation of the human female genitals, symbolizes fertility in general, and has done so for thousands of years. (see Chapter on the Oval, the Almond Shape and the Eye). That is why the Eye, as a symbol of the vulva which is a symbol of female fertility, without the phallos, its male complement, signifies the epitome of non-production and is therefore evil.

Abstract Symbols

One of the oldest identifiable symbols of the vulva is the triangle on its point, inspired by the female pubic triangle. It is found on cave walls drawn in the context of a female body (e.g., Grotte d'Angles-sur-Anglin in France), or alone often with a small slit bisecting the lower point. In that latter form, it became in fact the pictogram for "woman" in ancient Sumerian pre-cuneiform writing (fig. 28.1). The triangle on its base came to signify "male" because of the phallic triad or, as Inman calls it, the phallic trinity. The two triangles together, then, mean "life." Superimposed, we have the Shield or Star of David (or Seal of Solomon) (cf. fig. 27.2). The *Musaeum Hermeticum* published in Frankfort in 1625 and in 1678, shows in its frontispiece, a female on the left, a male on the right, each holding her or his appropriate triangular symbol, and Life in the center, holding the Star of David.[86] More rarely, the triangles are joined at the base, forming a diamond, which can then be assimilated to the oval.

The Egyptian *ankh* is also a double symbol. The small oval at the top of the ankh is the kteis and the cross below is the phallos. As a hieroglyph, it means: "life," "eternity," "fertility." The ankh is also known as *crux ansata*. By extension it is identical to the "mirror of Venus"—now the female symbol in biology—, except for the fact that the oval is a large circle, to which emphasis is given, the cross below being small (see figs. 27.3). Like the Celtic Cross, it is a combination of the kteic oval superimposed on a phallic cross. The orb, which originated in ancient Sumer, is a mirror of Venus, upside down (the cross is above; cf. fig. 27.3). All over the Orient, the lotus flower in its closed state is phallic and in its open state it is kteic. The *fleur-de-lys* symbol is a stylized version of the lotus, and as such it was a double fertility symbol. The calla lily and all flowers of the arum family, became double symbols (fig. 29.1 and 29.2). The ancient Egyptians, like the Hindu of today, had an elaborate system of fertility symbols woven into their rituals and beliefs, one of which, the Eye of Horus, will be discussed later. The menat, the sistrum, were also double fertility symbols (see fig. 30.1).

The alchemists of the Middle Ages extended the principle, "The Union of Opposites to Make One," represented by a mating couple, to the mixing of metals in the search for the Philosopher's Stone. The Chinese *Circle of Life*, made up of the female Yin and the male Yang (see figs. 27.1), is an ingenious and powerful device because it symbolizes visually the physical complementarily of the sexes, which in turn symbolizes life.[87]

The Statuettes

> This problem of how one "sees" in a cultural context is, in fact, one that research in "artificial intelligence" has not been able to adequately address. There is no better instance of the problem of how one sees than the persistent and changing efforts by an army of authors to interpret the complex and variable iconography and imagery of the Ice Age, the images that authors have for so long presumed to be the primitive "beginnings" of human art. Since we do not have the accompanying mythology or the antecedents of these traditions we are endlessly free to create mythologies and "origins" of our own. (Marshack, p. 404)

The statuettes found at archaeological sites all over the Old World, covering a period of tens of thousands of years, are probably the most misinterpreted of prehistoric symbols, and because of their abundance, these misinterpretations distort the image that we have of the people living in the type of society in which the Evil Eye was born. It is possibly our obsession with status and rank that has caused the prehistoric statuettes to be identified as "goddesses." We project into simple non-state societies, the ideas of feudal order and stratification which we feel are an inevitable part of life. That is why we see gods, goddesses, chiefs, paramounts and kings everywhere. Yet, the culture of pre-state societies does not include a concept of stratification or hierarchies, nor does it have centralization of authority. Therefore, their *Weltanchuung* does not include it either. People in simple societies are eminently aware of the powers of Nature, the most important of which is production and reproduction. The prehistoric statuettes, therefore, are not "goddesses," they are *Fertility* itself, they epitomize the mana of fertility, and they exhibit both elements of fertility: male and female, sometimes rather obviously. This has been recognized by some authors, but it is not the general rule. Jacquetta Hawkes, Anne Barstow, Sigfried Giedion, recognize the symbolic status of these objects. Giedion says:

"They were not goddesses but potent magic symbols, able to bring new life to birth and to renew the life of the dead, beside whom they were buried in later times."[88]

As a matter of fact, however, the figurines are not generally associated with burials. When they are associated with anything, it is with the living quarters of prehistoric peoples. We can infer what this means from the ethnographic record. Elsy Leutzinger makes a distinction between "the small personal ancestor figurine" and the fetish. But, she says, the dividing line is a blurred one. Rarely has the fetish any "artistic value." It is produced casually by a medicine man on the basis of traditional forms, and if it is ineffective, it is thrown away.[89]

The phallic character of some prehistoric statuettes, that otherwise seem to represent females is at times so obvious that it is surprising the fact has not always been noted. For comparative purposes and visual confirmation of this, the reader should look at illustrations 31 through 34. Double fertility symbols are abundant, although we do not always recognize their duality. The very early statuettes may exhibit characteristics identifiable as female, but most of them also have a remarkable phallic character. The "Venus" of Savignano is a good example (fig. 31.2). It is about 22,000 years old. The very fact that it has been named "Venus" means that it was identified as a female by those who first described it, but its "headless neck" and its "breasts" are so very evidently a portrayal of the phallic triad that it has been difficult to escape noticing this. Sometimes, those who acknowledge the phallic shape often seem to be unsure. Franck Bourdier, for example, although he presents it as a "phallic Venus," nevertheless hesitates by adding an interrogation mark after his description: "avec cagoule phallique?,"[90] as if the top part of the statuette could not possibly and frankly represent a phallic triad rather than a woman with a "hood" in the shape of a phallos. Marija Gimbutas seldom acknowledges the phallos, except in her chapter on the "column of life" (*The Language of the Goddess*) in which she correctly identifies the phallic trinity aspect of some statuettes. But it is only when the maleness is so evident as to be indisputable. Even then she has reservations. She says (p. 232): "Although the male element is attached, these figurines remain essentially female. They do not represent a fusion of two sexes but rather an enhancement of the female with the mysterious life force inherent in the phallus." As a matter of fact, on page 235 of *The Civilization of the Goddess*, in conjunction with a "female" figurine in the obvious shape of a male triad, she refuses to see the "buttocks" as testicles and she goes as far as granting the status of "symbol of life proliferation" to women's buttocks, but not to testicles: "Buttocks and breasts share the magical power of being double, while also being symbols of life proliferation." Coming back to Savignano, it is therefore not surprising that she should say that "on this Upper Palaeolithic figurine of steatite (or serpentine marble), the head is replaced by a featureless phallus." She does not point out, and yet it should be evident, that the "breasts" do double duty as testicles, therefore, the phallos is not featureless.[91] By "featureless," however, she probably means that, she, as an observer, expects a "head" to have nose, mouth and eyes, all of which are absent, since it is not a head. It is a phallos with testicles. Looking at Savignano, one could as well describe it as a phallic triad with an appended female body. Relative to each other, the phallos is enormous, while the body is small. But again, I do not think that this kind of comparison was intended. It is simply a way of representing in one single view, the triads emblematic of female and male fertility, blended into each other.

Twenty thousand years later, in the statuette from Late Zagros site of Tepe Sarab in Iran, dated to the early 6th millennium B.C. (see fig. 31.5), the style may be slightly different, but the phallic character of the "neck" and "breasts" is still unmistakable. The statuettes from Savignano and from Tepe Sarab (see figs.) are ideal symbols inasmuch as breasts and testicles become one, while yet not relinquishing the aspects of both male and female. Some archaeologists go to elaborate lengths to describe the "elongated stalk-like head" (there is no head) of the Tepe Sarab "goddess" (it is not a goddess), without mentioning that there is a male triad component that actually dominates the figurine.[92] This would be true of all the "pillar-headed goddesses" from prehistoric Central Europe, the Russian plains, the Cyclades, France, or from present-day Africa. They range at least over an extraordinary 29,000 years, from 27,000 years B.C. to the present (see figs. 31-34). There are archaeologists who do recognize the double identity of these statuettes, even in cases where the male aspect is not as evident as in the examples above, but, generally speaking, our culture's obsession seems to be congealed in the female fertility mode and in the idea that goddesses and gods are inevitable. Michael Dames in speaking of a "goddess" (illustration 31.1) from Cernavoda, Romania (ca. 5000 B.C.) says that the statuette "combines the two modes of the deity."[93] At first reading, I had no doubt that Dames had seen the phallic aspect of this neolithic "pillar-headed goddess," as well as her kteic nature, but on closer reading, it turns out that he was referring to the "Squatting-Mother" (i.e. giving birth) aspect of "the deity" as opposed to the Old-Hag (i.e. stagnant nature during the winter after harvest) aspect. He is not entirely wrong, but the phallic-kteic configuration of the statuette is so obvious that one would think that it would not have escaped him. Moreover, since Dames does say that we now know that Neolithic society in England "was totally classless and peaceful," it is highly unlikely that the forms to which he refers (and compares to the statuette) represent a "goddess." It is, again in the words of Anne Barstow, "a celebration of fecundity" without any necessary personalization of fecundity at all, let alone a supernatural personalization.

I agree with Martha and C. C. Lamberg-Karlosky who say quite accurately about a statuette found at the site of Tepe Yahya in Iran that "the sculpture was apparently intended to be a dual representation: a female figure imposed on a stylized phallic shape."[94] Sometimes the representations are a little more sophisticated, as in the necklace bead from the 27,000 B.C. site of Dolni Vestonice in Czechoslovakia identified as exclusively female by, for instance, Absolon, Marshack and Gimbutas who consider it simply as a pair of "breasts" under a conical "head," whereas it could easily be seen at the same time as the male triad (see fig. 31.3). Surely, the beads are not closer to realism in representing breasts and neck than they are in representing penis and testes. Marshack, who describes the beads by saying that "Each is the image of two breasts with a headless, faceless neck," belabors the "female only" interpretation (p. 293):

> It would seem that these breast images were both used and worn, not by the male hunter for erotic purposes, but by women, or else by a shaman or titual person performing for women, helping them to participate in the story whose symbol was the flowing breast, a process whose power and effect came with maturity and fullness, a fullness that is clearly depicted in the ivory images. This is not the large-bellied pregnancy image nor a menstrual or copulative image and, while we can assume that all these processes were storied within the unified myth and lore relating to women, the breast aspect could be separated from the whole as a distinct image with a separate story. We might conjecture that it was not worn by men, or by girls before menstruation, or by women before pregnancy, but we cannot be sure. Whatever its meaning, it was specialized.

Marshack, in spite of his extraordinary creative talents, is fixed in the "female" modal interpretation. If one thinks of the beads as representing penis and testes *as well as* the female neck and breasts, then Marshack's quandary disappears, because the figure is not "specialized," but, on the contrary, it represents both the male and the female aspects of fertility, and as such it was probably considered as "good luck" for everybody, especially, of course, for women in their role as genetrices.

In that same form as the beads, the double identity male-female, occurs in Mesopotamia (Modern Iraq) at the site of Arpachiya dated to some 22,000 years later, ca. 5,000 B.C. and identified by its discoverer as a "goddess." Given the existence of many "pillar-headed goddesses" at the time of discovery, it may be understandable that Goff should have identified this statuette as "a goddess," that is a female representation, but it looks so much like a phallic triad that, without this comparison, she would have had to identify it as a phallos (see fig. 31.4).[95]

Those figures which Gimbutas describes as having "pendulous breasts," may be, as she says, a symbol of the nourishing mother, but the breasts are prominent and "pendulous" not only because female breasts are obvious sexual markers, but also because their "pendulous" shape has to represent testicles as well, albeit on another scale. In that light, it may be significant that nipples are virtually never shown. On those fertility carvings and drawings that show a woman in childbirth with no intention of representing the male dimension of fertility (see the chapter on the Parturient Woman and the Sheelas below), the breasts are rarely given any emphasis, and when they are present, they are not necessarily "pendulous," that is, they do not have the appearance of testicles.

The site of Dolni Vestonice has another remarkable statuette. It is made with clay mixed with crushed ivory and fired (see fig. 32.5). It is identified as a female figurine, which it is. But it is difficult to overlook the fact that the "head" of the statuette has the shape of a glans. Yet, Marshack says of the "goddess" that it has "an unreal schematized face with slit mask-like eyes, a nose represented by a line drawn in the wet clay and the absence of a mouth." The fact is simply that, as in the case of Savignano, it is not a face. The "nose" markings go down to the breasts, so that Gimbutas sees "divine liquids" flowing from the eyes, where Marshack sees a nose. The markings, however, are more likely to represent the visible swelling of the male urethra on a penis in erection.[96] The "eyes" are the edge of the glans. This could be said also of the Aurignacian carved mammoth ivory pendant from Abri Cellier (France), which is presented in Randall White's *Dark Caves* as showing a "hair line" (his fig. 110). The edge of the glans as "hairline" is obvious in the megalithic stone figures at Filitosa in Sardinia (see Cles-Reden, plates 64, 65 and 66).

The "abstract" female from Petersfel in the "buttock style" mentioned by Marshack has an obvious phallic shape. That is, it is as much an "abstract" phallos (with the testicles blended here with the buttocks) as it is an "abstract" female (fig. 32.7). It may not be an exact rendition of a penis, but then it is not an exact representation of a female either. However, if the "artist" who carved it wanted to have his or her work represent both the female and the male symbolic dimension of fertility, he or she came up with a remarkable allegorical and stylized compromise. So is the small ivory rod from Dolni Vestonice, which both Marshack and K. Absolon identify as a female figure, Absolon, its discoverer, going to the extent of saying that its maker was "stressing his sexual libido only where the breasts are concerned," and calling it "diluvial plastic pornography" (see fig. 32.1). He further generalizes by saying that "the origin of these statuettes is due to sexual-biological, erotic motives."[97] This interpretation tells us more about Absolon's freudian frame of mind than it says about the original prehistoric sculptor. It is puzzling why Absolon thought of these artifacts as personal expressions of sexual libido, when he himself noted the similarities in styles between statuettes distributed in an area from Lake Baikal to the Atlantic. He also notes that almost all of them "neglect" the face, the arms and the feet. Marshack disagrees with Absolon, but he still thinks of the figure as exclusively female, in spite of the blatant male triad appearance of the "breasts and neck." Again, Bourdier classifies it as a phallic Venus, and again I don't see why it has to be a "Venus" rather than a representation of femininity and of masculinity all at once.

Georges Charrière, who is otherwise very perceptive, says of some phallic stone monuments from Ethiopia, that "when these megaliths are endowed with breasts, it is doubtful that we can call them Phallic."[98] What Charrière fails to consider is that these phallic menhirs with breasts may be considered as double symbols, both male and female.

If we are to compare the numerous Cycladic statuettes to such finds as the effigies from the site of Malta near Lake Baikal in Siberia, still identified as "flying birds" in the National Geographic of October, 1988, we can only come to the conclusion that these artifacts are not "flying birds" (fig. 33.3), but fertility amulets comparable to the phallic "females" with long "necks," no face and "negligible" arms, from the Aegean and elsewhere (see all figs. 33). Marija Gimbutas must be credited for saying that the "birds are anthropomorphized" (her page 4, figure 1. [8] a,b,c). Buffie Johnson speaks of "swan goddesses [which] combine the features of bird and female." Neither Gimbutas nor Johnson admit to seeing the phallic shape. Georges Charrière does reproduces the "flying birds" in a table of females statuettes without any other comment (his fig. 55-n, page 164).

Even Colin Renfrew, who is a well-known and respected archaeologist, looks upon the Aegean effigies as if they were portraits of humans, and he painstakingly looks for a head. In his "Introduction" to *L'art des Cyclades* he says of the so-called violin-shaped "statuettes" that: "A toutes il manque une indication claire pour la tête. Comme l'exemple néolitique de Saliagos, elles présentent une sorte d'excroissance allongée, dont la fonction est d'indiquer à la fois le cou et la tête." [Roughly translated it means: "There is no clear indication of a head. Only the presence of a kind of long excrescence serves the function of both neck and head."] But again, as we have said for Tepe Sarab, the "excrescence" is fundamentally a phallos, although it might satisfy the "functional" requirements of a neck or a head if one is looking for a neck and a head. In other words it is meant to represent a symbolic embodiment of both female and male fertility, kteis and phallos *combined*, rather than a person or an anthropomorphised "goddess."

At the very same time the Cycladic statuettes were being produced and used, there were also a large number of "pendant amulets" clearly in the shape of phalloi, but nevertheless often identified as "fly amulets" or "mushroom amulets," etc.[99] There are many such errors in interpretation. In the end the abundance of the visual evidence is so great that it would be tedious to go over it all.

None of the illustrations given here are unique, and there are variations on the theme: the dagger-like shape from Ghelaesti, Romania, dating to about the 5th Millennium B.C., is clearly phallic (fig. 35.2). So are the 5th Century B.C. statuettes from Priene in Asia Minor, with their "hair" in a double bun, which, with the phallic shape of the legs, present a picture of the male triad (see fig. 35.1). Hermaphrodite representation is frequent and is yet another way of symbolizing the duality of life. The same types appear over and over and over and again in various places. It is important to note that from Savignano to the

Aegean effigies of the Bronze Age, a period of at least 20,000 years, and ranging from the Ukraine to Persia and Western Europe, the statuettes share the common characteristics of "negligible arms" and no facial features.[100] The neck, or the body, or the legs, are generally phalloid. I would like to emphasize the length of time: conservatively, it is 20,000 years, and probably closer to 30,000 years, which is a long time in the history of the development of Culture.[101] When one thinks of the considerable changes that have occurred in the last two thousand years since, let us say, Julius Caesar, it is a wonder that this one single symbol has hardly changed at all in form over a period ten times as long. It is insignificant that in a few cases like Willendorf, the phalloid shape is less obvious. There are so many intermediary stylistic variations in the type that it is easy enough to establish a morphological gradation from, let us say, Savignano and Le Placard, to Dolni Vestonice, to Willendorf and Gagarino, on the one hand, or to Lespugne, Ghelaesti, and Priene, on the other hand. Moreover, given the evidence of occurrences throughout the ages, it is possible that the bent heads of Willendorf, Gagarino (several),[102] Lespugne, Lausel, Kostjenki (several), etc., might have had a phallic meaning for those who made them, or, it is even probable that these statuettes were accompanied by separate phallic symbols that were not found during excavation. An example of this kind of duality is illustrated in Robert Wernick's *The Monument Builders*; the caption of the photograph of the effigy reads: "An ample mother goddess made of chalk, the expendable material from which flint is extracted, once watched over an unproductive shaft at Grimes Graves, a neolithic flint mine in eastern England. Her imaginative creator set the four-and-a-half-inch statuette next to a chalk phallus, evidently in the prayerful hope of improving the output of the mine" (p. 94). The creator in question was probably not that imaginative. He was most likely following in the tradition of his people, a tradition which had lasted already for thousands of years, that is the idea of complementing the female element of reproduction with the male element in order to increase production even if the production is the output of a mine. Even then, La Barre's "archosis" might have already set in and our "sculptor" at Grimes Grave might not have given much thought to what he was doing, except that he may have had a vague, unidentifiable feeling that his actions would bring about good fortune. But then, it is pointless for us to speculate on the motives and the feelings of an individual who lived thousands of years ago. We can only observe what is left from their cultural activities and analyze it on that basis.

Of course, not all carvings, not all engravings that were made during these 20,000 years are necessarily fertility symbols, but it is extraordinary that so many of them were. Grimes Grave also shows the casualness with which sometimes these figurines were made. Analysts of primitive art have noted that there was a tendency for stone-age peoples to use the natural forms available to represent what they were looking for. Menhirs, customs associated with menhirs, the name of some still extant upright stones in Western Europe whose name leaves no doubts as to what they represent (see St. Vit, below). It is not unreasonable to assume, then, that any upright stone, for instance, could have been considered a phallos although it might not look like a phallos to us.

Finally, we can and should extend the continuity into the contemporary world. Fig. 20.9 is a Dogon Mask, one of many such fertility representations from West Africa in which the Parturient Woman has a phallic upper body which is as obvious as in the Savignano and Tepe Sarab statuettes, and where the breasts complete the male triad.

It may be because so many scholars project their own values into the life of early Homo *sapiens* and take for granted that the statuettes are portraits made by some early Michelangelos whose only concern was to create pictures as graphically exact as their technical means allowed. The result is that the debates concentrate on aesthetics, or on whether all prehistoric women were really endowed with the large buttocks (steatopygia) characteristic of some of the statuettes. Among the many, we could single out, for example Gomez-Tabera, who goes so far as to try to decide which statues are steatopygic and which are simply fat. Colin Renfrew, Doumas and Zervos discuss the *aesthetics* of it all. One wonders why these same scholars have not speculated whether some prehistoric women had any breasts at all, since they are absent (or almost) in most sheela-na-gig carvings (discussed below in Chapter XI). Prehistorians, art historians, even physical anthropologists, agonize over these questions. The opinions as to the significance of the statuettes vary from one extreme to the other: Richard Lewisohn says (1956): "not the slightest proof has been found that they represented goddesses of Love or Fertility goddesses" (p. 9). Many others feel that the carvings are among the first objects of worship. As in so many cases, the issue is made into a false problem because again we render a judgment on the basis of criteria that may have had very little significance for early humans. Marshack, in speaking of the "markings" on Upper Paeolithic objects, says that they should be considered "as aspects of symbol systems, rather than as 'art,' or aspects of 'style'" (p. 395), and he adds: "the 'style,' if there was any, was behavioral and it resided in the making and the use, not in the form or quality of the image" (p. 397).

I would carry his idea one step further. I believe we should think of the artifacts themselves, as symbolic means of communications. As such, they developed in the same way as writing eventually did, from pictograms to symbolic configurations that were not necessarily representational. If we keep in mind what has been said of the nature of symbols, the statuettes, then, like all symbols, represent what the conventions of the time say they represent and it does not matter that they are not an exact detailed picture of the material world. In that sense, it is totally irrelevant to discuss whether women of the palaeolithic were steatopygic or not. I would suggest that these artifacts, whether statuettes or graphic signs, including the symbolism of the Eye, are probably the closest thing to writing developed by early humans.[103]

Finally, it must be said that there are authors who, although they "read" divinities in ancient artifacts, will nevertheless concede, as Judith Ochshorn does, that "in no sense was divinity itself conceived as solely female or male."[104]

Summing up

The prehistoric statuettes are the manifestation of a great concern with the mana of fertility. They are the concretization, of the idea of fertility, the mana of which needs to be controlled. The earliest figurines exhibit both aspects of fertility, male and female. As we will see in the next three chapters, when the female dimension appears by itself, the symbolism concentrates on the vulva, particularly the vulva at the moment immediately preceding birth, when it takes on the shape of a near-perfect oval. The next stage of birthing that seems to have been greatly significant is the moment of crowning when the top of the baby's crown forms a circle at the center of the oval shape of the vulva, and which graphically can be compared to a large "eye." But the point to remember is the "ritual" importance that the statuettes seem to have had in the perpetual attempt to control the mana of fertility. As fertility symbols, the statuettes' similarity to each other in form is astonishing when one considers the wide area over which they were spread and the long period of time they lasted, all of which is also characteristic of the Evil Eye system of beliefs.

Chapter X

The Parturient Woman

When one gets away from the technicalities of physiology and genetics, it is difficult not to see the wonder and the sublime in the production of a new life. It has all the poetry and the sense of renewal one gets out of the surge of green plants and the explosion of color after the first warm breeze and the first gentle rain of Spring. A birth is a marvel even in its predictability, and yet, as a human experience, it is personal and unique every time it occurs. In this, especially among people in subsistence societies who rely on what they see in the real world, and despite the fact that they are well aware of the double value of fertility, male and female, the perception is that while men may have a primal and initiating function, that function is fleeting, whereas women's is long and elaborate. To them, the "natural" mettle of women differs from that of men precisely in the areas of procreation: menstruation draws attention to their genitals; a lengthy gestation occurs inside their bodies; they bear the children and give birth; they produce the milk which will sustain the babies until these are able to survive on solid foods. This special biological role of females may be, indeed, one of the reasons why we, ourselves, tend to see the female in double fertility symbols rather than the male, unless the duality is "obvious."

Giving Birth as Symbol

There is one type of symbol which is almost universal and occurs in all times and across the world. It appears sometimes alone, as the female principle, and sometimes it is accompanied by a symbol of male fertility. This is the one that represents what I shall call *The Parturient Woman* (figs. 17 through 24). Richard L. Anderson follows Douglas Fraser and calls the symbol "The Heraldic Woman." Both authors generally refer to those cases where the woman is flanked by two beings, human or animal. The universality of occurrence of this symbol puzzles Anderson and leads him to ask:

> The crucial question with regard to distribution of the motif is *why*? Why was this particular design so attractive to people in such diverse cultures that they were prompted to incorporate it into their own indigenous art styles? And why did it remain unchanged for nearly 3000 years? These questions are truly enigmatic. . . .
>
> The Heraldic Woman, for example, has turned up on four continents and throughout the Pacific, always seemingly associated with one of two sets of related meanings. . . .
>
> As far as speculation can carry us, however, it seems that the motif was always associated with one (or both) of two themes: either the figure was a symbol of fertility, renewal and regeneration, or else it was associated with a defensive power against sickness or danger in battle.[105]

Anderson's question is puzzling to him only because, first, he presumes that occurrence of the motif is caused by diffusion and, second, because he and Fraser narrow their study to the cases of a woman giving birth while flanked by two personages. Without this latter limitation, the "Heraldic Woman" would be even closer to universality in occurrence. The distribution is not primarily due to diffusion, but rather to function. That is, the stance of the Parturient Woman is the physical posture that women inevitably have to assume in preparing for childbirth.[106] Even in a changing technology, "test-tube babies" have to be gestated in a woman's body and are born in the manner meant to be described by the Parturient Woman symbol. First, to allow for the delivery, a woman's legs and thighs have to be spread apart, with knees bent. Given the anatomy of human beings, this posture is universal. Secondly, to give birth, she has to be either prone or in a squatting position; the latter is by far the most frequent in the history of parturition in the world, with the woman often supported by two individuals flanking her and holding her arms. She may be squatting, or in a birthing chair,[107] or yet again she may be hanging onto a branch or a bar above her head. In any case, whether the position is prone or squatting, her arms are usually thrust above her head. The configuration has been universally used always and everywhere to symbolize fecundity.[108] Illustration number 24.1 is the photograph, at the moment of crowning, of a woman giving birth.[109] Her posture is that of the Parturient Woman symbols.

The moment of crowning is the instant when the crown of the head of the fetus appears in the opening of the vulva. The child is said to be "coming into the world." But, as Paul Williams pointed out, in early belief systems "The term 'fertility' need not only be associated with offsprings or crops in that all transformations that take place may be looked upon as being the result of the union of fundamental sources of energy, and it is the moment when transformation takes place that is considered the most dangerous."[110] It follows that the symbolism of fertility can refer to the increase in the returns on money investments as well as to the increases of crops, domestic animals or people, but whatever the referent, the symbol often depicts precisely one of these natural moments of transformation mentioned by Williams: the birth of a child. The moment of crowning is therefore considered a critical instant in the continuation of life and as such it has become a symbol of fecundity. The oval, the almond and particularly *the eye* are the-part-representing-the-whole (*pars pro toto*) symbols standing for the Parturient Woman, and therefore all these symbols represent that same moment in the process of birth: the moment of crowning (see *The Moment of Crowning* in Chapter XII).

The characteristic design of the Parturient Woman is found on cave walls, on the prows of canoes, in the "corn dollies," the barrows and henges of England, in carvings and drawings at the entrances to buildings, on gemstones and jewelry, on weapons and shields, on utilitarian objects, and on ritual objects.[111] The woman flanked by beasts is a ritual stylization. As with other fertility symbols, anything that can, in the most remote way, remind one of the posture of the Parturient Woman, i.e. arms up and thighs asunder, has been considered a fertility symbol. Arms, legs and head make five protuberances, as in a pentagram. The theme can include a symbol for the child coming out of the womb, in which case there may be, below, an additional protuberance (6) representing the head of the child. Or there may be a replication of the head and the arms of the child (eight protuberances). There can be variations of seven or ten, rarely any other numbers. This is so pervasive that the generalized form of the posture is extended to the abstracted form of animals, or of tree leaves and flowers. Such are the pangolin (Africa), the turtle, the crocodile, the frog, the toad, even the bee. Among leaves, the ancient Romans favored the plane-tree leaf (*platanus* orientalis, not *platanus* occidentalis) because of its five lobes and its shape resembling that of the Parturient Woman (fig. 21.2). The grapevine leaf was a symbol for the same reason. When we keep in mind that the fig leaf was also a fertility symbol (because of its "heart" shape), it is ironical that the Vatican, in the 19th century, when it "discovered" that the statues from Antiquity were naked, covered the pubis with precisely those leaves. One wonders if any of the perpetrators were conscious of this. The flowers that represent the Parturient Woman are all of the composite family, made up of five, six, seven or eight petals. As a design on pottery or as architectural decoration, it is found all over the Old World and over a long period of time. Art historians call the design a "rosette." The rosette, incidentally is particularly frequent in Romanesque churches. In Western Europe, it is found as early as 2500 B.C. among the megaliths.

There is another category of fertility symbols represented by women in a birthing or coital posture that can be classified as a variation of the Parturient Woman. In this category, the woman, usually squatting, helps spread her own legs by pulling or pushing against her own thighs, or by pulling the labia open: the sheela-na-gigs discussed in the next chapter are the best example of this posture. The same posture occurs in the Tantric temples of India and Tibet. Or, again, the figure has her hands on her genitalia, as in the type represented by the numerous terracotta "Baubo" figurines of the fertility "cult" at Bubastis in Ptolemaic Egypt.

As for Anderson's last statement in the above quotation, the Parturient Woman symbol is protection in battle for the same reason the ktenes, or the phallos, or the eye, or anything that is a fertility symbol, are protection. Elsy Leuzinger says of the African figurines: "The fetish is an object endowed with magical powers for certain specific purposes, and employed in a defensive or offensive capacity. It gives protection against illness, on journeys, in childbirth, or during wars and hunting expeditions. Wherever there is danger, and there lurk evil sorcerers who cannot be dealt with by natural means, the fetish is brought into play. . . . They have no exalted religious function to fulfill."[112]

The Bucranium as Parturient Woman Symbol

Michael Dames has already made a case for the "reversible" ox-head representing "*also the divine woman, squatting in the birth position, with arms raised*" (his italics).[113] "Divine" may be the wrong qualifier, but support for his "reversibility" interpretation is abundant. Illustrations 22s are examples in point; 22.1 is from contemporary Africa. It represents generally a buffalo's head, but it clearly shows a phallic triad at the same time that, if the bucranium is turned upside down, it shows the Parturient Woman symbol. The same can be said of 22.3, which dates back to the 4th Millennium B.C. in Bulgaria, except that, here, the female dimension is emphasized in the incised dotted drawing of a woman.

I have done field work among cattle peoples in Rwanda, Africa. There, life and language were replete with the idiom of cattle. The king "mounts" the throne using the same word signifying that a bull "mounts" a cow. He is said to be the "bull of his herd." At the local level, the local feudal patron is constantly praised and flattered in being compared to the bull of his own herd. Once, when the actual bull of the baron's herd escaped the pen while in rut, the people glorified the havock that it created, and related its power and strength to the power and strength of its owner, who greatly enjoyed the whole episode and was flattered by the comparison.

A question could arise as to the origin of the bull's head as fertility symbol, but it is generally accepted that it came from the symbol of the horn as phallos and of the bull itself as power and abundance. Combining the bucranium and the Parturient Woman makes the design a classic double symbol of the male and female elements of fertility. The historical and archaeological evidence supports this conclusion.[114]

Chapter XI

The Sheela-na-gigs

Because the eye originated as a graphic representation of the vulva at the moment of crowning, it is pertinent to discuss the sheela-na-gigs, which themselves are depictions of that moment. Moreover, to quote Wright: "it is well understood that they were intended as protecting charms against the fascination of the evil eye."[115] The following discussion is also meant to illustrate the extraordinary power of fertility symbols to persist, generation after generation, from prehistory into history, in spite of all the deliberate attempts on the part of various institutions (like the state or the church) to do away with them. Whatever happened historically to sheela-na-gigs as symbols also happened to the Eye as symbol. Both icons came out of the struggle a bit distorted in meaning but still here, probably because of their ancient fertility/goodluck aspect, which includes the ability to protect against unproductivity, infertility and ill-fortune.

The Sheela as Parturient Woman

Given all the symbolic imagery discussed above, it becomes difficult not to accept the notorious sheela-na-gigs as ancient fertility effigies. If we think of the symbol of the Parturient Woman as representing both birth and coitus at the same time—and it is a fact that both are used as symbols of fertility—then the sheela-na-gig figure can be classified as an instance of the Parturient Woman symbol.

The sheelas are grotesque stone carvings of women presenting their genitals in the splayed legs position of the Parturient Woman symbol, from which they differ in that they are holding the labia open with their hands, (fig. 17.3 and 17.4 et al. etc.) rather than having their arms thrust above their head. Their most remarkable feature is their incorporation in churches and in castle walls, floors and doorways particularly of the Romanesque period, where they remained for several centuries without being particularly singled out or mentioned in contemporary records or in literature. It is only at the end of the 18th century and during the 19th century that clerics and scholars began to notice them and expressed their horror at the "shameless" and "indecent" poses of the carvings. They found themselves in the predicament of trying to explain in religious terms, the presence of these figures in religious edifices (see Appendix IV). The explanation they devised was one in which they speculated that clerics and monks of the early church meant to convey the ugliness of *sex as sin* to their parishioners by exhibiting naked women with tormented faces (see *The Elusive Grimace* below).[116] This is still the explanation advocated by recent scholars, such as Anthony Weir and James Jerman, or Jorgen Andersen.[117] It is always possible that the clergy of the medieval period thought that way, but there is no evidence that they did. Another explanation is much more probable. First, recent scholarship in medieval studies has shown that the peasants had a generally more robust view of life than the clerical chroniclers would have us believe. Secondly, the Church and the "establishment" did have great difficulties in getting the heathen peasants to accept the worship of a single male authoritarian and inflexible God. Ideology is simply a reflection of society. In her book, *Adam, Eve and the Serpent* (Random House, 1988), Elaine Pagels shows how the interpretation of the story of Genesis changed according to the historical circumstances of the times. She says: "I am not saying that religious ideas are nothing but a cover for political motives. . . . Instead, I intend to show that religious insights and moral choices, in actual experience, coincide with practical one." She concludes: "biblical *interpretation* is no more than ideology under a different name" (p. xxvii) [my emphasis]).

From prehistory to antiquity and beyond, the people of the land had inherited a sense of reverence for what folklorists and psychoanalysts (such as Neumann) call the Great Mother, in one form or another.[118] The fertility of the Earth was paramount in their minds and in their values. To ask them to be disloyal to that which they considered as the essence of their lives was an impossibility unless some concessions were made to their convictions. The Church did this by including some of the ancient symbols of fertility in the new church buildings. Some of these were the "sexual carvings" such as the sheela-na-gigs, most of which are likely to have been executed in pre-Christian times but incorporated later. This seems to have soothed the sensibilities of the people in their need for protective icons. This kind of symbolic gesture was also used in other circumstances by the Church. Gantner and Pobé explain the building of

Romanesque churches upon foundations built of ancient Roman columns and capitals by saying: "In creative ages the monuments of by-gone times are used for building material—not treasured as museum pieces."[119] Be that as it may, dominant ideologies often build temples or churches *symbolically* on the ruins of the temples they have displaced. Michael Dames points out that: "The erection of the Avebury [Christian] chapel from fragments of shattered Stone Age megaliths, neatly epitomizes a turning point in human affairs on this planet. As Max Weber says: 'That great historical process . . . the elimination of magic from the world . . . came here to its logical conclusion'" (Dames, p. 116). Throughout Greece, all temples to Helios (the sun) have been replaced by churches and monasteries dedicated to Saint Elias. Christian churches built at the time of the arrival of Christianity on the Aegean Islands incorporate pieces of white marble from ancient temples. This was done, not because of lack of building material (there is stone enough all around), but rather as an intentional symbolic transformation of belief absorbed by a "greater truth." The same could surely be said of the menhirs like that of St. Duzec in Britanny on which Christian symbols have been carved, or of the Celtic Cross at Kilkieran, County Kilkenny in Ireland, which is topped by a magnificent glans (see fig. 25.1). This seems to be true also of the many ancient "crosses" of England. Longworth says: "Many of the oldest examples are not *crosses* at all, but *pillars*, and some of them would seem to have been fashioned at first to resemble the phallus." This position is carried one step further by Alexander Stone regarding the "Celtic Crosses": ". . . the ancient so-called Keltic cross, which, aside from symbolizing the male generative organ, depicts also the *pudenda* of the female by means of the circle which is a component of the whole."[120]

The Church was trying to eradicate old fertility beliefs associated with the menhirs. The new creed nearly always had to contend with lingering "pagan" beliefs. Everywhere, the Church and the clerics sought to destroy or christianize them. Their efforts at eradication were often in vain and they had to resort to absorbing the old pagan gods in order to change them into beings subordinate to the Christian God. Franck Bourdier illustrates the "union of pagan and Christian traditions" with some small scale carvings showing representations of Christ and Mary intermingled with old pagan ktenes and phalloi, and at least one Parturient Woman symbol.[121] During the first three centuries of Christianity, there seems to have been a concerted effort by the Church to create saints that never existed. The story of these saints were often based upon old pagan myths. The warrior saint, Martin, is the descendant of the Roman god of war, Mars (Mars/Martis in Latin). Sainte Venise (the name of a town in France) was Venus. Even the Greek Earth Mother, Demeter, became a male Saint Demetrios.[122] Another case in point is the cult of Mary which at first the Church sought to suppress as a remnant of a cult of Mother Earth. When peasants continued to revere Mary in preference to the now official male God, she was incorporated into the system and demoted to a secondary role.[123] Berger in her study of the development of the goddess notes: "Reluctant to abandon such a deeply rooted mythic figure, early medieval peasants sought ways to retain the grain protectress while rendering her innocuous to the church hierarchy. . . . Accordingly, some of the earliest female saints—Radegund, Milburga, Macrine, Wilpurga—as well as the Virgin Mary, were mythically to take the place of the grain goddess in one locale or another." Yet, to this day, Mary is still revered by Greek peasants who call her Panagiya (Παναγια), "All Holy," with seldom a reference to the Orthodox "Theos." While working in Greece, I heard the name of God (Θεος) invoked only once in twelve months and that was in response to a question that I had asked. Otherwise, the constant references to the supernatural were directed at the Panagiya.

With this in mind, it is small wonder that in the Celtic area the pagan sheela-na-gigs—if indeed (as seems highly probable) they were fertility symbols—were incorporated into the new Christian churches. The gesture was a concession meant to placate the peasant, as was the acceptance of Mary as part of the hagiology of the Church. Weir's contention that "no mason would have been allowed" to carve figures of such indecency "unless his work had been done with the connivance or direction of his patrons," may be true but he jumps to a doubtful conclusion.[124] The intent of the clerics was more likely to have been, not to horrify peasants but rather, to conciliate them. Moreover, the possibility that some sheelas may have been pre-Christian artifacts incorporated into the building of churches, does not exclude the likelihood that the tradition of carving sheelas was perpetuated, conserving the ancient style as in the early examples. Some art historians dated the sheelas according to the age of the Romanesque churches in which they were found. But many sheelas are carved out of stone that is different from the stone of the buildings. Moreover, the style of the carvings, except in later times, is quite different from that of the rest of the sculptures of the churches in which they occur. This has led other art historians to conclude, more logically, that the early sheelas were old Celtic carvings that were incorporated in the Christian churches. This interpretation is most likely if indeed the figures were fertility symbols central to the belief system of the old Celts, whom we know to have had a strong fertility worldview (see Appendix IV).

In later times the sheelas became stylized as in the double-tailed mermaids, or for that matter, Bernini's carvings on the outer faces of the four pedestal of St. Peter's baldachino in Rome (see below). That is not to say that "the anti-femininism of the twelfth-century Church"[125] did not play a role in the inclusion of sheelas in churches that were built at that time. It is always possible that the clergy, who advocated the idea of women as sexual beings created for the perdition of men, thought of the "ugliness" of the carvings as being horrifying, but this does not mean that the peasants, who had venerated fertility symbolized by sheelas for generations before the coming of Christianity, did not demand that their ancient symbols be exhibited for protection against the evils of infertility. In that sense, the two attitudes are not mutually exclusive.

In the Tantric temples in India, there are many carvings of women in the sheela posture. This indicates that the "ugliness" of the sheelas has nothing to do with the "horror of sex," on the contrary, if we may infer from the contemporary Tantric rituals, the "ugliness" seems to be aimed at diverting the attention of worshippers from beauty (see below) to that part of the body which is symbolically important: the entrance to the female reproductive organs. In the Tantric rituals there is a ceremony called *stipuja* in which a woman is especially selected and trained by the guru. Then, according to a description by a European observer of the beginning of this century: "The woman is seated on an altar with legs spread wide apart to display the sacred symbol, the yoni [vulva], which the priest kisses and to which he offers food and libations in sacred vessels called *argha*, which are shaped like the yoni. After these offerings have been consecrated by touching them to the living yoni, they are distributed among the worshippers and eaten."[126] John Allegro, who cites the above, adds: "The woman thus honored is not necessarily selected for her youth, beauty or virtue. Often she will be repulsively ugly and ill-formed, or chosen for her low-caste or depraved and debauched character. The idea is to concentrate the attention of the worshippers on the vulva itself as the prime embodiment of the female sex principle, to the exclusion of all consideration of beauty, birth and breeding."[127]

The sheelas, then, may be considered as a variation of the Parturient Woman, that is, Woman preparing for delivery. All this also explains the "enormous" vulva of some sheelas. It is "enormous" because it is a representation of the vulva at the time of parturition. Referring again to illustration photograph number 24.1 of a woman giving birth: the process is fixed by the camera at the very moment of crowning. The vulva is dilated to give way to the head of the child, and, at that particular instant, the vulva can be considered "enormous." It is also in an almost perfect almond shape (see Chapter XII, on the significance of the oval), and the face of the woman, like the face of the sheela-na-gigs, expresses the pain and the stress of childbirth.

The Elusive Grimace

Kirchhoff, in his article on *Woman's Posture During Childbirth* shows two figurines from the Taranto area of Italy. They represent women giving birth and are dated to the middle of the fourth century B.C. and the first century B.C. respectively. Both statuettes have "painfully distorted faces" to which the author attributes the intention of turning away evil. But again, the "distorted faces" simply identify The Parturient Woman, and it is as Parturient Woman symbols that they are apotropaic, and not because of the distorted faces.[128] Latter-day carvings representing women in parturition plainly feature the facial grimace of pain. Witkowski describes a sculpture in St. Etienne cathedral in Sens (Yonne, France). It depicts a woman giving birth (his fig. 551, p. 453). The head of the child is beginning to emerge, and Witkowski says: "Effectivement, les traits de la parturiente son convulsés par l'acuité de la douleur." ("Effectively, the features of the parturient woman are distorted by the intensity of the pain.") So are the features of the woman in illustration #24.1 and so are the features of all grimacing sheela-na-gigs.

There is a photograph by Wayne Miller in Steichen's *Family of Man*, which shows the grimace of a beautiful woman in the pains of childbirth.[129] Another shot of a woman showing the grimace of the pain and effort of childbirth is found in the film produced by Lennart Nilsson called *The Miracle of Life* and in his book *A Child Is Born* (fig. 17.8). This latter photograph is particularly illustrative because it exhibits the same quadrangular shape as that of the Cavan sheela's mouth and others. This contorted facial expression appears as symbol in art. The eight outer faces of the four pedestals of the famous baldachino in St. Peter's basilica in Rome depicts the stages of birthing in a sequence of relief carvings by Bernini for Pope Urban VIII. The artist uses the shape of the heraldic shield to represent a woman's body. The "middle base" of the heraldic shield is in the shape of the vulva at various stages of the process of birthing. Witkowski describes this as follows:

> . . . la partie inférieure représente les organes génitaux de la femme, avec les détails anatomiques les plus complets et variables suivant les phases de l'accouchement. (p. 256)
>
> . . . the lower part [of the eight carvings] represents, in complete anatomical detail, the state of a woman's genital organs in the various phases of the birthing process. (my translation)[130]

Witkowski discusses the Bernini work quite freely, but he wonders how Bernini could have gotten away with this "espièglerie d'atelier" (workshop mischief). It may well be that Bernini was familiar with the symbolism of the Parturient Woman, and I suspect it meant more to him and to Pope Urban VIII, than just a practical joke. Given the widespread and quasi-archetypal quality of the symbol, the Parturient Woman explanation is certainly much more plausible than that of a monumental "espièglerie d'atelier." Accordingly, the shield is surmounted by the head of a woman whose facial expression changes from serenity to agony as she proceeds to give birth. At the climax, her expression is, in a technically more sophisticated way, the same as that of the Lepenski Vir carving (see below), that of many of the sheelas, and of the gorgoneia.

The Gorgon's face, especially the early representations such as the well-known Etruscan Gorgon, exhibits the pain of childbirth, the only difference being the technicality of having the grimace curl up instead of down. One of the Gorgones, the Medusa, is to be taken as a fertility symbol, and "the hideously grotesque original type of the Gorgoneion, as the Gorgon's head was called, was used generally as an amulet, a protection against the evil eye," particularly, I might add, as protection in war on the shields of Greek warriors (see below, the section on Gorgon.)[131] The grin that strikes terror in the soul of art historians is the symbolic grimace of the Parturient Woman at the significant and critical moment of delivery, and is meant to protect against adversity.

A Possible Historical Origin of the Sheela-na-gigs

I would suggest that there may be a possible historical connection of the sheelas with some of the carvings found in Lepenski Vir, Yugoslavia.[132] That the people of Lepenski-Vir venerated fertility is almost certain in view of the carved vulvae. I shall single out two of these. One of them cannot be mistaken.[133] It clearly represents the vulva in the process of birth *just before* the moment of crowning and is described as such in the final report (see fig. 13.1 in this book). The other, fig. 13.2 in this book,[134] is labeled "a fish" by the author, but even a superficial glance at the two carvings will reveal their similarity, so that if figure 13.1 is the representation of a vulva, so is figure 13.2, the only difference being that the latter is a vulva *at* the moment of crowning. It is puzzling that Srejovic, the author of the report, did not see the similarity.[135]

Most significantly, however, in the Lepenski Vir II level, house XLIV, there is found a carving (his fig. 53 or Plate V, shown in this book as fig. 17.6) which the author inexplicably identifies as a male. It has all the characteristics of a sheela, beginning with the obvious genitalia, the positioning of the hands, the ribs, the diminutive breasts and the grotesque face. Marija Gimbutas restores her sex and calls her a "fish Goddess" because of the shape of the mouth. The facial grimace of the Lepenski Vir statue should indeed be compared to that of the known sheelas such as the Cavan sheela in the Dublin Museum (fig. 17.7). The shape of the mouth in the latter is remarkably like that of the Lepenski Vir statue, yet no one has interpreted the Cavan sheela as a fish goddess. In both cases, it is more likely to be the face of a woman expressing the pain of childbirth. By the same token, I think that the figure from Capdenac-le-Haut (c.4000 B.C.), shown by Gimbutas, and classified by her as a "bird goddess," ranks closer to the Lepenski Vir sheela (c.4600 B.C.) (see fig. 17.5).[136] If, as Gimbutas argues, the criterion for classifying the Capdenac figure as a bird goddess is based solely on the presence of three-fingered hands, then, the Lepenski Vir figure is also a bird goddess, because, it too, has three fingers (a fact recognized by Gimbutas in her latest book). Still, because of the subjectivity of the evidence, and because there is no precedent in the ethnographic literature, whereas there is a great abundance of evidence for a grimace in parturient women, it seems most unlikely that either is a "goddess," or a fish or a bird. Each represents *fertility* in a remarkable similarity of style. The fact that they are represented with three fingers may be puzzling but is probably not significant. The best known of the sheelas, Kilpeck, has four fingers, and that fact is probably insignificant also. The distorted mouth of the Lepenski Vir figure has probably more in common with all the other distorted-mouth sheelas and gorgones than with the possibility that the inhabitants of the Lepenski Vir site may have had a fish economy. Like the sheelas, the Lepenski-Vir effigy and the medusas, all women do express the pain and effort of childbirth with a grimace.[137]

Lepenski Vir is dated between 5600 B.C. and 4950 B.C. It is in the proximity of the area which has been proposed as the place of origin, at a much later date, of the Celts. It is possible, therefore, that the idea of the sheelas, once created, was diffused into the areas of later Celtic occupation. Nevertheless, some scholars have attributed the sheelas to an era contemporaneous with the building of Christian Churches on the grounds that they were found in church structures. The arguments used to support this contemporaneity are tenuous. I think as good an argument can be made for the pagan Celtic origin of sheelas (see Appendix IV). First, as stated above, the figures may have been a concession to peasants who were Celts. Many figures are in fact to be found imbedded in walls and floors of castles in Ireland. Second, the area of distribution of sheelas corresponds to the area of diffusion of Celtic Culture. Lepenski Vir, of course, is not exactly in the area of assumed Celtic origin. The site is older by several millennia and precedes the occupation by any people we could give a name to. Nevertheless, the area is close enough to that which is deemed to be the center of Celtic origins, so that cultural contact is possible. In the instance of *fertility* symbols, the reality of persistence over time and space is well established. One needs only to show that it applies to sheela-na-gigs. This has been done, in my opinion (and it is not an adamant opinion), by evidence of the great morphological similarities in the style of the Lepenski Vir/Capdenac-le-Haut carvings and the sheela-na-gigs, and their congruence with the assumed distribution and spread of Celtic Culture from an area around the Danube in Central Europe to Western Europe.

Chapter XII

The Eye As Symbol

The Oval Shape

As symbols, the oval, the almond shape and the eye cannot be separated from each other. Each represents the kteis, which, in turn, is the part representing the whole Parturient Woman. The most common graphic fertility symbol is the oval, which appears in the rituals of almost all religions. It recurs in church art as a mandorla (or Mandala). The word itself is from the Latin and Greek words, (*amygdalum*, *amygdalon* respectively) meaning almond. It may have stemmed from an even older Semitic term, amygdala, which, according to Yarden, "means conceivably Great Mother—a prototypical, apparently Mesopotamian fertility goddess."[138] As the essence of femininity, it appears in the name Magdalene. The almond, because of its shape, was a symbol of fertility in antiquity and it still is in the northern Mediterranean area where sugar-coated almonds (confetti) are distributed at weddings and baptisms. The oval shape or almond shape in oriental art is "a schematized representation of the cosmos," but it also occurs in western religious art.[139] It is often referred to as *vesica piscis* and has been a symbol for the vulva in both eastern and western antiquity. As fish symbolism it survived into Christianity, with its meaning modified. Greek Christianity turned the term ιχθυς (ichthys: fish) into an acrostic: Ιησοῦς Χριστὸς, Θεὸῦ υιὸς, Σωτὴρ (Jesus Christ, son of God, Saviour) (fig. 2.1 from Kythnos.) The fish has long been a fertility symbol in all areas affected by the Evil Eye syndrome. Probably for several reasons. First because of the apparent fecundity of fish, but mostly because of their shape. Generally, the fish is oblong in shape. Therefore, the generic symbolic form is an oval, which itself is a classic symbol of the vulva, and therefore a symbol of fertility. Alexander Marshack, in the latest edition of his book (1991), says that he has found that the representations of fish in cave art is of far greater occurrence than had been reported (see Marshack, pp. 398-401).

Even fish that are not properly "oval" in shape, such as the dolphin, represented, at least in the Mediterranean, the uterus, a fertility symbol. It is interesting to note that in Greek the uterus (or more properly: the womb) is δελφυς (delphys), a name obviously related to two other fertility symbols, the sow, which is δελφος (delphos), and the dolphin, which is δελφις (delphis, later: δελφιν [delphin]). Also, the temple complex at Delphi was said to be *the* navel of the world.

A frequent representation of Christ in Romanesque art is a Christ "in majesty," issuing from a mandorla, the side of which are pulled open by two angels. It is worthy of note that Mary has an almost equal status with Jesus in that posture. Ordinarily, no saint is accorded this privilege in Christian iconography. Other instances give us clues to that meaning; there is, for instance, a mandorla from the sarcophagus of Doña Sancha in Spain, dating from the early 12th century, depicting two angels pulling at the sides of the oval inside which there is a child, who, presumably, is coming out of the womb (fig. 11.1).[140] Or again, in McLean's *Contribution à l'étude de l'iconographie populaire* there is the photograph of a graffito showing an uncontestable vulva in the shape of an almond, inside which there is a child. Granted that in this latter case, the intent must have been prurient and not traditional art, nevertheless the comparison to the Doña Sancha sarcophagus is inevitable. It is in the nature of things that it should be difficult for individuals to make a distinction between the lofty ideals of αγαπε ("agapes" or spiritual love) and the more earthy needs of ερος ("eros" or physical love). The species *as species* does not have a morality that will put a value on either of the cultural categories mentioned. That is why the same forms recur over and over and again, whether it be to express love or lust, fertility or prurience, the distinction being an intellectual and cultural exercise made by people. For the same reason, it is interesting to note that the phallos which accompanies the kteis in McLean's work is winged, as were so many Roman apotropaic frescoes and protective "mobiles," to use an Alexander Calder word (cf. McLean's figures 207, a, b, c). A guess, then, at the original symbolic meaning of the Christ "in majesty" is that it was intended to signify that Christianity is the birth of a new life. Another type of clue is offered by a "maternity plate" from the Italian XVth century in which is shown a naked woman in a mandorla, who is, if not "in majesty," certainly in glory (fig. 11.2). She seems to represent "maternity" rather than a particular woman. There are rays emanating from her kteis directed at six males who look up from below in reverence. The vignette here is very much reminiscent in spirit of the numerous Roman bas-reliefs showing an "eye," called "the much-suffering eye" by Otto Jahn, surrounded by phallic symbols (figs. 8 all). Both consist of a kteic center of attention surrounded by numerous phallos. It is also reminiscent of the modern Catholic medals (to be worn around the neck), oval in shape, depicting the "Immaculate Conception" in majesty, with rays emanating from the palm of her hands. (The palm of the hand is a kteic symbol. See below.) Finally, many of the Parturient Woman figures, including the sheela-na-gigs, exhibit an almond shaped vulva, as do live parturient women at the moment of crowning (see fig. 24.1).

The Egg Shape

The oval in three dimensions is the egg, which itself, is an obvious fertility symbol. Its shape was used as a mandorla in alchemy during the Middle Ages (see the Alchemical egg-vessel from the manuscript, *De Lapide Philosophorum*, England, XVIth Century, in which the mandorla, although it is called "The Cosmic Egg," is even surrounded by hair).[141] The egg-shape was already present in the Upper Palaeolithic as is evident in a remarkable carving from the Abri Pataud in France. It is made out of a rough pebble in the shape of a vulva; the cleavage in the middle contains what seems to be a clitoris personified by a slender female figure which itself has a phallic shape.

The egg-shape is also male, in as much as the testicles are egg shaped. Grains of cereals such as wheat or rice and cowrie shells (because of their resemblance to the vulva, and because of their egg shape) have been universally used as fertility symbols. That is why grains of rice and wheat are still thrown at newlyweds. By extension, other forms, such as that of the coco-de-mer in South Asia, or for that matter, the link of a chain, have come to symbolize the same thing.

The Eye as Symbol

The idea of the eye as a symbol for the vulva—and by extension, for female fertility—is not a new one. Among scholars, it was suggested by Dulaure (1805) who quotes Knight (1786). Both of them hint at a relationship between "the worship of Priapus" and protection against the Evil Eye. In later times, Reither (1913) and Deonna (1965) among others have suggested, in passing, that the eye is a symbol for the vulva.[142] Catherine Johns points out that in art history "The first association of a phallos with another object which comes to mind is that of the phallos and an eye or a pair of eyes" (p. 66).[143] The eye in direct association with the phallos is encountered in ancient Rome, and is placed at the entrance of homes to protect the household and make it prosperous. Two striking examples appear in mosaics, one from Moknine, Tunisia shows a phallus directly pointed at an eye (fig. 39.1), the other is from Susa in Tunisia also (fig. 39.2), the design of which is almost identical to the Moknine mosaic, but the phallos is flanked by two explicit vulvae and is connected to one of them by a line representing a highly probable ejaculation. In comparing the two mosaics, there is no doubt that the eye and the vulva are equated. Symbols of fertility are not always that graphic, but these two samples do provide unmistakable evidence that the eye is symbolically equated with the female pudenda. From ancient Rome again, there are innumerable bas-reliefs, engraved gems and medals (all apotropaic against the Evil Eye), representing an eye towards which are pointed a great number of varied known phallic symbols: the scorpion with its erect tail, the lion and a lion's paw, a clove of garlic, the bull and its horns, lizards, dolphins, birds, usually with a long neck, detached phalloi, spears, Jove's bolts, arrows, tridents and in the case of at least one wall carving in Leptis Magna, Roman Libya, a Centaur's phallic nose (figs. 8.2), (see also Elworthy, pp. 130 & 131 for medals and engraved gems). Bonner Campbell, who wrote *Studies in Magical Amulets*, is puzzled by the diversity of animals surrounding this "much-suffering eye" (see pp. 97 & 98), and he comes to the conclusion that: "Efforts to find a religious or symbolic meaning in the choice of these animals seem to me futile" (p. 98). No need to say that if Campbell had reviewed the literature on fertility cults, he would have understood the meaning. In the context of the eye as a kteis, it being surrounded by phallic symbols (including animals) makes sense. There is even the bas-relief, referred to as the Bedford (or Woburn) Marble, showing what is alleged (by Jahn, among others) to be "a man" defecating over a large disembodied eye (fig. 8.3).[144] Kirchhoff, who has made a study of the posture of women giving birth, points out, on the basis of his data, that the "posture of defecation" which is seen by some in many Baubo and related figures, really represents a woman in the squatting birthing posture of the time.[145] In the case of the Bedford-Woburn marble, the eye is her kteis, and as in so many Roman bas-reliefs, medals and engraved gems, it is surrounded with phallic symbols (a scorpion, a lion, two birds, Jove's bolt and a trident, the latter two being held by a man).

Either the kteis, or the phallos, by itself, is unproductive and therefore "unlucky" or "evil." Perhaps it is in that sense, that "spinsters" are considered to have the Evil Eye (see Distasi, pp. 18-19). Given the complementarity of the sexes, one has to be coupled with the other in order to achieve the only thing that counts: fecundity, which is inevitably equated with productivity.

Isis and Osiris were the God and Goddess of fertility. Horus, their son, was the yearly product of their fertile union. The ultimate symbol of fertility became the design called the "Eye of Horus," which is a hallmark of Egyptian art (fig. 12.3).[146] In the light of what we now know, the eye proper is female and the shape below is phallic. Charrière reproduces an Egyptian drawing of a mating couple in which the man's exaggerated penis has the same stylistic shape as the line under the Eye of Horus.[147] The "eye shadow," which may originally have been an attempt to emulate the Eye of Horus, was and still is protection against the Evil Eye in Egypt and many parts of the Orient (see fig. 5.1). Hasluck reports that in Macedonia, women spotted their face with cosmetic markings so that "first remarks made by passers-by" would be on the markings rather than on their beauty, even if, as Hasluck says: "the ladies are quite aware of how these patches enhance their charms."[148] The same thing is true of Indian women and children in Veranasi, India (see above), who wear lampblack around their eyes to protect themselves against the Evil Eye (fig. 5.1). Whether Indian women are secretly aware of the fact that the dark patches "enhance their charm" is a moot point, but they certainly explicitly state that the purpose of garnishing their children's eyes (including the boys') is to disorient any Evil Eye curse. It may be significant that women, who are traditionally among those who have to be "protected" against the Evil Eye, are the ones who generally wear cosmetics. It may also be that there was originally an affiliation between the two meanings of the Greek word "cosmos" (κοσμος) which means both "Universe" and "ornament." From ethnography and from prehistory, we have collections of statues (particularly in Africa), and sometimes even skulls (from the prehistoric Middle East and from contemporary New Guinea), where the *eyes* are represented by cowrie shells, which are also known to be fertility symbols because they represent the vulva.

The Moment of Crowning

The oval as symbol of the vulva (i.e. as kteis), can be classified into two categories based on two moments of the birthing process. These two moments seem to hold great significance in what I may call the Universal Code of Fertility symbolism, from perhaps as old as 25,000 B.C., to as recently as the European 12th Century A.D. and later, if we include the "ethnographic" world outside of Europe. These instants are:

1-The state of the vulva *immediately before* the moment of crowning, and

2-The state of the vulva *at the moment* of crowning.

The vulva, just before birth when the fetus starts its descent and the orifice of the vagina is beginning to open, takes on an oval shape that is quite characteristic of the moment. There are very old prehistoric effigies whose "enormous" vulvae exhibit unmistakably "the moment of crowning." As examples, we have already mentioned the Lepenski-Vir carving of a vulva at the pre-crowning stage, as well as the gorgones and the sheela-na-gigs (especially Oaksey and Cavan), but there are others. One of the oldest is a statuette 5½ centimeters tall found at Monpazier in the Dordogne (fig. 16.2). Another is a larger than life statue which was still the object of a cult at the end of the 17th century near Couarde (Morbihan) in Brittany. It had a "vulve démesurée" (a "disproportionate vulva").[149] The claim expressed by Hadingham about the lack of attention to the vulva on most statuettes must be due to the fact that he ignores Lepenski Vir, Capdenac-le-haut, the sheelas, particularly the ones from Oaksey and Cavan (fig. 16.1 & 17.7), and such palaeolithic figurines as Monpazier, Soulosses, Couarde and several of the Balzi Rossi cave (Grimaldi) statuettes.[150] The "enormity" of the vulvae is explainable by the fact that they represent the pre-delivery moments. Figure 13.1 is from a site in Yugoslavia, Lepenski Vir, level dated to 4600 B.C. It shows the status of the vulva just before crowning, and figure 13.2, from the same site, shows it at the moment of crowning. These designs seem to have diffused through a widespread area and become traditional. They were probably present in Celtic statuary, and one of them may have been incorporated in a church as were the sheelas. It is now called "The Eye of God" and is situated on the tower of Ste Mary's church in Newchurch-in-Pendle, England (see illustration No. 12.1). According to local legend, it was placed there to protect the parishioners "from witches" i.e. against evil. This Eye of God has all the appearances of the vulva at the moment of crowning. Certainly the designs still appear in Romanesque carvings of the 10th, 11th and 12th centuries, a good example of which is found on the stoup in the St. Barthélémy-de-Farges church in the Department of Saône-et-Loire, France (fig. 14.1 & 14.2). The worshippers must wet their fingers and make the sign of the cross over their body. Wetting a finger to touch a symbolic vulva was, and still is in some places, a symbolic fertility gesture. On the outer side of the stoup at Farges, there are incised figures in which one can see the birthing progression of the vulva on the three leftmost carvings, ending with the wide-open kteic "eyes" of the grotesque central figure. The authors of *The Glory of Romanesque Art*, however, identify the first as "plant-like ornaments," although they do grant that the style of the "plant" designs correspond to the style of the "eyes" that are also represented. (They do not explain the face: on the basis of what we have said of the faces of sheelas and of the Gorgo, there is a possibility that the "grin" was meant to represent, awkardly to be sure, the grimace expressing pain and effort in childbirth, a fact that seems to have been traditionally important.) Given what we know of the sequence of shapes that the vulva takes as it approaches the moment of delivery, these "eyes" seem to be a representation of the vulva at the moment of crowning, and they look remarkably like some of the "eye goddesses" from Mesopotamia, which were considered as protection against the Evil Eye. Illustration 14.4 shows a gypsum figure "eye goddess" from Tell Asmar, late 27th century B.C. The "plant-like ornaments" cannot be taken for anything but ktenes, especially if one is to compare them not only with reality, but also with the known ktenes on Roman lamps, or to the Roman kteic carving on the column base from Nîmes, or to the "flowers" on Hindu carvings or the lotus petals on the pedestal of Hindu deities. We have here an aspect of birth that is repeated over and over and again in fertility symbolism. The vulva is represented at the moment immediately *before* crowning. In the case of the "eyes" of the head on the stoup, it is a representation of the genitalia *at the moment* of crowning. Those "eyes," as the authors say, are in line with the other designs and it is beside the point to try to imagine why the stone-cutters, carving a sequence of ktenes from pre-crowning to moment of crowning, should carve a grotesque face around the last two, which, after all, "look like eyes." Moreover, the kteis was possibly still a symbol of fertility at the time of carving. This is all the more plausible because the gesture of wetting the fingers in the stoup at the entrance of a church is repeated at the entrance of Tantric temples, where the finger is wetted with saliva, for the purpose of touching the vulva of the goddess as a fertility gesture. "In recent times in India visitors to many ancient shrines used to have symbolic intercourse with stone-cut female deities by thrusting their fingers into deep touchholes, worn by generations of finger-thrusters, at the deities sexual centres."[151] The "sheelas" in the Celtic areas often show the kind of wear consistent with this type of activity. This could be the "pagan" origin of the Catholic custom, not through India, of course, but through the Celts. Incidentally, one might argue that the Mezuzah is likely to have been the same kind of fertility symbol. It is placed at the entrance of the house, and it is made up of a small oval similar to the ankh's, below which is a rolled up phallic scroll. Upon entering the house, one has to wet a finger and touch the oval (see also under "Spitting and Saliva": apotropaics against the Evil Eye).

In the Middle Ages, the idea of "creating" life (or gold, or whatever) was symbolized by a mating couple, but it was also symbolized in the Alchemical Egg which in its graphic two-dimensional representation is a kteis at the moment of crowning.[152] In present-day Greece, the symbolism of renewal, of new life in Spring is expressed when at Easter, a red egg is baked in a swirl of bread dough in the shape of the Moment of Crowning (fig. 14.5). Dulaure reports that bread loaves (*miche*) shaped like phalloi and ktenes were still baked in his time in France.[153] The same reverence, the same awe felt by early peoples faced with the moment of crowning seems to be evident again today in, for instance, "The Birth Project" described by Elizabeth Durbin and Doug Bradley in an article called "Women's Work" (*The Progressive*, March 1986.) One of their illustrations is a photograph of a tapestry by Judy Chicago, called "The Crowning." It represents two things that have been symbols of the female dimension of fertility: the Parturient Woman and the vulva at the moment of Crowning. One finds the former everywhere, in Africa, in Melanesia, in Ptolemaic Egypt, in Celtic Europe, in India, in Australia, and in the New World. The symbol comes in a variety of forms, sometimes realistic and sometimes highly stylized but always recognizable; it always represents fertility. The oval and the Eye cannot be separated from the Parturient Woman symbol. It is the part that stands for the whole.

The variations can include an oval truncated at both ends with a line in the middle (see figs 15, 15.2, 20.3). This truncated oval is found from the cave walls of the palaeolithic to present day Tanzania and Nigeria, where it still represents the vulva.[154] With this shape in mind, it behooves us to re-interpret the symbols bossed on the Gundestrup bowl. Stove and Kraig say: "One of the most brilliant piece of Celtic art, the Gundestrup bowl found in a Danish peat bog, shows a God placing a warrior in a cauldron head first. This is thought by some to mean warrior sacrifice. More likely, it is related to the myth of Dan Cecht and symbolizes a return to life." Given the truncated-oval shape and form of the "cauldron," it is more likely to be a kteis and the "warrior" is more likely to be a child just delivered from its mother's womb, and in that sense it could, indeed, be the return to life of Dan Cecht. By the same token, the "god" is unlikely to be a "god," rather, the total picture could be a representation of fertility, as is the symbol of the Parturient Woman.

To sum up: for those who live close to Nature, barren women, barren domestic animals and barren fields are among the great tragedies of life. An untended field spells misfortune, because it will not be productive. This neglect portends lack of food and therefore is *evil*. The fields must be plowed and the seed must be sown. The eye as kteis, then, is as much a symbol for the fertility of the fields as it is a symbol for the fecundity of people or the bounty of any productive (or reproductive) activity. Given the consequential role of the female in reproduction, a kteis by itself is sterile, and therefore portends evil. To create life, the power potential of the kteis must be complemented with the power potential of the phallos. Hence the apotropaics against the Evil Eye are generally phallic. Sometimes there may seem to be a contradiction in having a kteic symbol be used as an apotropaic against the Evil Eye, which itself is kteic, but we must remember that *the original intent was fecundity*, so that the sexual character of the apotropaics can be either kteic or phallic.

The malignant character of the unheeded eye can be aggravated by the negative character of the envy that emanates from those who might resent the "good luck" quality (prosperity, fecundity, affluence) of one's own mana. These individuals disrupt social harmony. The protective devices are then brought to bear upon these unfortunate individuals: the apotropaics are directed at them. But, this is only one facet of the strategies of protection.

In the end, symbolically speaking, whether it is an oval, or a heart, or a phallos, or the Alpha and the Omega, or an Eye, or a prehistoric statuette, or the Circle of Life, or a lotus flower or a calla lily, etc., it is all one: all these symbols represent the same thing: the impersonal mana of fertility. The possibility of its absence is what is considered "evil." The Eye is a symbol of the female dimension of fertility, and when it stands alone, it is bound to be unproductive, therefore evil. Hence, its remedies are symbolically phallic.

The Ultimate Eye

Thou hast ravished my heart, my sister, my bride;
Thou hast ravished my heart with one of thine eyes,
With one chain of thy neck.[155]
[The Song of Songs, 4/9. King James version]

The Song of Songs is an erotic love poem. The text teems with words and images that can best be described as fertility symbols. Solomon, or whoever wrote the text, must have used the symbols that were current in his time and understood by everybody. These symbols are no longer intelligible to us and we cannot understand them, unless we place them back in the context of what it meant to love, to mate and to be fertile in Solomon's time.

The verse quoted above from the King James version of the Song of Songs (chapter 4, verse 9), has puzzled translators of the Old Testament. "With *one* of thine eyes"? If we are to take the words literally, it almost seems to be a caricature. In a love story, how can one be enraptured by the beauty of one eye only? Some of the recent translations try to get around the problem by saying: "you have ravished my heart . . . by one *glance* of your eyes." But the original Hebrew text clearly says: "With one of thine eyes."[156] The question then becomes, ultimately, which eye? In order to make the text intelligible, let us place the symbol in the context of a world in which the eye is a fertility symbol. I suggest then that the line addressed by Solomon, the Lover, to the Shulamite woman refers to the only eye that counts, the eye that defines prosperity, abundance, fertility and well-being, the ultimate symbol of female fecundity and charm, that which, in mating, attracts its male counterpart, and well should have fascinated the lover in the Song of Songs: her vulva.[157]

Chapter XIII

On the Endurance and Tenacity of Fertility Rituals

Phallic and Kteic Saints

Fertility symbols are as enduring as they are abundant. There is among peasants, who are by definition close to the land, a compelling force that drives them not only to identify with the earth, but also to have an almost awesome respect for the fertility of the soil. Joanna Hubbs wrote an article on "The Worship of Mother Earth in Russian Culture."[158] What she brings out, although that is not her principal intention, is that Russian peasants, in spite of Christianity, in spite of Bolshevism, in spite of any ideology, can still wax lyrical when it comes to the love of the land. I am not "of the land," but I do remember from my childhood being impressed, perhaps without understanding, by a farmer standing in front of an open field, looking over a piece of land that had just been plowed, picking up a piece of soil, crumbling it delicately in his fingers, looking at it almost tenderly, carefully probing its odor and its taste, after which he declared it good and ready. Over the years, this image has stuck with me. It does make it possible, I think, to empathize with all the peasants who may have venerated the earth and personalized Fertility. It helps in explaining the dogged persistence of fertility beliefs, and therefore of the Evil Eye. And it helps perhaps in understanding why the folk of the past were overwhelmed by the coming of a new creed, Christianity, which spread among the slaves and the destitute and which arose probably as a means of defeating oppression, unfair and cruel treatment, and inadequate distribution of resources. Christianity at that time was able to help the deprived by giving them a sense of solidarity. In the end, however, this could be done only by displacing the old fertility "gods and goddesses." The peasants could certainly understand the defeat of oppression, but it is likely that the new single God, who demanded exclusive rights to their loyalty and devotion, remained an enigma for them. Nevertheless, peasants are pragmatists and they probably generally understood instinctively the political role of the Church, albeit without being able to articulate this understanding. They saw no contradiction in continuing their veneration of what they perceived as life itself.[159] The renewal every Spring of the grain crops they planted had always occurred without the intervention of a despotic God. In their intimate relationship with the soil, with the earth, there endured always the hope that the mana of fertility would descend upon the fields, the domestic animals and upon themselves. Centuries upon centuries of experience and rituals had taught them that a respectful and harmonious relationship to the land was essential for producing a good crop. Displacing all their devotion and attention exclusively to the new God must have seemed like a betrayal for which Nature would surely punish them. The peasants, then, continued to place their faith in the forces of Nature, which were certainly more palpable than an absentee Lord-God who, it was said, was responsible for the mana of their fields, and yet by-passed the forces of nature, ignored them in fact.[160] The co-existence of the two attitudes is not unknown in present-day ethnography: Partha Mitter says that "There exists in Hinduism a whole range of attitudes from the belief in an abstract *Upanisadic* supreme Deity to simple animism at the village level."[161] But be that as in may, in Europe and in the face of the resistance of the peasants, the Church compromised by converting old "gods" and "goddesses" into "saints" who were said to intercede for the peasants, to obtain those very things that the peasants wanted.[162] Many of these new "saints" changed in name only. There were many saints, such as St. Ildefonse in Normandy, against whom sterile women rubbed their "abdomen" (probably a euphemism) in the hope of becoming fertile, as in many other places women rubbed against menhirs for the same purpose.[163] The peasants simply (and possibly slyly) projected the characteristics of the old "gods" and "goddesses" of fertility onto the new "saints," including all the pertinent symbolism of phallos and kteis, including the Eye. If necessary, the phallos of a fertility figure could be referred to as "the big toe" of a male saint, as was done for Saint Cosmos in Isernia, Italy, in the 18th century.[164] Phallic and kteic saints persisted well into the 19th Century in Europe. Sometimes they were found under the form of "relics," such as the foreskin of Christ (at least at a dozen places), or the vulva of Ste. Gudule (two places).[165] Most often, however, the "saints" were found in churches and monasteries under a number of suggestive names. The most common of these was a Saint Foutin found throughout France. The meaning of the name is derived from the French vernacular verb for coitus.[166] Sterile women who wished to become pregnant would visit the statue of the saint who was provided with a large phallos, sometimes replaceable, from which they scraped bits of material that they mixed in water and drank. The material of the phallos was stone, wood or leather, depending on whether the statue itself was made of any of these materials, and depending on whether the phallos was replaceable or not. Saint Foutin and the other phallic saints were often associated each with a kteic saint, who is not always recognized as such. There is, for instance, a St. Foutin in the church of St. John in Lyons, France,[167] associated with a Ste. Blandine, whose name is a derivative of the Latin adjective *blanda* which means one who is cajoling, caressing, alluring, pleasing, charming or enticing. With such a name, and with such associations, she may well have been a Gaelic "Venus" transformed by the Church into a "saint." There were probably at least as many kteic saints as there were phallic saints. More of the latter have been recorded however, probably because of the male-orientation of medieval Christianity. It is interesting to note that the name of other kteic saints and heroines like Gudule, Godelva (whose vulvae were venerated as "relics") and probably Godiva, whose virtue was celebrated in her nudity rather than in sainthood, share a Germanic prefix, *god-*, *gud-*, having the same meaning as the Latin *blanda*, that is: alluring, pleasing, enticing, sweetly sensuous, most often referring directly to sexual gratification. Fernando Henriques in volume II of his *Prostitution and Society*, says:

> Whatever interpretation is given, this strange association of sexuality and religion in terms of Christianity remains an enigma. It was a tradition which persisted in different forms right up to the nineteenth century. The festivals of St Pharaildis at Ghent, of St Balbine at Liège, of St Godeleva at Longuefort, and the Drunken Vespers of St Berlindis near Brussels are all reminders of this association. There is evidence to suggest that many of these early female saints were connected with phallic and nature worship. (p. 19)

Gode, godin, godinet, godine, godinette, godel, godelureau, goder, godiller, godaille, godemine, godemiché, gaudriole, and other words in French, *godesco, godible, godir* in Spanish (the latter has become *joder* in some areas). The principal meaning of *godir* is indeed "to have something that is tasty, pleasing and agreeable," but it has an even more interesting secondary meaning: "to know a woman carnally (*conocer carnalmente a una mujer*)" and is undoubtedly related to the modern French *jouir* which carries all these meanings, and to the old French term *goder*, or still older *gauder* and *gaudir*. *Goder* can also, sometimes, have the meaning of "to have an erection." *Godine, godin, godinet, godel, godelureau*, are people who enjoy sexual activity, *gode* is an adjective, *goder*, a verb, *godaille* and *godemine* refer to the collective world and behavior of *godins* and *godines*. In German there are the terms *gut* and *gott*, which, as the English good and god possibly share a common origin (even if through "borrowing") with *gaudium, gaudere* in Latin (see also Appendix V).[168]

Another name which appears in Eastern and Central France, with a certain frequency, is that of St. Vit (or Avit, or Wit or Vith). The term "vit" was a popular designation for the penis in Medieval French, as well as a derivative from the Latin, *vita*, meaning life. Surely the contemporary French slang term of "bitte" to designate the male organ, must also be derived from this. There is a menhir in Saint-Germain-Lambron, in the Department of Puy-de-Dôme, called Vit-de-Chal, upon which infertile women rub their bellies.[169] St. Wit (pronounced "vitt"), (aka St. Fix) was venerated in a grotto near Saverne in Alsace. There is near Saverne, a town named Phalsbourg. Because of its proximity to a fertility shrine, its name might be taken for something that it is not. It was founded in 1570 by a Prince of the Pfalz (The German Palatinate) from whence it derived its German name: Pfalzburg. There are, however, phallic Saints by the name of St. Phal in at least two French communities away from the Palatinate, one of them being in the Department of Deux-Sèvres, which is situated near the Atlantic coast. We must keep in mind that many towns and burgs of Medieval Europe were under the protection of fertility figures, which were transformed into patron saints by the Church.

A curious case which associates eyes with fertility, while at the same time emphasizing the persistence of symbols in the minds of the populace, is the case reported in the *Revue des Traditions Populaires* (V. XVII, 1902, p. 386) by Léo Desaivre. The church in Champdemers (Deux-Sèvres) had been consecrated to St. Pierre before the French Revolution, but his statue, having disappeared, was replaced by a statue of St. Roch. Pierre in French means stone and Roch(e) means rock. The Department of Deux-Sèvres is situated in an area of menhir worship, that is where these megaliths were, and perhaps still are, visited to promote fertility. This new statue, which had been commissioned by the parishioners, was termed indecent by a new parish priest who was appointed there in 1872. It seems that the saint was represented as lifting up his tunic, presumably to expose his genitals, but the objections of the curate seems to have been directed to the "lust" expressed in the eyes of the statue, so that he had a coat of wax spread over the eyes. His parishioners, however, objected to this so strongly that he had to have the wax removed "to keep the peace." Dulaure mentions a Phallic saint by the name of St. Arnaud, whose "veil" had to be lifted "to expose the symbol of fecundity."[170]

Another recurrent phallic saint from France is Guignole, whose variations are Gignolé, Guignolet, Guénolé, Cunolé, Guerluchon, Greluchon, Greluchot. The basic name, Guignole, shares a common radical with "*guigne*" which is a sideglance, but also means bad luck. As a verb, *guigner*, means to maneuvre deviously to obtain something because of envy. It also means *to covet*, *to lust after*. More immediately, the etymology of the name is probably derived from the Latin, *gigno, genui, genitum*, which means "to give birth," "to engender" or "to cause." The meaning may be related to the Greek word for the act of generating, i.e. "generation" (γενεα). All of these meanings, desire, yearning, luck, engendering, begetting, envy, producing, are symptomatic of the syndrome of the Evil Eye. There is an interesting etymological analysis of this name to be done. Dulaure, may be on the right track, but he is misled and misleading. He seems to think that there is a term, "gignere" (he does not say in what language) which means "to engender."[171] There is no such word in French. To engender, in French is "engendrer." Dulaure may have meant "guigner," which is formally more likely, but *guigner* does not mean to engender. It does, however, refer to looking askance with an eye of envy or lust, which meaning might be of some interest. The word "gignere" does exist in Italian, but it means genus or gender. To engender, in Italian, is *generare*.

There are less frequent names such as Gorgon, Fort, Firmin, etc., but there must have been as many kteic saintes also, and if the list is not as long, it is probably because they were not recorded. It must be pointed out that the Church did not absorb all phallic or kteic figures. Some, like Perceval (whose name was germanized as Parsifal) and Guenevere passed into popular legend. Perceval's name is from the French meaning "he who pierces the valley." His alternative name leaves no doubt as to the meaning of his first name: it is "Perceforest," that is: "he who pierces the forest."[172] It must also be noted that Latin, Spanish and Italian commonly use verbs meaning "to pierce" to refer to sexual penetration, such as *ficcare*, in Italian, or *futuere* in vulgar Latin.

The *Conte du Graal* (the Romance of the Grail) by Christian de Troyes (12th century), about Perceval, was never finished by him, so that we do not know if Christian ever meant for Perceval to find the Grail. XIVth century and later additions deem that Galahad is the only knight worthy of looking for it). In any case, in terms of fertility symbols, Perceval should have been the one to find the Grail, since the Grail is a vessel, which in terms of sexual symbolism is the equivalent of a valley.

I do want to mention one last one from France, and that is Saint Gorgon, a fertility Saint related, at least by name, to the Greek Gorgones, one of whom, the Medusa, in my opinion, was originally a fertility figure, which explains why it was used as an amulet against the Evil Eye. Athena, the protectress and warrior goddess of Athens, wore the emblem of Medusa (Gorgon) on her shield. The shields of warriors in ancient Greece, customarily were decorated with apotropaics against the Evil Eye. Even the Goddess was not exempt.[173]

There are many more kteic and phallic saints, but these should suffice to demonstrate, first, that there is a dogged persistence of these remarkable personae and what they represent, and second, that they are all somehow related to fertility and the Evil Eye. A belief in the Evil Eye persisted along with the veneration of the principle of fertility. It was so strong, as a matter of fact, that in 1675 a virulent disquisition against the Evil Eye beliefs of the common people was published by a cleric, Johann Christian Frommann, in which he manifested his revulsion at what he considered the scandalous relationship between the Evil Eye beliefs and things sexual, although, he, himself is quite explicit.

Dulaure also, with more scholarly intent than Frommann, speaks of the lasting custom of wearing *fascina*, at the same time that he speaks of the endurance of the old phallic "gods" under the guise of "saints." He says: "The *fascinum*, that species of phallic amulet that women and especially children, wore about their neck or shoulders, was in use among the French for many centuries."[174] He goes on to say that the amulets were, until recently of the same nature as the old Roman ones, that is a phallus, meant to ward off "glances of envy."[175] Dulaure certainly knew and could have mentioned that the term *fascina* comes from "fascination," which itself comes from the Greek word for Evil Eye (βασκανια).

John James Blunt correctly points out the striking similarities between saints venerated by Sicilian Christians (i.e., at the time Blunt observed them at the beginning of the 19th century) and the old pagan gods of antiquity.[176] He makes a particularly good point in describing the rituals of Santa Agatha at Catania in Sicily, which have replaced those of Ceres, who, it is to be remembered was a goddess of fertility, equivalent to the Great Mother, Demeter in Greece. The Sicilian rituals, he says, are still (1818-21) essentially the same as those pertaining to the cult of Ceres, which makes Agatha a kteic saint, although her sex is not defined by her pudenda, but by her breasts. Another saint favored by the Italians is Santa Lucia, who offered her eyes to her pagan Roman suitor. In view of the symbolism of the Eye, and in view of the fact that she was invoked for fertility, I suggest that in the original, it was not her organ of sight that Lucia was offering, but that which symbolized "*felicitas*," abundance, prosperity, fertility and happiness. The details about preserving her chastity were possibly just another re-writing of tradition by the state or the Church.[177]

Blunt also noted the substitution of white crosses in the fields to replace the ancient fertility effigies of the notorious god of fertility, Priapus. These effigies are still with us in the form of scarecrows (see Deubner, p. 436),[178] as in India, the fields are protected by phallic poles upon which kteic pots, painted white, are placed.

Gestures

Among the gestures or rituals designed to insure the fertility of fields and gardens, is the custom of ritual coitus in the field (West Africa), or the sowing of the seeds by a naked person (Central Europe and Scandinavia).

Presenting one's rear end while bending over is a "female" gesture and was probably originally the equivalent of the act of covering one's genitals with the hand for a male. A symbolic image of the genitals protects against the Evil Eye but so do the genitals themselves. It is both a protective gesture and a show of contempt at the same time, as are the obscene hand and finger gestures that are more familiar to us. In Europe, still in the seventeenth century and probably later, a woman uncovering her genitals was considered as "scaring the Devil away." In present day India, women will display their genitals in front of a fire, as a protection against the Evil Eye. Mary Ellen Mark in her photographic essay, *Falkland Road*, has a photograph of an Indian prostitute lifting her skirts to expose her pubis above a fire on the floor. The caption reads: "Every Saturday and the first day of every month, the girls perform a fire ceremony to ward off the evil eye."[179] Indian peasant women, while they are working in the fields, will bend over and direct they backside toward passing strangers, to protect the fields against the Evil Eye. The custom is ancient. Waterman quotes Pliny (p. 142) who says that a "storm can be avoided if a woman uncovers herself before it."[180] In Italy, a most effective gesture for a man is to cover his genitals with his hand, which is probably the equivalent of a woman uncovering her own to ward off evil. In any case, like raising the middle finger, it is both a gesture of contempt and protection. The same gesture of covering one's genitals was a protective symbol among the Maori males of New Zealand.[181] I suggest that the fact that some Scythian male burials had their hand stitched to their pubic area, may have been meant to ward off the Evil Eye even after death. In passing, we might mention that there is, at the Lepenski-Vir site, an unusual burial. It is labeled "male" by Srejovic, but it is in a sheela-position, which in the context of what we are suggesting could be re-interpreted as the skeleton of a female buried ritually in a position of parturition, which is so often graphically used as a fertility symbol. The fact that the site has yielded so many fertility carvings, increases the support for this re-interpretation. But another re-interpretation could be based on the analogy of the Central Asian males who were buried with hands stitched to their crotch, in which case the Lepenski Vir burial could be a male in the posture of protecting himself against the Evil Eye by covering his genitals with his hands, a protective gesture that is customary among the living in contemporary Italy and elsewhere in the Mediterranean.

Swearing an oath on the genitals has a long history. Lee Alexander Stone quotes Hannay ("Symbolism in Relation to Religion"):

> "Everywhere," says the author, "in the Bible we find a special regard paid to the organ of generation. As I have already pointed out, their oaths were taken on the phallus; as when Abraham swore his servant, he said: 'put, I pray thee, thy hand under my thigh,' Gen. xxiv, 2 and to show that this was no isolated case let me recall the passage in which Jacob swears Joseph in the same way, Ibid. xlvii, 29, also Chron., xxix, 24, mistranslated, 'submitted themselves unto Salomon,' when it really means 'placed their hand under Salomon,' the usual way of taking an oath or testifying."

> "The custom has lasted amongst the Arabs until the present day, and there is little doubt that the Latin word testiculi, refers to the same custom, as the phallic word 'testes' is the basis of testis, 'a witness.'" (pp. 61 and 62)

If displaying the genitals can be both protection and a gesture of contempt, so then are many gestures—and idioms—that are still in use amongst us today. Raising the middle finger has such a significance. The gesture was already in use among the ancient Romans, as well as both the *mano cornuta* and the *mano fica*, all of which, then, protected specifically against the Evil Eye (figs. 3). With us, still, the middle finger gesture is often accompanied by a statement which leaves no doubt as to the meaning of the gesture. But the statement too is protective as well as a show of contempt. James Noel Adams, in his book on *Latin Sexual Vocabulary*, points out that obscene sexual idioms and vocabulary were used to express contempt as well as for protection, using the same word or words that are in use today to accompany offensive gestures.[182] Another finger gesture was the one used by one of my informants in Greece. He expressed the same meaning by placing his index finger over his median, in the form that we refer to as "cross-fingers." I have no doubt as to what he meant because, as we often communicated in gestures, he used this sign once to tell me that he was going to breed his ewes to this particular ram. It may be that our own "crossed-fingers," which after all is protective, originated in this same fertility symbolism.

Spitting and wetting the finger with saliva are other gestures considered as apotropaic against the Evil Eye. Spitting has all the characteristics of Evil Eye apotropaic gestures. It is used in the same circumstances, directed at the same people and objects and it is both protective, aggressive and a gesture of contempt. The only attribute which seems to be absent is the sexual character, but the sexual aspect can be restored if we think of spitting as a symbol for ejaculation (RE: Selare in Dundes.) We have already mentioned the touching of effigies in Tantric temples, the dipping of fingers in stoups to make the sign of the cross, wetting the fingers to touch the Mezuzah, spitting at gifts in Greece, etc. Other more concrete examples follow: Eugene McCartney quotes G. F. Lyons, a nineteenth century traveller who shows that wetting the finger was used in North Africa to exorcise the Evil Eye. "The 'Evil Eye' is of all other mischiefs the most dreaded. For a stranger to express particular admiration of a child, a horse, or any other valuable, is to bring on it or its possessor certain misfortune; this may, however, be averted by passing over the object a finger wetted with saliva, or by the equally efficacious charm of an open hand, either attached to the clothes as an ornament or tattooed on the skin."[183] McCartney also brings the testimony of G. Henderson who says that the Scots counteract the anticipated effects of the Evil Eye by wetting a person's eye with finger and saliva.[184] Distasi reports: "Another antidote commonly used against evil eye is spittle. I first heard of this from my mother, who was born in Hungary. When her mother, suspected that a child had been hit by evil eye, she would lick the child's eyelids, spit away, and then dry the baby's eyes with the inside of her undershirt."[185] It is mentioned by Crooke as a gesture for "scaring" the Evil Eye in India.[186] Unwin says that the Nandi from Kenya in Africa spit at the moon "for good luck," and William Crooke quoting J. C. Lawson says that: "In modern Greece 'at a baptism . . . the priest opens the service by exorcising all evil spirits and influences from the four corners of the room by winging his censer, but the midwife, who usually knows something of magic, or one of the godparents, accompanies him and makes assurance doubly sure by spitting in each suspected nook.'"[187] Crooke then later mentions that spitting is a mode of repelling the Evil Eye, not only in Greece but throughout the world (p. 102).

To illustrate the extraordinary tenacity of fertility customs, I will quote, without comment, part of the report by a journalist of a trip to Paris, during the course of which he visited the Père Lachaise Cemetery. The following is extracted from *The New Yorker* of October 27, 1986, p. 110.

> A few steps farther on, I came to another grave that wasn't on my map, but a grave of which I had very much heard. It was a grave of peculiar celebrity and a grave peculiar in itself. It was the grave of a French journalist named Victor Noir, shot dead at twenty-one, on a Paris street on January 10, 1870, in an altercation with Prince Pierre-Napoleon Bonaparte, a cousin of Napoleon III. Noir lies in a life-size bronze on a large slab of white stone as he lay dead on the street—flat on his back, arms outstretched, pantalooned legs slightly apart, his top hat capsized at one knee. It is a grim depiction and more. The sculptor, in his realism, approached (by accident or design) the surrealistic, and endowed Noir with an enormous genital bulge. Noir's grave for this reason is widely revered as a shrine. Barren women visit it in search of fertility and touch that anatomical freak: their visits over the many years have polished it to the gleam of brass.

Hinduism and Fertility

With the development of state society, both in India and in western Europe, religion became as complex as their respective political organization. Goddesses and gods were created and personalized. Temporal and supernatural worlds became highly centralized and hierarchical. In Hinduism, however, the fertility cult—the word "cult" this time is used advisedly—remained much more in evidence than in Christianity. Partha Mitter says that "there exists in Hinduism a whole range of attitudes from the belief in an abstract *Upanisadic* supreme Deity to simple animism at the village level."[188] As in western Europe, however, there was one moral code for the upper echelons of society and another for the lower. In both cases, as the upper classes became more and more removed from production, their supernatural world became peopled with fanciful and authoritarian figures, justifying and maintaining the class and caste systems that allowed them to dominate and exploit the lowers classes. At the same time, the commoners who remained close to the land retained their devotion to the fertility of the Earth Mother. In Europe we have seen what form this devotion took among the peasants. In India, the divergence was not as great—at least superficially—inasmuch as all castes carried on rituals designed to uphold the great phallic God of fertility (most often Siva) and his relationship with the great cosmic yoni Goddess (most often Parvati) under each their various "aspects," and made offerings over altars of interacting lingam and yoni (i.e.: phallos and kteis, the one inside the other. Fig. 6.1). In the same way that "phallic saints" persisted in Europe long after the advent of an integrating Christianity, so too, in India, "gods" such as the ithyphallic Bhaironnâth have persisted long after the coming of Hinduism. Curt Maury in discussing the "Folk Origin of Indian Art" explains that the various manifestations of "gods" in the Hindu pantheon are not always clear. The peasants call the figures of their worship Balaji, but so is Siva, Balaji. He says: "Shiva is no more a proper name than 'Balaji.' Like the latter, it is an epithet, a euphemistic appellation applied by the Aryans. . . ."[189] Balaji is qualified as "deva" as if the term were co-terminus with "mana," and with what Maury calls "the power beyond," (pp. 18 & 19).

This cult of fertility is also expressed in symbolism drawn on the walls of houses, for protection against the Evil Eye (see fig. 23.2). Also, as in Medieval Europe, there has been a movement in India set in motion by the secular authorities (made up of upper caste gentry) to ban that which would not be acceptable to western foreigners' sense of propriety while at the same time serving purposes of control by these same authorities. Paul Thomas documents the cases where the various overlords prohibit *devadasis* (temple ritual "prostitutes"), or certain festivals, considered offensive to Western sensibilities.[190] Temple prostitution and the festivals, nevertheless, persist to this day under other names, just as the veneration of phallic and kteic saints continued in Europe even after centuries of prohibitions. There is a difference, however: the core of Hinduism is fertility manifested in the intercourse between the great phallic God, Shiva and the great yoni of the universe, whereas Christianity tried, though with limited success, to get away from Fertility symbolism entirely.

As this work was going to press, there appeared, in the *Chicago Tribune* of November 16, 1993, a report by Joel Simon on another of these extraordinary instances of persistence of fertility worship. In San Francisco's Golden Gate Park, there is an abandoned traffic barrier shaped like the linguam (phallos) in Hindu temples. It has been turned into a shrine to Shiva by the resident Hindu community. People come to pray and leave offerings and libations.

Chapter XIV

Other Significant Symbols

The Heart Shape

The Heart has become an almost universal symbol of love. Greeting card companies certainly make the most of this come St. Valentine's day. A tentative explanation for the symbol is that the Ancients thought of the biological heart as the seat of life and therefore the seat of all emotions. It is a good explanation except for the fact that the symbol has a much more earthy origin. The fig leaf, which we think of as heart-shaped, was considered in Antiquity, not as a representation of the anatomical heart, but rather as a representation of the vulva, and therefore a symbol of the female dimension of fertility. Richard Lewinsohn who wrote *L'Histoire entière du coeur* (The Complete History of the Heart), after looking for but finding no heart symbols in prehistory, says of later periods that:

> "D'autres images en forme de coeur représentent l'accès aux organes génitaux de la femme; on les trouve quelquefois à côté d'un phallus."[191] (p. 12)

> "Other images in the shape of a heart represent the entrance to the female genital organs; they are sometimes accompanied by a phallos."

What we call the heart-shape, in that sense, can be considered as a variation of the pubic triangle. During the Middle Ages, the heart shape appears with a rift in the middle, which fact is indicative of its origin (cf. fig. 36.1). Lewinsohn speaks of the oldest of the heart shaped watermarks figured in C. M. Briquet's book on medieval watermarks. It is the oldest of the heart-shaped marks:[192]

> "C'est un triangle étiré aux coins arrondis et dont les deux extrémités supérieures sont séparées par une profonde échancrure. La figure est coupée en son milieu par deux lignes pointillées." p. 88

> "It is a stretched-out triangle with rounded corners, whose two upper extremities are separated by a deep rift. It is split in two by a broken line." (My translation.)

Because of this center line, the author concludes that it must be the representation of a tree leaf, an error made in at least one other case, as seen above, when those who described the stoup at Farges, mistook the kteic designs for "plant-like ornaments." The error is understandable if one keeps in mind that certain tree leaves, because of their shape, are also kteic symbols. If Lewinsohn had a fig-leaf in mind, he should have known that, it too, represented the vulva at one time. Papermarks from the European Middle Ages invariably feature fertility symbols of one sort or another. According to Harold Bayley (*The Lost Language of Symbolism*, 1912), papermarks were originated by Albigenses papermakers, who used them between 1282 and 1600 A.D. The fact the great majority—and perhaps all—of the papermarks are fertility symbols, is quite consistent with Albigenses beliefs. Many of the marks are variations on the heart theme. Some are clearly kteic, some are phallic and some are both. At the turn of this century, W. L. Hilburgh reported that the Portuguese still wore heart-shaped amulets as protection against the Evil Eye.[193]

Strangely enough, in some contemporary graffiti, one finds the heart shape with a rift in the middle. The intentions of the street-wise urban virtuosi were probably prurient, and what they intended to draw was most likely to be a vulva rather than a heart, but the fact of the matter is that whatever the intention, the representation is heart-shaped. William McLean, in his work on popular iconography has a section on the heart, accompanied by many photographs of wall graffiti. The majority of these hearts have a separation in the middle and are often elongated as in the medieval watermarks. Some are pierced with a phallic arrow and others have drawings of realistic penises directed at them. Figure 66, in McLean's book is the photograph by Brassaï of a grafitto (fig. 36.2). It is remarkable for the spontaneous re-invention of a phallic heart overlapping a kteic one. Note that the upper heart is a kteis with a separation in the middle, and the lower heart is "upside down" and has the shape of a phallic triad. As if to make his point clear, and for good measure, the "artist" drew another phallos aimed at the cleft. This being a grafitto on the wall of an industrial district of Paris at the beginning of this century, it is highly improbable that the perpetrator was conscious of using a conventional design, and it is unlikely that his immediate goal was to represent fertility, but he was, in the end, willy-nilly, using the basic elements in the symbolism of fertility.

Another photograph, by McLean, reproduced in his book, is one he refers to delicately as that of a "venus" drawn presumably by soldiers on the wall of a lavatory in a now abandoned barrack. It is of vast proportions: it covers an entire wall. Its intent is obviously prurient. But the most remarkable thing about this magisterial graffito is that it is, constitutionally, the re-invention of some of the prehistoric statuettes with a long neck, a bulbous head and large breasts that make the upper part of the body look like a huge phallos. Her posture, moreover is exactly that of a sheela-na-gig. To make this masterwork even more remarkable, the kteis of the sheela is surrounded by phalloi, all directed at it, in the same manner that the "eye" on Roman bas-reliefs is surrounded by phallic symbols directed at it. Even if one is not a Jungian, one cannot help thinking of Jungian "archetypes." However, I still would rather explain this phenomenon in terms of Bachoffen's "Psychic Unity of Mankind"; that is, in general, given the same circumstances, people tend to think of the same things and re-invent them.

The Alpha and the Omega

At a very early date in the Ancient Mediterranean world, we find the complementary Alpha and Omega. Alpha is the Bull's Head, and is generally considered male because of the horns. The letter itself originated in Phoenician writing as the pictogram of the head of a bull (aleph), representing the sound of the first letter of the alphabet, which, in Greek, came to be known as alpha. Omega is the vagina, open at the bottom, ready to give birth, and is considered female. However, each contains an element of the opposite sex. The Bull's Head, turned upside down, represents the posture of a woman in parturition, whether it be a prehistoric representation from the Northwest Ukraine of the 4th Millennium or whether it be a modern West African specimen (figs. 22). The Omega shape turned upside down, in turn, represent the horns of the bull. It is found all over the Mediterranean and of course in Crete. Among the Egyptians who were more particularly intent in protecting themselves against the Evil Eye, the omega *shape* appears in many forms, all of which were used as apotropaics. It is seen in the Egyptian TJET (or, eventually, the Coptic TOTE), which, in amulet form, represented the genital organs of the goddess Isis, who, although she may have reached the status of "goddess" by the time of Ptolemy, certainly represented fertility in the earlier Egyptian civilization. Waterman says:

> One of the earliest and most universal emblems of the female creator is the mystic sign of the horseshoe. The famous head-dress of the Egyptian goddess Isis was a horseshoe, and there are numerous divinities in different parts of the world who are represented with similar devices upon their heads. In Rajputana, India, there are temples constructed on the plan of a horseshoe for the reason that the symbol of life is one of the sacred emblems of the deities therein worshipped. p. 17

The Omega was present also in the *sistrum* and the *menat*, which protected Ancient Egyptians against the Evil Eye. The sistrum was a kind of rattle formed in an Omega shape, crossed by loose metal bars which made a sound when shaken. Not only did the sistrum have an Omega shape, but it represented explicitly the virgin uterus. It was, moreover, decorated with phalloi and it was complemented by a phallic handle fixed at the bottom opening. The sistrum was used in religious ceremonies celebrating the end of female virginity. The sistrum, in that sense, is comparable to the *hortus conclusus* (enclosed garden) of the virgin bride in the Song of Songs:

> A garden inclosed is my sister, my spouse,
> A spring shut up, a fountain sealed.

The menat, or whip amulet, consisted of an Omega shape linked by a chain to a phallic shape. It was worn as a necklace to ward off the Evil Eye. The Omega is still with us in the form of horseshoes nailed above the doors of barns and stables and in the form of lucky wishbones. Cattle horns are hung in these same spots, as well as above the doors of houses in Spain and Portugal. In Texas, cattle horns appear everywhere, in and out of houses, certainly because it is the traditional thing to do, but also with a vague feeling that this brings good luck and is a sign of prosperity and power. None of this is expressed in terms of fertility symbolism, but it is worthy of note that some catalogs that cater to a "country-western" clientele sell swagger sticks made of genuine bull's penises hardened in plastic.[194] So is the horn contemporary in such expressions as being "horny" and in the "mano cornuta," and all the "horns of power" symbols. The Spanish and Portuguese "lunar crescent" amulets have an Omega shape and are meant to protect against the Evil Eye.[195] The crescent moon (never waning) is a variation of the Omega, which, turned points down, is the female sign and, points up, is the representation of the male horns. The crescent moon is a widespread symbol. It prevails particularly in Muslim areas, where it is often displayed on national flags, on which the fertility symbolism is re-enforced by the presence of the pentagram, a Parturient Woman symbol. The alpha and the omega appear regularly in medieval iconography, flanking a representation of God. The Church interprets the biblical declaration: "I am the Alpha and the Omega, I am the Life,"[196] to mean: "I am the beginning and the end," from the fact that Alpha is the first letter of the Greek alphabet and Omega is the last. It could very well mean that, indeed, but in view of the symbolism discussed here, it probably and primarily means "I am both the male principle (Alpha) and the female principle (Omega) of Life. I am fertility." This seems to have been the view of the very early Romanesque artisan who produced a brass plate in which the Alpha, is clearly phallic and the Lower Case Omega (ω) is as clearly a stylized Parturient Woman symbol (see fig. 38.1).

In his book on *Symbols, Signs and their Meaning*, Arnold Whittick, under his entry for *Alpha-Omega*, has a photograph (Plate XLIX) which shows a modern Lutheran church of the Trinity in Hamburg, Germany. Whittick says: "It was only when seeing the design on a sketch that he (the architect) discovered in the plan the omega of the church and the alpha of the belfry." To us, in the context of what we are discussing here, the effect is remarkably like the representation of a kteis and a phallos. The symbolism, however, has been recognized before. Lee Alexander Stone remarks: "However ignorantly employed, towers and steeples, columns and minarets have a connection with the phallus, while the horizontal buildings or enclosed surfaces from which they spring trace back to the kteis."[197] Stone goes even farther on his page 82, where he says: "The reproduction of a pagan temple, presided over by a Scotch Presbyterian minister, proves conclusively to my mind, that while paganism was condemned by Christians, they did not hesitate to borrow from pagans the beautiful designs of their temples."

"The church steeple is a phallic symbol, just as much so as is the obelisk, and in the construction of the interior of the church the anatomy of the female genitalia is taken into account."

The Gorgon

The Gorgon figure of the ancient Mediterranean has been discussed in many ways, but it is a symbol that was already old at the time when written documents began to appear. It is therefore subject to interpretation. The evidence, however, seems to indicate that the Gorgon was ultimately derived from a Parturient Woman symbol. The Gorgones are one of a number of female trinities such as the Harpies, the Keres, the Erinyes, the Graiae and the Gorgones, who, like the *neraides* of Greek contemporary folklore, "seize" men, not women. The imagery is all the more significant when we consider each of the trinities as aspects of a single symbolic female (as Jane Harrison does). The Gorgon turns men to stone with her eye, and the Graiae have one single good eye coveted by Perseus. The very early Gorgon is best exemplified by the "Etruscan" Gorgo (ca. 540-530 B.C.) now housed in the Munich Alte Pinakothek. It is a bronze plaque for the front of a war chariot and probably meant to be protection against the Evil Eye in combat. It represents a Gorgon in a Parturient Woman posture, and a grimacing face as in a sheela. Moreover, if the principle of multiple re-enforcing symbols holds, it has a kteic mouth and a phallic tongue. Harrison says: "These . . . images were also called *βασκάνια* or by the unlearned *προβασκάνια*, charms against the evil eye; and if we may trust the scholiast on Aristophanes, they formed part of the furniture of most people's chimney corners at Athens. Of such *βασκάνια* the Gorgon mask was one and perhaps the most common shape."[198]

The Horn

The horn has been mentioned continually as a male symbol. It surfaces as the male symbol par excellence in the same way that the eye is the female symbol. We have mentioned already that anything, but anything that could, in the most remote way, be interpreted as looking like a penis (even a straight line), has at one time or another been used as a phallic symbol. On that basis, the bull's horn became a classic symbol, possibly even before the time of cattle husbandry. By extension, anything that resembles a horn became a phallic symbol. This accounts, in the world of material culture, for the abundance of amulets made of elk's teeth, carnivore's canine teeth, feline retractable claws, eagle's talons, or amulets made in the shape of these. It also accounts in part for the universal Mediterranean use of cloves of garlic as apotropaics. In some parts of Africa and Asia, the rhinoceros' "horn," reduced to powder, is considered as an aphrodisiac, as cure for certain ailments, as well as a protection against misfortune. One might consider the possibility that the lore of the unicorn, which is said to be peculiar to the

European Middle Ages, as perhaps being related consciously to fertility symbolism. The unicorn was, after all, a wild one-horned male beast that could be captured only by a young woman who would first attract the animal, and then would seize him by having him sleep in her lap.

The generic horn is a symbol of the penis (phallos); to agonize over whether the horn is from an ox, a billy goat or a ram is superfluous. It might (or might not) be significant in other contexts, but in the context of the breadth of meaning of fertility symbolism, it would be vain intellectual gymnastics to go through such an exercise.[199] To use an analogy: the Romans had a special term for the male membrum: *mentula*, but the common familiar "slang" expression was *penis*, the primary meaning of which in Latin is "tail." They used this term outside of the context of fertility symbolism. It would be as pointless to agonize over whether *penis* referred to a bird's tail or a dog's tail, as it would be to agonize over the modern anglo-saxon term "tail" used in exactly the same way. That the horn is also a symbol of power is not a contradiction. It is consistent with the "polysemantic" character of most fertility symbols.

Cowries

There was a long drawn-out debate, during World War II, lasting from October 1939 to December 1943, in *Man*, the British ethnographic journal, over the meaning of the cowrie shell. One of the protagonist compares it to the dispute between Christian philosophers while Byzantium was under siege over the proposition as to whether Adam and Eve had navels. The essence of the more recent debate revolves around the question: does the cowrie represent an eye, or is it the vulva, or is it simply an apotropaic against the Evil Eye? The exchanges are almost amusing in their naïveté. Most of the protagonists maintain that if the cowrie is one thing, it cannot be the others. Even the venerable authority on witch cults, Margaret Murray, fights a losing battle to "prove" that cowries are eyes and not symbols of the vulva. As proof, she presents a battle helmet from Formosa decorated with cowrie shells and she argues: "The shells are set horizontally giving the effect of an eye. It is very clear that here they are used merely as luck charms, for no warrior would go into battle wearing the representation of the female genitalia."[200] What Murray does not seem to know is that it is precisely *because* the cowrie represents the female genitalia that it is protective and a bringer of good luck. It does not mean, either, that it cannot be considered as an eye also, since the eye represents the vulva. Moreover, Murray did not notice that the helmet was also decorated with tusks, symbols of the phallos, which are apotropaic as the cowrie-vulva is. As a matter of fact, the combination of kteis and phallos is the most powerful symbol of all. In the debate, only J. H. Driberg says essentially that the cowrie can be regarded as all that, i.e. eye, vulva and apotropaic if one is to assume a belief in the power, or the forces, or the energy of Nature. He "hesitates," he says, to call it "mana," whereas I do not hesitate to define mana in its broader inclusive sense. What Driberg does not state, though it has become obvious, is the equation cowrie = eye = vulva. As symbols, all three are as one and they are meant to encourage production and reproduction, and in that sense they are a protection against "bad luck," whether called "evil eye" or not. Therefore, from the greatest antiquity, to the present day, heads and skulls and statues have been provided with cowrie eyes in order to promote production, reproduction and protection. Because of their shape, grains of rice, wheat, barley, rye and oats play the same role as cowries.

The debate probably has been settled now and its conclusion summarized by Rawson, who says that: "At the present day cowries are used in the clay sculptures of West Africa to indicate the vulva as well as the eyes. Eye-shapes, where schematically rendered, may also be used to symbolize the vulva" (pp. 14-15). Finally, given the predilection of people to express their immense concern with fertility by creating symbols that express fertility and ideas associated with it, in many ways, it is surprising that no one has pointed out that cowries (and the grains mentioned above) are egg-shaped, and that they are therefore comparable to testicles. Hence, cowries (and grains) are both male and female at the same time, and as such they are complete symbols of fertility.

Chapter XV

On the Great Abundance of Fertility symbols

Ktenes Without the Eye

Finally, because the constructs of the Evil Eye are so intimately bound to the constructs of fertility and fertility rituals, it becomes impossible to separate them from each other in the real world. It is only in a systematic analysis that they can be conceptually segregated. They have persisted with each other, and alongside each other for millennia and have left a trail of symbols, all of which were meant to keep "the Eye" productive, whether it came to refer finally to a gravid woman or invested capital. Production cannot be left to chance. Somehow it has to be controlled, or at least people seem to need to have the feeling that they control it. A belief in the Evil Eye (or today we would be more likely to think of "Luck") provides such an opportunity. Protective fertility symbols have saturated the world through the ages and, as such, they have all been used to protect against the Evil Eye. They are still all around us. Like specters of a long-gone past, outdistanced by change, they haunt us and insist on perpetuating their outmoded role as protectors against sterility and poverty, and, by extension, against misfortune in general. It should be obvious by now that if the eye is simply one of the numerous symbolic representations of the vulva, then, there should be equally numerous representations of the female genitalia as fertility icons without the symbolism of the eye. We do not always recognize them for what they are. The greater part of the most ancient symbols have been subjected to *post facto* interpretations which make them all the more difficult to recognize for what they originally were. Lilies of the Araceae family (Calla, Arum, Diffenbachia), with their large spathe and their large enclosed spadix, have been an almost obvious symbol of fertility (figs. 29). The lily symbol was brought into Europe under the form of the fleur-de-lys, at the time of the Crusades. It was later adopted as an emblem by French Bourbon Royalty in the sixteenth century and by the British Boy Scouts in the twentieth. The lily is still an acknowledged fertility symbol in Africa.[201] Its meaning has been turned by Christianity into its opposite: the symbol of the purity of the Virgin Mary. Nevertheless, the original meaning of the calla lily was still extant in the Middle Ages. To wit: a students' song quoted by Symonds:

> Neath the waist her belly turneth
> Unto fulness, where below
> In love's garden lilies grow.[202]

All the "obscene" sculptures in Romanesque churches were in all probability fertility symbols rather than a statement on the ugliness of sin (see the section on sheela-na-gigs). Easter, the rabbit, eggs, Spring, sleighbells, are all fertility symbols. We no longer think of them as such. Like Christmas, they have become a merchandising opportunity. In some parts of Europe there is still the distorted legend that the eggs are brought from Rome by the pealing Easter bells. Eggs are fertility symbols because of their shape and because of what they are. Bells were an old fertility symbol in ancient Rome, still extant in India, with the bell itself being kteic and the clapper, phallic.

The hand (kteis) and its fingers (phalloi) are an ancient fertility symbol. According to Elworthy, "The earliest example we have of the hand as an amulet against fascination . . ." are from early Etruscan tombs.[203] The protective medals worn today show, for instance, Mary in a Mandorla, with rays emanating from her open hands. The *form* is that of a kteic amulet. The hand being a kteic symbol, one can extend an open palm in the direction of someone in the same spirit of protection (see Marcadé, p. 20). It would be interesting to find out if the "fascist" salute of the Roman Legionnaires had that same protective meaning. More recently, it is still prevalent among the arabs and related peoples, who, if they are Muslims, will refer to it as "the Hand of Fatima," which for good measure in protecting against the Evil Eye, has an eye in the palm. It should also be noted, for whatever it is worth, that there are customs like hand-kissing and idioms like "asking for a woman's hand in marriage," that could well derive from a fertility hand symbolism. The foot and the sandal, for reasons rather obscure to us, are ancient fertility symbols. Some authors think that there is "natural" tendency to succumb to the "sensuality" of the foot, hence the relationship of the foot symbol to the shoe or sandal symbol.[204] I will not argue for or against this particular thesis, but the fact is that the sandal and the foot have been fertility symbols. There is a rather well-known statue of Aphrodite and Pan, from the first Century B.C., found at Delos. Aphrodite has taken off her left sandal and is said to be playfully threatening Pan with it. In view of the kteic symbolism of the sandal, and in view of the characters in the group, it is possible that Aphrodite is not rejecting Pan, she is symbolically inviting him. Allan Edwards, in his *Erotica Judaica*, discussing Hebraic documents says: "*Ragle* or *rigl* (foot, leg) and *ragli* or *riglim* (feet) are familiar euphemisms for the pudenda."[205] Sir William Hamilton in his letter published in Knight relates that in 1780, "I did intend to have been present at the Feast of St. Cosmos this year; but the indecency of this ceremony having probably transpired, from the country's having been more frequented since the new road was made, orders have been given that the *Great Toe* of the Saint should no longer be exposed" (Knight, p. 5). The Great Toe, of course, is the phallos. The church authorities were systematically trying to destroy the cult of phallic and kteic saints, which were still extant in peasant Europe at this time.

The list of fertility symbols is so extraordinarily extensive and diversified that no list could ever be exhaustive. Beyond those already mentioned, one can mention the unicorn, the stag, the donkey, the bull, the ram, any buck, be it deer, goat or rabbit, the horn and anything that looks like a horn, claws, canine teeth, the bear, the sow, the fig which represented not only the vulva but also the virgin uterus, as opposed to the pomegranate which symbolized the gravid uterus,[206] peach, apple, flowers (the lily, the lotus, the orchid,[207] the rose), leaves of certain trees,[208] the mistletoe, the elongated rounded evergreen leaf of which, along with two berries, represented the male triad; hence the custom of maidens being "kissed" under the mistletoe. Birds, especially in antiquity, deserve a special mention. They were symbols of fertility, especially those that could be outlined in soft round curves, like the dove, certain types of parakeets and the goose. The dove as a symbol of peace may have been derived from this. The rooster and the peacock, the former in western Europe, the latter in India (eventually imported into the Roman Empire. The Gaelic rooster is still with us in the vernacular "cock" to designate the penis. The wings of birds seem to have been considered as kteic, which led to the development in Rome of effigies made up of winged phalloi, often having the head of a bird or the tail of a bird (figs. 8.4 and 40.3). Other symbols were, hunchbacks, hermaphroditic figures, umbrellas, peppers, the anchor (derived from the Parturient Woman symbol), maypole (and dance), spinning, spitting (as symbol of ejaculation), dancing, snakes, fish, doors (and the entrance to things in general), towers, fawns, lions (and the lion's paw), the scarab (*scarabeus sacer*) which was considered as androgenic in ancient Egypt, the scorpion (because of its oval back with a line in the middle and its erect tail), scepters and orbs, swagger sticks, wands, staves of office, amber, bronze, red, blue, horse-shoes (fig. 2.3) and the horseshoe crab, cloverleaves, vases, actually any vessels, especially those made to receive liquids, pentagrams, fleur-de-lys, the crescent moon, shells, coral, pearls, mandrake, ginseng and ergot of rye, as much for the ithyphallic shape of its sclerotium as for its ecstatic effect when ingested.[209]

Then, there are those symbols that are dependent upon the analogy of the interaction of the male and female membra during sexual intercourse, requiring two complementary referents. The sacred writings of Hinduism, the Vedas, for instance, makes frequent use of the sexual symbolism of the *mortar and pestle*. The same metaphor is used as an educational tool in initiation rites among the Bambara (West Africa).[210] *The plough and the furrow* analogy has been in use in most agricultural societies where the plough is in use, the plough being male and the furrow being female. The Greeks still use the verb "to plough" as one of their directional terms to refer to coitus.[211] The agricultural analogy is extended to the seed spent into the ploughed earth. The Latin *semen* and the Greek *sperma* referred to seed of plants as well as to the male genital secretion in both languages. The sword and the sheath (or the wound); the dagger and the scabbard (vagina means scabbard or sheath in Latin). This over-abundance of sexual symbols has caused strange mixed metaphors to arise in unexpected places: Shakespeare in *Anthony and Cleopatra* has Agrippa vociferate against Cleopatra:

> "Royal wench!
> She made great Caesar lay his sword to bed:
> He plough'd her, and she cropp'd."[212]

The heart and the arrow: we have already probed the symbolic significance of the heart shape; it follows that if the heart is female, then the arrow is a phallic counterpart; the tongue and the mouth; the horn and the eye; the key and the keyhole; the fingers and the hand as well as the finger and the ring at weddings, or the crown and the head in Greek marriages and in the *svayamara* ceremony in India.[213] All of these double components have been, at one time or another, symbols of the interacting sex organs: phallos and kteis, which themselves are symbols of fertility. The wedding ring is kteic and the finger is phallic. That may be why it is still such a powerful symbol of marriage. We have already mentioned rice thrown at the newlyweds, but confetti can be substituted for rice and confetti is the Italian word for sugared almonds, which themselves are a fertility symbol. Figure 37 shows tombstones in Arussi decorated with concentric circles, which, according to Azaïs et Chambard, represents the vagina.[214] All these symbols are meant to encourage prosperity and give protection against ill happenings.

Many of the above symbols and a few more were mentioned by an Arab historian of the Crusades, Imad-ad-Din, who is speaking of the female contingent accompanying the Crusaders to the Holy Land. He gets carried away and, as is so often the case with fertility imagery, he piles on the euphemisms for what the ladies have to offer:

> they invited swords to enter their sheaths, they razed the terrain for planting, they made javelin rise towards shields, excited the plough to plough, gave the birds a place to peck with their beaks, allowed heads to enter their antechambers and raced under whoever bestrode them at the spur's blow . . . caught lizard after lizard in their hole . . . guided pens to inkwells, torrents to the valley bottom. They contested for tree trunks, wandered far and wide to collect fruit and maintained that this was an act of piety without equal.[215]

Today, the old symbols often go unrecognized, but they may still occur in association with such things as courtship, marriage, love, births, baptisms, or as traditional designs on such mundane things as pots, wooden shoes, Easter eggs, bells and as industrial logos. And all have been used as apotropaics against the Evil Eye. As Hocart said about the Evil Eye, the only thing we have culturally retained is the strong feeling that somehow they mean good luck, so that we keep on using them, most often unknowingly. Sir E. A. Wallis Budge says about the decorations on a horse collar that: "It is tolerably certain that the brass bosses and ornaments which decorate the harness of cart horses and shire-stallions were, like the great brass horns which rise from their collars, originally intended to protect the animal from the Evil Eye; but this fact has been forgotten. . . ." Budge could have added that the horns are phallic symbols and the bells, which we know now only as sleigh-bells, are kteic. Blunt said it also when he spoke of bells around the neck of domestic animals in Sicily: "The custom has survived the consciousness of its origin."[216]

Dance

Because the sex act is, for most people, an ecstatic experience, certain activities that induce a state of comparable ecstasy seem to become associated with the sex act, and therefore with fertility. The dance may be such a thing. The "whirling dervishes" do become ecstatic by whirling rhythmically. Sacred dances, have been and still are part of many sects. The Spanish flamenco dances and the Greek and Turkish "belly dance" originated in movements celebrating mating. Unlike those performances in cabarets and movies, the belly dance involves a man and a woman, who end the dance by falling to the floor in a state of high sexual excitement.

During a year's residence in Greece, I discovered that the dance has a certain sacrality that is mystifying for an outsider. It certainly has a symbolic value of sorts, that, I must admit, I have not been able to decipher. When I asked a neighbor what he would look for in a prospective husband for his daughters, his immediate and unhesitating answer was: "That he dance well." I am, of course, well aware that peasants have a sense of humor, and misleading outsiders is part of their bag of tricks, but in this case, having evaluated critically all the circumstances, I don't think that he was being facetious, although the phrase may have had a hidden symbolic meaning, of which the informant himself was unaware. All those present agreed that a man who would take the time and make the effort to please by developing a dance routine called a Zembekeiko, must be energetic, enterprising, creative and a man who cares about his neighbors. The meaning of the dance probably goes beyond this, and it is possible that the statement has symbolic overtones of sexuality, but what is important for us is to note that the people of the island had a very strong feeling, about the value of the dance.

Like sacred dances, there are substances that induce a state similar to ecstasy. They too have been associated with fertility "mystery" cults of Ancient Egypt, Rome and particularly of Ancient Greece. Wasson, Hofmann and Ruck make a good case for the ingestion of ergot of barley in the "mysteries" rituals at Eleusis.[217] Ergot of rye was involved in the "dance epidemics" of medieval Europe, which produced St. Vitus' dance.[218] St. Vitus, as we have seen was a phallic saint. It must be remembered however, that this ergot-induced state was not necessarily needed for the performance of dances celebrating fertility activities during the Middle Ages. A case in point is the Feast of Fools or the Feast of the Asses, both of which were celebrated in churches in spite of the objections of the Church to the lewd character of the performances.

Idioms

There are many idioms in European languages which are used as a matter of course, without questions. However, in some cases, if one stops to analyze them, they are puzzling until one places them into the context of fertility symbolism. A few have been mentioned in previous chapters: asking for a woman's hand in marriage, could be explained in terms of the kteic symbolism of the hand. The idiom "a snake in the grass" may now refer to the hidden dangers of a devious individual, but in conjunction with the polysemantic origin of symbols, it might also refer to the penis amidst the pubic hair, as it does in the language of the Pangwe, who refer to it as "the snake in the reeds."[219]

Summing up

The concern for prosperity and for that which produces it is universal. Or in other words, the concern for production and reproduction is universal, hence the symbols for production and reproduction have been with us universally and at all times. The paramount symbol, The Eye, is still with us.

Chapter XVI

Conclusion

The Fascinating Eye

The word "fascination" comes from the Greek *vaskania* (*βασκανια*) whose primary meaning is "Evil Eye," but it also signifies "fascination," that is, the act of mesmerizing with the eyes, like a serpent with its prey, and, by extension, it means to enchant, to charm, to captivate attention through the agency of something seductive. In that latter sense, the Evil Eye is figuratively a fascinating topic. It is seductive because, in fact, in its 5,000 years of proven existence, it still is imbued with overtones of sexuality and fecundity, which, as facts of life, are not only inevitable and delightful, but are necessary if the species is to perpetuate itself.

Sexuality and fecundity remain "fascinating" and popular topics in spite of the distortions that they have been subjected to in the last millennium or so. The misrepresentations, however, are also the cause of wanton neglect on the part of such venerable institutions as the Church and Academe. Marx and Engels said that the Church in the Middle Ages had created a morality for exploitation. If indeed it did, it accomplished this by, among other means, forcing sex into a category of things that were opprobrious, turning the very thought of sex into something shameful, ugly and abject. Yet, the strong urge of individuals to mate, the necessity for the species to reproduce itself and survive, and the fact that the people, the peasants especially, identified reproduction with production, make it so that propagation was of primordial importance. In the pragmatic philosophy of the world of subsistence, not only are production and reproduction undistinguishable, but people tend to identify with the rest of nature. They view the reproduction of the grain in the fields, of the animals, wild or domestic, and of themselves as essential for their survival. In this atmosphere of dire need to produce and reproduce, fecundity came to be the nexus of life and the object of awe. It was sacralized and symbolized by an infinitely great number of emblems that represented the nexus of reproduction, coitus, sexual organs, and parturition. These emblems were used as talismans (as the cross is worn today by christians) and were used strategically to encourage fertility. The most obvious symbol of human fecundity is the act of reproduction, which itself, is best symbolized by the visible generative organs of both sexes (kteis and phallos). In time these came to be stylized and represented by graphs, abstract designs or by objects that resembled them superficially. It is surely significant that the eye was for a long time one of the chief symbols of fertility, although it seems that the original symbolic meaning was eventually lost, whereas the *literal* meaning of "eye" was retained. The Evil Eye became the ultimate conundrum: an enigma, the answer to which is a play on words. The Evil Eye is virtually the persistence of the symbolic representation of the principle of female fertility which, combined with the male fertility principle, perpetuates life and protects all those things that are considered essential in the eternal struggle to survive.

It is, culturally speaking, not so much a question of a desire for mating as it is a question of urgent fertility, therefore of productivity. That is not to say that on a personal level, people have ever lost their interest in sex, they have not, or else we would not be here to tell the tale, but it does mean there is a generic societal law that says that fecundity must be promoted if life is to go on. In the conflict between the State-Church sponsored morality, and the doggedly conservative tendencies of people to hold onto ancient beliefs, the characteristics of such arcane and hallowed systems of beliefs as that of the Evil Eye have undergone transformations, but it is the language that was transformed rather than the beliefs. The beliefs and the symbols persisted with as much power as they ever had, and they came to be applied to things that were produced but were no longer directly related to Nature. That is why, to insure the "fecundity" of a business or of an artisan as artisan, a fertility symbol based on *human* imagery can and will be used.

If all this is true, then the phenomenon that we call the Evil Eye ought to exist outside of the symbolism of the Eye. It does. The Parturient Woman (including the sheelas) is such an instance. It is as widespread, if not more so, than the eye symbolism. The eye motif (and the oval and the almond shape) is simply a *pars pro toto* (a part standing for the whole) symbol of the Parturient Woman symbol. The Parturient Woman symbolizes not only childbirth, but also coitus, both being symbolic of fertility. The so-called sheela-na-gigs, as well as all Baubo figures and the figures at the entrance of temples in India and Nepal, exhibit ktenes which have to be complemented by a figurative phallos in the form of a wet finger. Somehow, the power (or mana) manifest in these symbols is pervasive and, in some areas of the world, it is accepted unquestioned, and is often integrated into the religion of State, as it is for the Evil Eye in Greece or in India.

Without saying that the culture of state societies possesses a clear concept of mana, it may be argued that the people in them do believe in the mysterious powers of Nature, often impersonal as in mana. It takes on the form of a belief in luck, good or bad, and/or of a belief that "the forces of Nature" are manipulated by some equally mysterious, but higher, personalized authority, operating from an overseeing supernatural world, and who can be reached by means of various rituals, often of an occult nature. Finally, it must be said that if apotropaics encourage life, they also protect life. That is why the shields of warriors, their helmets, their equipment are often covered with symbols that can be recognized as being the same as those which protect against the Evil Eye (think of the "Glamour Girls" painted on WWII plane "noses.")

Now that most of us no longer exact our subsistence directly from nature, the need for a protective device such as that of the Evil Eye has lost its meaning, but it has retained its emotional power. In some quarters, indeed, especially among people who are only one step removed from subsistence agriculture, and who rely partially on nature to survive, there remains the strong feelings associated with the necessity to encourage "good luck" to settle upon direct or indirect subsistence activities. These people often cling to the traditions that, in their cultural past, used to ritually guarantee abundance and security. The Evil Eye is one such tradition: it has lost its original meaning, but what remains is the powerful feeling (and only the feeling, not the understanding) that somehow a belief in it provides abundance and security.

Envoy

Certainly, abundance and security is what we still seek, and in so doing we believe in things that are the generic equivalent of the Evil Eye. We too, are obsessed with production and reproduction, the object of which may no longer be the land, the animals or ourselves, but it is still those things that we think make us prosperous: industrial capital, profits and jobs. On an individual level, we have lost our respect for nature and have come to worship that which is produced rather than that which produces. The Gross National Product has become the measure of our well-being, if not of our happiness. We have come to transcend personal values and, "rugged individualism" notwithstanding, we have assumed a "global" perspective, so that, collectively, we still feel that our productive-reproductive system is under threat—not from the Evil Eye, that explanation is too personal and no longer sufficient—but from some vaster and still mysterious Evil Force against which we feel compelled to protect ourselves by pointing at it the equivalent of phallic horns. Unfortunately, one would be hard put to find a meaningful kteic complement to re-establish a truly cosmic equilibrium. The ancient kteic symbolism of dove, olive leaf and rose somehow are no longer pertinent, and neither is the Lonely Eye.

Appendix I

Our "reality" is culturally molded. Other peoples' "reality" is given form by the culture they live in. They can be every bit as ethnocentric as we are. Their knowledge is determined by that culture and their perception of things and events is also determined by that culture. That is why to a person in a pre-industrial, pre-political world, the cure of a headache by swallowing an aspirin (given by an outsider from the industrial world) is of the same nature as the cure of a headache by having the local shaman ritually suck an object out of one's head. It is perceived as the same thing. One is the outsider's way, which might or might not control the ache, and the other is the indigenous way, which, also, might or might not control the pain. I once had a neighbor in Africa, who came to me for treatment of a terribly inflamed wound on his foot. He had treated it himself with a white powder, because he had seen someone in an outsider's imported clinic being quickly cured with white powder (sulpha). His own attempt had been very obviously unsuccessful. So, not being able to rely on himself, he had come to me, an outsider. I evaluated his problem on the basis of my own culture, which had produced the DDT powder with which he was unwittingly poisoning himself. I took care of his problem successfully. To him the only difference between his treatment of his wound with white powder and my treatment of his wound with white powder, was the person who administered the medicine. He concluded that the power to cure, then, lies with the person. On the basis of his experience and his knowledge of his world, he was, of course, perfectly correct and his logic was impeccable. We might say that he should reconsider his premisses and his postulates, but that is beside the point here, the point being that he used the postulates at his disposal to come to a logical conclusion.

Appendix II

Regarding the Word "mana."

Unfortunately there is room for confusion. First, with the Latin word "manes." There is a concept of the *mana of the family* certainly in all lineage societies, and probably in all societies where organization is based upon some sort of "family" structure. The confusion comes from the fact that the Roman *manes* is quite similar in character. According to Frederick Stanley Lusby, the cult of the *manes* "involved the tendance of all the dead of a particular line. The dead individual as such was not the object of worship, but the life-force or genius [of the family group involved]" (*Encyclopaedia Britannica*, 1963, V. I, p. 881). Yet *manes* is a Latin word, whereas *mana* is a Melanesian word, and there is no evidence that the two words are historically linked.

Another word which may lead to confusion, is the Kinyarwanda term *Imaana*, which also, as we have seen in Chapter VI, has something to do with power. And here, also, there is no evidence that there is a historical relationship between Kinyarwanda and Melanesian.

A third word, perhaps more remote in meaning, is *manna*, the food miraculously supplied to the Israelites in the wilderness (Exodus 16:14-36).

A stone lying on the ground partakes in its own way of that power with which the Universe is imbued. The combination of stone and the end of a man's arm will result in a multiplied increase in mana. Cultural factors such as carvings on the stone, or the status of the man wielding the stone will change the potential. A chief has the mana of his rank permuted with the mana of the position he occupies in the network of his society, and the mana of his personal experience which molded his personality. In a sense, the concept of mana is to subsistence societies what the concept of a High God is to state society. The term High God is used by folklorists, students of comparative religions and anthropologists, to refer to a supernatural being who is at the top of a hierarchy of beings created by himself and who has authority and power over all and everything below him. It is a concept that does not occur in non-stratified societies.

Appendix III

As an aside, we might point out that belonging to a corporate group does not necessarily deprive one of individuality. As a matter of fact, belonging to a small family corporate group, which exists as an environment for the well-being of the individuals that make it up, is much less deteriorating to individuality than the situation which occurs when an individual has to survive by selling part of himself, his labor and his talents, to an industrial special purpose corporation whose primary goal is to show a profit for those who own the means of production. Production of goods or services becomes a means to that end. To achieve solidarity and cohesion, the industrial special purpose corporation expects to receive as a gratuity, a third part of the persons whose labor and talents they buy: loyalty. This is manifested most often in conformity and anonymity. To maintain the system, it is necessary to keep the individual fragmented in this way. Whereas the primary goal of the general purpose family group is to assure the individual of a secure environment and an opportunity to cultivate and maintain the integrity of his or her personality. The loyalties accorded to such a general purpose corporation are self-serving and reciprocal.

Appendix IV

Jorgen Andersen seems to think that the sheela-na-gig figure "was first developed by Romanesque carvers." He explains the disparity of style between the sheelas and the rest of the Romanesque carvings in any one particular church, by suggesting that the sheelas were carved deliberately without style to make them "ugly." The argument does not stand. The Romanesque stone workers were entirely capable of "doing" ugliness with style. Not only should this be an argument against his thesis, and in favor of the Celtic origin of the sheelas, but there are, in fact, other carvings from the Celtic period, which, stylewise might link the sheelas to a pagan past. One of these might be the Braunston Church carving, which has been identified as a 2,000 year-old Celtic relic. It was placed outside the church, but against the church wall. Other "pagan" items have been included in the building of churches but not identified as such. An "Eye of God" on the tower of St Mary's Church, at Newchurch-in-Pendle, seems to be a vulva at the moment of crowning, comparable to the vulva of some sheelas, and comparable to the carvings on the stoup at Farges.

Andersen nevertheless also says that the sheela is "sometimes interpreted as a fertility figure of pagan origin." He also admits that it is "associated with lingering pagan beliefs."

It is to be noted that there are other explanations, such as those of Georges Devereux, whose interpretations are all completely freudian in character. Others explain the occurrence of sheelas in terms of diffusion from a center of origin, usually Ancient Egypt, cf. M. P. Nilsson for example.

Appendix V

It might be revealing for linguists to investigate the origin of the term "miche" as in *miché or godemiché*. *Miche*, in modern French, can refer to either a chunk of bread or to a large round loaf of bread, but until the nineteenth century, at least in southwestern France according to Dulaure, *miche* referred to the breads baked in the form of phalloi or ktenes at certain ritual times of the year celebrating fertility (see Dulaure, page 158). According to *Le Grand Larousse* dictionnary, "miche" is from the Latin *mica* meaning bit, piece of, morcel or crumb, which is the same Latin root as for *mie*, the soft internal part of a loaf of bread (as opposed to the crust); but *mica* also means alcove, that is, a vaulted recess in a room-wall such as that which served to accommodate a bed for instance. In modern French slang *miché* refers to a prostitute's "trick" or "john," or more broadly, to a man who services a woman, either for his or her sexual pleasure. Miché, which has the grammatical form of a past participle, could well refer to a man who has been "alcoved."

Le Petit Larousse dictionnary, which is not quite as reliable as *Le Grand Larousse*, gives a different origin for *miche*. It is, it says, from the Dutch *micke* referring to a large round loaf of bread. I would suspect that the Dutch word was borrowed from the older French word of "miche" referring to Dulaure's ritual bread loaves.

There could be also several etymological interpretations of the word *godemiché* (dildo). Barnhart's Dictionnary of Etymology says that there is "some confusion" in the origin of the association between "god" and "good." Good Friday used to be spelled "God Friday" and "ungodly" still means "not good" rather than "ungodlike." Ménage (1750), in analyzing the name "Godhead" finds the radical god in Germanic languages and in Greek and Latin (p. 682). He also adds a French meaning of the word "godard" which refers, in the popular vernacular, to a man whose wife has just been delivered of a child.

Larousse hesitantly attributes the radical "god-" to Celtic (see under entry "gode," p. 326). Littré says that Dies also suspects a Celtic origin (see his p. 1891, under "godinette"). Dulaure's *The Gods of Generation* has a rather broad interpretation. See Dulaure's note No. 3 for Chapter XI, p. 257.)

In the end, given the above and all that has been said about the radical *god-* in chapter XIII, the fact seems to be that the underlying meaning of "good," "pleasant," "agreeable," etc., remains. Thus, the semantic derivation of *godemiché* is "pleasure-john," i.e. dildo.

According to the Robert dictionnary, however, *godemiché* is derived from the Latin *gaude mihi* (which can be paraphrased as "pleasure to myself").

Endnotes

[1] See Siegfried Giedion. His entire opus is devoted to this thesis. See more particularly p. viii (V. 2) and p. 79 (V. 1).

[2] Read, John. "Chemistry," in James R. Newman's *What is Science*?, 1955, fourth paperback printing, 1962, p. 166.

[3] Even among the textbooks on beliefs, only *Magic, Witchraft, and Religion* by Arthur C. Lehman and James E. Meyers offer some insights on the Evil Eye. See the second (1989) and third (1993) editions, Mountain view, CA: Mayfield Publishing Co.

[4] This is confirmed by Paul Williams who says: "The term 'fertility' need not only be associated with offspring or crops in that all transformations that take place may be looked upon as being the result of the union of fundamental sources of energy, and it is the moment when transformation takes place that is considered the most dangerous." Williams, Paul. *Primitive Religion and Healing*, p. 76. We will discuss this further in the text, particularly in the chapters involving "the moment of crowning."

[5] Hasluck, Margaret, p. 163. Note that the term "to overlook" (overlooking) used by Margaret Hasluck is the term used in the British Isles to refer to the act of casting the Evil Eye.

[6] Random House Dictionary, p. 768.

[7] According to Winifred Blackman, the Evil Eye in Egypt is referred to as "the eye of envy." Blackman, Winifred S. *The Fellahin of Upper Egypt*. London: George Harrap and Co., 1927, pp. 71 & 218.

[8] Elworthy, F. T. "Evil Eye" in *Encyclopaedia of Religion and Ethics*, James Hastings, ed. Vol. V. New York: Charles Scribner's sons, 1955, p. 608.

[9] Elworthy, op. cit., p. 608.

[10] Mauss, Marcel. *The Gift*, New York: W. W. Norton and Company, Inc., 1967.

[11] Cf. Simmons, Leo W., ed. *Sun Chief: The Autobiography of a Hopi Indian*. Published for the Department of Sociology by Yale University Press, New Haven, 1942. Don C. Talayesva, the protagonist in this work, would have been considered as having the Evil Eye, had he lived in Europe, because he disrupted the Hopi social order by not

abiding by the rules of reciprocity. Instead, as he would have, had he lived in Africa, he was considered a witch, which is the equivalent of having the Evil Eye, without the fertility dimension.

[12] Elworthy, Frederick Thomas. *The Evil Eye*. From the facsimile of the 1895 Edition, p. 3. Sir E. A. Wallis Budge repeats the exact same phrase in *Amulets and Talismans*. New York: University Books, 1968, p. 356. This latter book was originally published in 1930, thirty-five years after Elworthy's.

[13] The term High God is used by folklorists and students of comparative religions to refer to a God who is at the top of a medieval and supernatural hierarchy of beings created by Himself, and who has authority and power over all and everything below him, including beings in the natural world.

[14] Mellaart, James. "The Beginning of Mural Painting." *Archaeology* V. 15, No. 2, June 1962, p. 11.

[15] Note that Harrison uses the term *vaskania* here to refer to apotropaics. Its proper meaning is "Evil Eye."

[16] See CHAPTER XIV, under *The Horn*.

[17] Blue, red and black are the protective colors almost everywhere, but one color usually prevails in each area. In Turkey the color is blue. In Italy, it is red. In India it is black.

[18] See Gubbins, p. 196.

[19] See "spitting" in the chapter on Other Significant Symbols.

[20] Distasi, Lawrence. *Mal Occhio. The Underside of Vision*. San Francisco: North Point Press, 1981.

[21] Meccia, Neil. *M.A. Star Paper*, Department of Anthropology, Northern Illinois University, 1978.

[22] *Chicago Tribune*, Sunday, October 5, 1986.

[23] Donaldson, Bess Allen. "The Evil Eye in Iran." *The Evil Eye*, edited by Alan Dundes, University of Wisconsin Press, 1981, 1992, pp. 66-77.

[24] Sachs, Lisbeth: *Evil Eye or Bacteria. Turkish Migrant Women and Swedish Health Care*. Stockholm Studies in Social Anthropology. 1983.

[25] Lindquist, Eda. "Rue and the Evil Eye." *The Moslim World*, 26, pp. 170-175, 1936.

[26] Westermarck, E. *Ritual and Belief in Morocco*, vol. 1, p. 471. Quoted by John Abbott in *The Keys of Power*, 1974, p. 132.

[27] Abdelsalam, Sharafeldin Elamin. *A Study of Contemporary Sudanese Muslim Saints' Legends in Sociocultural Contexts*. Ph.D. Dissertation, Indiana University, 1983. Reference: abstract from OCLC.

[28] Patai, Raphael. "T'Khelet - Blue." Chapter 6 in *On Jewish Folklore*. Wayne State University Press, 1983.

[29] Eliade, Mircea. *Patterns in Comparative Religions*, p. 333.

[30] Vuorela, Toivo. *Der böse Blick* . . . Helsinki, 1967, p. 61.

[31] Castañon, Luciano. *Supersticiones y Creencias de Asturias*. Ayalga/Ed., Salinas, 1976. "Ojo" also means clove of garlic.

[32] W. L. Hildburgh. "Lunar Crescents as Amulets in Spain." MAN XLII, #42, p. 77.

[33] Waterman, Philip. Op. cit., p. 142. Lee Alexander Stone also mentions it in his *Story of Phalliscism*, pp. 91-92, although his attribution of the origin of the Omega symbol to this particular custom is doubtful.

[34] See below, Chapter on Mana; and see also Monica Wilson's *Good Company*, pp. 96-104.

[35] LeVine, Robert A. and Barbara B. *Nyansongo: a Gusii Community in Kenya*. New York: John Wiley & Sons, 1966.

[36] Burton, Richard F. *The Lakes Region of Central Africa*. New York: Horizon Press, 1951, p. 116. The original was published in the mid-nineteenth century.

[37] Roberts, John B. Letter from the field, Spring 1990. John B. Roberts did field work in Uttar Pradesh, in India. Varanasi is also known as Benares. John B. Roberts is not to be confused with John M. Roberts, who wrote an article on the Evil Eye in Maloney.

[38] This kind of use of a strong universal emotion may be characteristic of the "extra-processual events" (cf. Bohannon) that occur spontaneously in State societies, where control of individual behavior becomes the focus for social and political control.

[39] Anand, Mulk Raj. *Kama Kala*, 1963, p. 5.

[40] Budge, E. A. Wallis. *Amulets and Talismans*. New Hyde Park, New York: University Books, 1968, p. 356.

[41] Budge, op. cit., p. 359. Budge spells it "Baskainon," but it is probably a typo. *Baskanion* does mean Evil Eye.

[42] Kern-Ulmer, Brigitte. "The Power of the Evil Eye and the Good Eye in Midrashic Literature." *Judaism*, Summer, 1991.

[43] Dundes. See pp. 259-262 of the 1981 edition.

[44] There is strong evidence for the recent existence of such a cult. Duerr discusses this thoroughly, but one should also read Ernest Tappolet, "La survivance de 'Diana' dans les patois Romands," and Felix Stähelin, "Aus der Religion des römischen Helvetien."

[45] According to Elworthy, this was also Plutarch's view. Elworthy, p. 13.

[46] The reference to these works will be found in the Bibliography.

[47] Elworthy, F. T. op. cit., and Inman, Thomas. *Ancient Pagan and Modern Christian Symbolism*. 1876.

[48] Maloney, Clarence, ed. *The Evil Eye*. New York: Columbia University Press, 1976.

[49] Dundes, Alan, ed. *The Evil Eye. A Folklore Casebook*. New York: Garland Publishing Co., 1981.

[50] Carroll, Michael P. "On the Psychological Origins of the Evil Eye: A Kleinian View." *Journal of Psychoanalytic Anthropology*, 7/2, Spring 1984. [Psychoanalytical interpretation based on the conditioning of children by the "fact" that the tip of the breast of the mother, "looks like an eye."]

[51] Siebers, Tobin. *The Mirror of Medusa*. University of California Press, 1983.

[52] Knight, p. 4. The style, the spelling and the punctuation are those of the cited edition.

[53] Thomas Wright seems to have been a rather energetic character. He not only was the editor of Knight's work, and the author of an accompanying essay, but he also was the founding secretary of both the Camden Society and the Percy Society, and he was, according to Sir James Holt, "the first editor of the political songs of medieval England,"

in the course of which he expressed the opinion that the Robin Hood legend was probably mythical. See Holt, J. C.: *Robin Hood*, 1989 edition, pp. 54 & 55.

[54] Dulaure, Wright, and Westropp, who each published works on the same topic in 1805, 1865 and 1885 respectively, all refer to the *Confession de Sancy* by Agrippa d'Aubigné (1699) which was a satire based in part upon another earlier satire by Henri Estienne (1566). Both Agrippa and Estienne were Huguenots with a bias against the established church. My question here is not to make a critical evaluation but rather to bring attention to the fact that by the nineteenth century the subject matter was in the hand of men who were concerned with a relatively objective analysis of society rather than in the hands of satirists.

[55] Cf. Rousseau, G. S. "The Sorrows of Priapus" (see Bibliography).
Niemoeller says that Robert Alan Campbell's *Phallic Worship* was plagiarized from Dulaure. At a later date, Sanger Brown seems to have plagiarized Knight's work in his *Sex Worship and Symbolism:* his illustrations have been taken directly from Knight's book yet he makes only a passing reference to him (see Bibliography). The name of A. F. Niemoeller was obtained from A.M.S. Press, Inc., the successors of Panurge Press, through the courtesy of Ms. Luanne Parker of the editorial department.

[56] Brandt, Paul Hans (pseudonym: Hans Licht), p. 64.

[57] See Chapter I under "Contemporary Folk Perception."

[58] Hocart, A. M. "The Mechanism of The Evil Eye." *Folklore* 49, 1938, pp. 156-157.

[59] A subsistence society is a society characterized by the fact that the people tend to produce for their subsistence and not necessarily for a market.

[60] Wax, Rosalie and Murray. "The Magical Worldview." In *Journal for the Scientific Study of Religion*, 1: 179-88, 1962.

[61] See Douglas, Mary. *Implicit Meanings*.

[62] Wilson, G. "An African Morality" in *Cultures and Societies of Africa*, edited by Simon and Phoebe Ottenberg. New York: Random House, 1960, p. 353.

[63] One is reminded of the vocabulary that we have inherited from the yippie generation of the 1960's: from some people one gets "good vibrations" from others, "bad."

[64] Cf. *Sun Chief. The Autobiography of a Hopi Indian*, edited by Leo W. Simmons. Yale University Press, 1942. Sun Chief was a Hopi Indian who was considered a witch

by his neighbors because he did not conform to the norms of Hopi society. His people thought he exuded "bad vibrations."

[65] See Waterman, pp. 15-16.

[66] Unwin, J. D. *Sex and Culture*. Oxford University Press, 1934. Cf. p. 131.

[67] Nurse and Spears.

[68] Colson, Elisabeth. "Ancestral Spirits and Social Structure Among the Plateau Tonga." See Bibliography.

[69] All quotations from p. 51.

[70] Barstow, Anne L. "The Prehistoric Goddess." *The Book of the Goddess Past and Present*, edited by Carl Olson. New York: Crossroad, 1988, p. 13.

[71] Oates, Joan. "Religion and Ritual in Sixth-Millennium B.C. Mesopotamia." *World Archaeology*, X, 2, 1979, p. 122.

[72] The implication, from our "scientific" understanding, is that in viewing the sperm as seed, people would think of the male contribution as being the substantial one, while the female has "only" a nourishing role. But that is not necessarily so. The belief, among some East African agriculturalists for instance is that the woman, during coitus, has her own flowing discharge which contributes to the "making" of a child (see *The Tree of Iron*).

[73] Already quoted above is Anne L. Barstow who made the point that on the prehistoric Persian Plateau, the rituals were not addressed to a goddess, but were rather *a celebration of fecundity*. Robert Ballon in *The Nature of Religion* quotes Jacquetta Hawkes as saying that prehistoric statuettes "portrayed not woman but fertility."

[74] Montaigne, Michel Eyquem de. *Autobiography*, edited and translated by Marvin Lowenthal. New York: Vintage Books, 1956, p. 55.

[75] E. W. Smith and A. M. Dale. *The Ila-Speaking Peoples of Northern Rhodesia*, 1920, ii, p. 35.

[76] Giedion quoting Winthuis, J., 1928, p. 12. See Bibliography. It is to be noted, as we will discuss later in the book, that Winthuis had run across universal symbols representing the sexual *membra*, particularly the omega-shape, which he calls sickle-shape.

[77] See St. Leger-Gordon, Ruth E. *The Witchcraft and Folklore of Dartmoor*. New York: Bell Publishing Co., 1972, p. 156.

[78] Actually, *volva* in Latin refers to the womb or uterus and the Romans did have a word for the female external genitalia, which is *cunnus*. This latter is obviously the word we should use, but after due consideration, I have opted for *vulva* (with a "u") to avoid offending the sensibilities of those who would recognize the Anglo-Saxon derivative as being "vulgar." Moreover, the definition given by Webster's II (Riverside Publishing Co., 1984) is quite close to the meaning I mean to convey: "Vulva. The external female genitalia, including the labia majora, labia minora, clitoris, and vestibule of the vagina."

[79] For example, "kteis" is used by Hodder M. Westropp's *Primitive Symbolism* first published in 1885 (p. 31), and by Lee Alexander Stone (who was a physician, as was Westropp) in his *Story of Phallicism*, (1927).

[80] Cf. Gimbutas, Marija. *The Language of the Goddess* her fig. #480, nos. 2 and 3.

[81] Brault, Gérard J. "Isolt and Guenevere: Two Twelfth Century Views of Women." In Morewedge, Rosemarie Thee ed. *The Role of Women in the Middle Ages*. State University of New York Press, 1975, pp. 41-64.

[82] Lee Alexander Stone quotes this passage (p. 90) and attributes it to "an antiquary" without giving any author or title. This may be due to the fact that when Wright brought out R. P. Knight's work on the *Worship of Priapus* in 1865, he gave credit to Knight, but did not acknowledge his own added contribution, as a consequence of which the authorship of the "Essay of the Worship of the Generative Powers during the Middle Ages" remained obscure, and may still have been so when Stone's *The Story of Phallicism* was published in 1927. Since then, however, authorship has been attributed to Thomas Wright.

[83] Waterman, Philip F. *The Story of Superstition*. New York: Alfred Knopf, 1929, p. 142. Given what Waterman says, the heraldic shape of a shield may have been a development from the female pubic triangle symbol. For confirmation of this, see Imand-ad-Din's quotation: ". . . they [the female camp followers] made javelins rise towards shields. . . ."

[84] See bibliography under Schmidt, Peter R.: "The Tree of Iron," a film about smelting directed by Peter R. Schmidt. See illustration Number 21f for an example of an ancient symbol used on a modern product.

[85] Andrews, E. A. *Copious and Critical Latin-English Lexicon*. New York: Harper and Brothers Publishers, 1856.

Andrews could have added *fero, ferre*, which means to bear, to bring, to produce, to be pregnant with. I would suggest that etymologists look into the possibility that the word *fetish* may be derived from this root also. After all, a fetish is most often a fertility figure, and although the origin of the word is supposed to be Portuguese, certainly the Portuguese could have derived from Latin.

[86] See Walker, Barbara G. *The Woman's Encyclopedia of Myths and Secrets*. Harper & Row, 1983. Hexagram, p. 401.

[87] The circle of life is also in the Japanese *futatsu domoe* symbol. It is associated with the Japanese *magatama* beads, which are referred to as "comma-shape" for the one and "ear-shaped" for the other. The former is almost certainly a phallos, and the latter is a kteis. Although Donald A. McKenzie says that: "The comma-shaped, or claw-shaped magatama had evidently a close association with the ear and with the life giving shell" (p. 151, *The Migration of Symbols*, 1926).

[88] Giedion, S. *The Eternal Present*. Pantheon Books, 1962, p. 74.

[89] Leuzinger, Elsy. *Africa. The Art of the Negro Peoples*. New York: McGraw-Hill, p. 26.

[90] Bourdier, Franck: *Préhistoire de France*, 1967, p. 280.
The phrase is translatable as "with phallic cowl?"

[91] Gimbutas, Marija A. *The Language of the Goddess*. New York: Harper and Row, 1989, p. 230, fig. 356.

[92] Rawson suggests: "It seems quite probable—though the more genteel archaeologists may rebel at the suggestion—that the heads of these figures were actually inserted into the vulvas of women or girls in the course of initiations, for example, to 'incorporate' them with the image of the Fertile Mother" (p. 18, PEA). The suggestion is not far-fetched since we know that until recently ritual defloration was practiced in India and Africa.

[93] Dames, Michael. *The Avebury Cycle*. Thames and Hudson, London, 1977, p. 31, cf. also p. 131. Dames, incidentally, offers explanations that are quite consistent with what we are saying in this book.

[94] C. C. and Martha Lamberg-Karloski. "An Early City in Iran." *Scientific American*, June 1971. Reproduced as article No. 20 in *Avenues to Antiquity. Readings from the Scientific American*. The reference is from p. 204.

[95] Cf. Goff, Beatrice Laura. *Symbols of Prehistoric Mesopotamia*. New Haven: Yale University Press, 1963.

[96] Cf. Marshack, op. cit. fig. 41 and Gimbutas, op. cit. fig. 86, p. 51.

[97] Absolon, Karel. "The Diluvial Anthropomorphic Statuettes and Drawings, especially the so-called Venus Statuettes Discovered in Moravia." *Artibus Asiae*, XII, 1949, pp. 208 and 204 respectively.

[98] Charrière, Georges: cf. "La signification des représentations érotiques . . .," p. 174.

[99] See Sapouna-Sakellarakis, Efi, in *Art and Culture of the Cyclades in the 3d Millennium B.C.* University of Chicago Press, 1977, pp. 127 and 128.

[100] For another perspective see Ucko and Bartel.

[101] Much longer if we include Monpazier dated at 25,000 B.C.

[102] The site of Gagarino is interesting because it includes statuettes in the style of both Willendorf and Lespugne.

[103] For those interested in stone age semantics, refer to Alan Forbes and Thomas Crowder: "The Problem of Franco-Cantabrian abstract Signs: Agenda for a New Approach." *World Archaeology*, vol. X, No. 3, 1979, pp. 350-367. See also last page (233) in Layton, Robert: "The Use of Ethnographic Parallels in Interpreting Upper Palaeolithic Rock Art."

[104] Ochshorn, Judith. *The Female Experience and the Nature of the Divine*. Indiana University Press, 1981, p. 33.

[105] Anderson, Richard L. *Art in Small-Scale Societies*. Englewood Cliffs, NJ: Prentice-Hall, second edition, 1989, pp. 75, 83 and 73.

[106] Since it is also a position that women may assume for coitus, it remains possible that some of the occurrences (in cave art for instance) were made by individuals with prurient intentions. That is, however, improbable. First, because coitus itself was a symbol of fertility, and, second, the fact is that we know the symbol occurs everywhere in a highly ritualized context (cf. Charrière, 1970). By inference, therefore, we can safely assume that the symbol is ritual. But to be considered is also Rawson's statement from his Primitive Erotic Art, p. 18:

> the public value of fertility and the private value of sexual enjoyment were not separated. [. . .] This is why any argument as to whether these images are religious or erotic is beside the point. They are both. In the primitive context desire was not separated from power.

[107] Many of the amulets described by Campbell Bonner in his *Studies in Magical Amulets*, feature gemstones that have been inscribed with parturient women sitting on a birthing chair. See Bonner, 1950.

[108] Cf. H. Kirkhoff. "The Woman's Posture during childbirth." *Organorama*, 14: 14-19, 1977.

[109] The photograph was originally published in the French edition of Dr. Orent's Book *Birth Reborn* (Pantheon Books, 1984). It also appears in Milinaire, Catherine. *Birth*. Revised and updated, New York: Harmony Books, 1987. The 1974 edition of this work features the photograph of another woman in childbirth. She is lying on her back, her arms are up in the position described as that of the Parturient Woman.

[110] Williams, Paul. *Primitive Religion and Healing*, p. 76.

[111] And, in one case, as a mark of ownership on goat pasture boundaries in Lozère (France). Cf. Van Gennep, Arnold: *Revue des Traditions Populaires*, v. 18, 1903, p. 591. (See illustration xx in this book.)

[112] Leuzinger, op. cit., p. 26.

[113] Dames, Michael. *The Avebury Cycle*, 1977, p. 181.

[114] Dorothy Cameron, Marija Gimbutas and Buffie Johnson offer a rather flighty interpretation for the origin of the bucranium, which would not deserve even this mention were it not for the currency of Gimbutas' books.

[115] Wright, Thomas. *Essay on the Worship of the Generative Powers*, p. 133. (See R. P. Knight.)

[116] For example, cf. Audierne, [abbé] François George: "Notice sur les églises du Département de la Dordogne." *Bulletin Monumental*, Vol. 1, No. 5, 1835, pp. 187-211. See p. 208.

[117] Weir, Anthony and James Jerman. *Images of lust. Sexual carvings on Medieval Churches*. London, 1986.
Andersen, Jorgen. *The Witch on the Wall. Medieval Erotic Sculptures in the British Isles*. London, 1977.

[118] Neumann, Erich. *The Great Mother*.

[119] Gantner, Joseph and Marcel Pobé. *The Glory of Romanesque Art*. New York: The Vanguard Press, 1952, p. 57 from the caption for Plate 74.

[120] Longworth, T. Clifton. *The Gods of Love*. Westport, CT: Associated Booksellers, 1960, p. 60.
Alexander Stone, in *The Story of Phallicism*, 1927, p. 84.

[121] Bourdier, Franck. *Préhistoire de France*. Paris, Flammarion, 1967. Cf. figure 148, p. 362.

[122] Cf. Saintyves, P. *Les saints successeurs des dieux*. 1907.

"Metera, mitera" means "mother." Demeter was the Earth itself inasmuch as she provided mortals with crops and subsistence. Hence, she was "Mother Earth." Gaia (or Ge) was "Earth" only inasmuch as she produced the World (including Demeter). To oversimplify the very complex mythology of the Greeks, one might say that Demeter, as Gaia's offspring, was a facet and a manifestation of Gaia. The divine role of Gaia was remote, that of Demeter, immediate. Demeter was comforting, Gaia, not.

[123] Cf. Berger, Pam. *The Goddess Obscured*, p. 3.

[124] Weir, Antony and James Jerman. *Images of Lust*, p. 20.

[125] Weir & Jarman. *Images of Lust*, p. 20. (See Bibliography.)

[126] O. A. Wall, *Sex Worship*, London, 1909, p. 480, cited by John Allegro.

[127] Allegro, John. *Lost Gods*. London: Michael Joseph, 1977, p. 110.

[128] Compare the grimace to figures 24c and 24d. Compare the pelvic area to figure 14b and to 19 b&c.

[129] See Steichen, Edward. *The Family of Man*. The Museum of Modern Art, New York, 1955, p. 22. There are also several photographs of women's faces at the same moment in Michel Odent's Birth Reborn. For Nilsson's photograph, see fig. 17.8 in this book.

[130] Cf. Witkowski, G.-J. *L'art profane à l'église*, V. II, Étranger. Paris: Jean Schemit, 1908, pp. 254-257.

[131] *Encyclopaedia Britannica*, Vol. 10, p. 531, 1963 edition, under the title of "Gorgon." See also Jane Harrison, op. cit.

[132] Srejovic, Dragoslav. *Europe's First Monumental Sculptures: Lepenski Vir*. New York: Stein & Day, 1972.

[133] In the site report, it is figure 38 from house #51, at level Lepenski-Vir Ic. (See figure 13.1 in this book).

[134] Figure 41, is from the same level, in house #45. (See figure 13.2 in this book).

[135] As a matter of fact, fig. 13.1, which represents unmistakably a vulva, graphically looks more like a fish than fig. 13.2 which is labelled a fish, but looks more like fig. 13.1, which is a vulva.

[136] Gimbutas, Marija. Op. cit. 1989, figure 50, p. 33.

[137] There is certainly a universal philosophical statement to be made here: the pain and agony of childbirth accompanying and contrasted with the advent and joy of a new life.

[138] Yarden, L. *The Tree of Light. A Study of the Menorah*. Ithaca, NY: Cornell University Press, 1971, p. 41.

[139] Random House Dictionary, p. 870.

[140] Zarnecki, George. *Art of the Medieval World*. Prentice Hall 1975, p. 271, fig. 269. Sarcophagus of Doña Sancha. Early 12th century. Originally in the convent of S. Cruz de la Seròs; now in the Monastério de la Benedictinas, Jaca.

[141] The Cosmic Egg is reproduced in Neumann, p. 170.

[142] Reither, Rudolf. "Zur Augensymbolic." In *Internationale Zeitschrift für Artzliche Psychoanalyse*, 1:159-61, 1913, quoted by Dundes.

Deonna, Waldemar. *Le Symbolisme de l'oeil*. Paris, Editions E. de Boccard, 1965, p. 25.

[143] In terms of statistical frequency, the association is by far the greater with one eye only.

[144] Elworthy, more accurately, calls it "part of the Woburn Marbles in the collection of the Duke of Bedford" (p. 138). He also quotes, as Jahn did, Pomponius, who was simply saying that people squat in order to defecate. It is not a proof that the Woburn Marble shows a defecating man. Jahn also tries to make much of the fact that the eye is a left eye. Elworthy responded to this false assumption by counting singular eyes appearing in collections of ancient art. He found more right eyes than left, but as he says, that fact is not significant either.

[145] Kirchhoff, H. "The Woman's Posture During Childbirth, from Prehistoric Times to the Present." *Organorama*, 14, 1977, pp. 14/19.

[146] See among others, Elisabeth Goldsmith: *Ancient Pagan Symbols*, p. 211.

[147] Charrière, G. The figure in Charrière is number 64g, p. 176.

[148] Hasluck, Margaret, p. 163.

[149] For the uncertainties regarding these two specimens, read Hadingham p. 220 for the former, and Charrière (1970) pp. 165 and 167, for the latter. Charrière has a line drawing of a hypothetical reconstruction of the Couarde statue, p. 171.

[150] Hadingham, Evan. *Secrets of the Ice Age*. See Bibliography. Hadingham's concerns, like the lack of attention paid to feet and arms, may not have been those of palaeolithic humans. Hadingham ends his list of doubts by saying: "Could they just be amulets to bring good luck?" (p. 225). The answer is "yes," that is probably exactly what they were: goodluck charms. One need not have a "cult" built around symbols. But it is important to remember that all "good luck" amulets, even today, are traceable to fertility symbols.

[151] Rawson, *PEA*, p. 12.

[152] Cf. The Orphic World Egg of the Orphic Mysteries in ancient Greece. See Jane Harrison.

[153] Dulaure, p. 158. See Appendix V.

[154] See fig 15.1, drawn from the female loincloth from the Chagga in Tanzania in Dames, p. 132. Dames comments that the pattern of cowries "repeat the shape of the genital organ and also resemble eyes." See the headdress from the Koko-Ache in Nigeria in Leuzinger (see fig. 20.3). Note the similarity between the Nigerian headdress and the Oaksey Sheela-na-gig.

[155] From the King James translation of the Bible. The Song of Songs, 4/9.

[156] This was verified by my friend and colleague, Professor Arnold Fox.

[157] It is to be noted that King James used the verb "ravished" and not the verb "fascinated." The meaning of "ravished" is "to take forcefully," to rape. Now it remains to be found if the original Hebrew term had the same meaning.

[158] Hubbs, Joanna. "The Worship of Mother Earth in Russian Culture." In James L. Preston, ed. *Mother Worship*. University of North Carolina Press, 1982, pp. 123-144.

[159] Although one has to be cautious in accepting her opinion, Margaret Murray commenting on the sculptures in Romanesque churches says: "I am inclined to see in them the remains of that ancient worship which was too strongly rooted among the people to be destroyed by Christianity, and whose emblems survived even in the sacred places of the new religion." *Man*, August 1929, item 98. Harrison, would probably agree. In her *Prolegomena of the Greek Religion*, she made the point that the Greek religion that came down to us through ancient literature, was the Golden Age sophistication of more "primitive" times, before the forces of nature were personified.

[160] See Berger, Pamela. *The Goddess Obscured. Transformation of the Grain Protectress from Goddess to Saint*. Beacon Press, 1985.

[161] Mitter, Partha. *Much Maligned Monsters. History of European Reactions to Indian Art.* Oxford: Clarendon Press, 1977, p. 17.

[162] Saintyves, P. *Les Saints Successeurs des Dieux.* Paris: Emile Nourry, 1907.

[163] See Boue-de-Villiers, Amaury-Louis R. *La Normandie superstitieuse. Le pélérinage de la fontaine Sainte Clotilde-aux-Andelys. Les Saints grotesques.* Paris, A. Le Chevalier editeur. Rouen, Lanctin, 1870, p. 43 [Rubbing of abdomen on statue of St. Ildefonse at Pacy-sur-Eure by barren women]. See also Callet, Daveluy and Louradour in bibliography.

[164] See Knight, Richard Payne. Chapter III.

[165] Longworth, T. Clifton. *The Gods of Love.* Westport, CT: Associated Booksellers, 1960, p. 131. Longworth probably obtained his information from Dulaure, regarding the dozen prepuces. Augsburg in Germany has the distinction of having both the prepuce of St. Bartholomew and the pudenda of ste. Gudule.

[166] The verb is *foutre*, which itself is derived from the vulgar Latin *futuere*. cf. Adams, James Noel: *Latin Sexual Vocabulary.*

[167] In this case there are two variations of the name: Pothin or Photin. In other places, Foutin appears as Fouti, Fostin, Fotin. It may be significant also that the church was St. John's. St. John, for some reason unknown to me, seems to be constantly associated with fertility and renewal.

[168] Cf. 1-*Dictionnaire d'ancien français*, Larousse.
2-Supplément au Robert en 6 volumes. *Le Robert, dictionnaire alphabétique et analogique de la langue française*, (p. 228).
3-Littré, É. *Dictionnaire de la Langue Française.* Paris: Librairie Hachette et Cie., 1883.
4-Ménage, Gilles. *Dictionnaire étymologique de la langue française (1750).* Slotkin Reprints, Genève (suisse), 1973.
5-Huguet, Edmond. *Dictionnaire de la langue française du seizième siècle.* Librairie M. Didier, Paris, 1973. (Volume 4.)
6-Barnhart *Dictionnary of Etymology.* The H. W. Wilson Co., 1988.

[169] See Francis Pérot, p. 97.

[170] Dulaure, op. cit., p. 167. Read Dulaure also for more on phallic saints.

[171] See Dulaure (translated and edited by Niemoeller), p. 262, endnote No. 15 for Chapter XIII.

[172] Cf. Taylor, Jane, ed. *Le Roman de Perceforest.* Genève: Librairie Droz, 1979.

[173] See Chapter XIII, under sub-heading: Gorgon.

[174] Translation from the American 1934 Panurge Press publication, *The Gods of Generation*, pp. 155-6.

[175] Dulaure, pp. 155-6 and p. 158.

[176] Blunt, John James. *Vestiges of Ancient Manners and Customs, Discoverable in Modern Italy and Sicily*. London: John Murray, 1823. Blunt was a Fellow of St John's College, Cambridge. The preface of his book includes a disclaimer, viz. that he is not "about to renew the warfare against the Church Of Rome, which Dr. Middleton waged so vigorously." He took two trips to Italy and Sicily in 1818-1819 and 1820-1821.

[177] Although I must admit that I don't know, then, what to make of the numerous instances from outside the Western World. See Williamson, Marjorie: "Les Yeux Arrachés." *Philological Quarterly*, 11: pp. 149-162, 1932. Nevertheless, the Agatha and Lucy legends are similar to each other and have probably a common origin. This is reinforced by the fact that some tellers of the tale attribute the same name to the Roman suitor of each woman: Quintianus.

[178] Deubner, Ludwig August. "Charms and Amulets (Greek)." *Encyclopedia of Religion and Ethics*, Vol. III, edited by Hastings. See p. 436.

[179] Mark, Mary Ellen: *Falkland Road*.

[180] Waterman, Phillip. Op. cit., p. 142.

[181] See Eldon Best (No. 89).

[182] The verbs *subigo* means to bring under, but was widely used as a euphemism for sexual intercourse. *Efutuitis* is a passive form for the same thing, and was used also.

[183] Lyons, G. F. *A Narrative of Travels in North Africa in the years 1818, 19 and 20*. London, 1821, p. 52. Quoted by McCartney, Eugene S. "Praise and Dispraise in Folklore" in Dundes, 1981, p. 16.

[184] Henderson, G. *Survival in Belief among the Celts*. Glasgow, 1911, pp. 27-8. Quoted by Eugene S. McCartney in Dundes p. 25.

[185] Di Stasi, L. *Mal Occhio*, p. 44.

[186] Crooke, Wm. Volume II, p. 22.

[187] Lawson, J. C. *Modern Greek Folklore and Ancient Greek Religion*. Cambridge, 1910, p. 15f. Quoted by W. Crooke in *Encyclopaedia of Religion and Ethics* XI: p. 101.

[188] Mitter, Partha, p. 17.

[189] Maury, Curt, p. 39.

[190] Thomas, Paul: Kama Kalpa, 13th Edition, 1963.

[191] Lewinsohn, Richard. *Histoire entière du coeur*. Plon, Paris, 1959, p. 12.

[192] Briquet, C. M. *Les filigranes: Dictionnaire historique des marques de papier dès leur apparition vers 1282, jusqu'en 1600*. 1907.

[193] Hildburgh, W. L. "Notes on some Contemporary Portuguese Amulets." *Folk-lore*, XIX, No. 2, London, June 1908.

[194] See The Sportsman's Guide, Golden Valley, MN 55427, Mail order catalog, 1988, p. 81, sold as "Genuine 'Bull' shafts" [sic]:

"The entire reproductive organ of a full-grown bull has been permanently preserved with a high-gloss polyurethane finish in all its extended glory."

[195] Cf. Hildburgh, W. L. "Lunar Crescents as Amulets in Spain." Item #42 in *Man*, July-August, 1942, pp. 73-84.

[196] Revelation. Chapter 21 and, variously, verse 5, 6 or 8.

[197] From Stone, Lee Alexander: *Story of Phalliscism*, p. 6.

[198] Harrison, p. 191.

[199] See Herzfeld, 1984, p. 449.

[200] Murray, Margaret. "The Cowrie Shell in Formosa." *Man*, Oct. 1940, item 188.

[201] See Talbot, p. 54.

[202] Symonds, John Addington, ed. *Wine, Women and Songs. Mediaeval Latin students' Songs*. Thomas Bird Mesler, 1918, p. 117, song Number 34.

[203] Elworthy, p. 241.

[204] Rossi, William A. *The Sex Life of the Foot and the Shoe*. Ware, England: Wordsworth Editions, 1989. (First published 1977.)

[205] Edwards, Allen. *Erotica Judaica*. Julian Press, 1967, p. 51.

[206] See L. A. Stone, pp. 25-26.

[207] From the Greek "orchis" which means "testicle."

[208] Not only the already mentioned plane tree leaf, but the olive leaf (Minerva-Athena), the myrtle leaf (Aphrodite-Venus), the laurel leaf (Daphne), or, for that matter, the "good-luck" leaf sold to tourists in Hawaii.

[209] Cf. Wasson et al. *The Road to Eleusis*.

[210] Zahan, Dominique. *Sociétés d'initiation Bambara, le N'Domo, le Kore*. Paris, 1960.

[211] I use the term "directional" to mean that a man ploughs a woman and not the other way around.

[212] Anthony and Cleopatra, Act II, scene 2, lines 234-5-6.
My colleague, Ralph Bowen brought this line to my attention and his wife Susan suggested that Agrippa was turning swords into plows.

[213] See Barbara Walker, p. 311.

[214] Azaïs et Chambard: p. 217.

[215] Imad-Ed-Din in *Arab Historians of the Crusades*, trans. Francesco Gabrielli, and trans. from the Italian by E. J. Costello, pp. 204-6, quoted by Andrew McCall in *The medieval Underworld*. New York: Dorset Press, 1991, p. 187.

[216] Blunt, John James. Op. cit., p. 162.

[217] Wasson, R. Gordon; Albert Hoffmann and Carl A. P. Ruck. *The Road to Eleusis*. Harcourt, Brace & Jovanovich, 1978.

[218] Backman, E. Louis. *Religious Dances in the Christian Church and in Popular Medicine*. London: Allen & Unwin, 1952, pp. 303-327.

[219] See Talbot's "schlange im Schilf," p. 54.

Bibliography

The following bibliography has been culled from some 1500 original entries. It may still be long, but it is made up of only those works that either have been cited in the book, or works from which illustrations have been taken or referred to.

A

Abbott, John. *Indian Ritual and Belief: The Keys of Power*. New Delhi, Usha 1984 (first publ. 1932). [ch. IV on Evil Eye].

Abdelsalam, Sharafeldin Elamin. *A study of contemporary Sudanese Muslim Saints*. PhD. dissertation. Indiana University 1983.

Absolon, Karel. "The Diluvial Anthropomorphic Statuettes and Drawings, Especially the so-called Venus Statuettes, Discovered in Moravia." *Artibus Asiae*, XII, 1949, pp. 201-220.

Adams, James Noel. *The Latin Sexual Vocabulary*. London: Duckworth, 1982.

Allegro, John. *Lost Gods*. London: Michael Joseph, 1977.

Allegro, John Marco. *The Sacred Mushroom and the Cross. A study of the Nature and Origins of Christianity within the Fertility Cults of the Ancient Near East*. Doubleday, 1970. [See Jacques, John H.]. Allegro is certainly imaginative but probably too much so. There are bits of interesting information, however.

Anand, Mulk Raj. *Kama Kala*. Some notes on the Philosophical Basis of Hindu Erotic sculpture. Nagel publishers, Geneva, 1963. See also Paul Thomas and Jean Marcade.

Andersen, Jorgen. *The Witch on the Wall. Medieval Erotic Sculpture in the British Isles*. London: George Allen and Unwin, 1977. [This book is on sheelah-na-Gigs from Ireland and England. Andersen lacks sophistication. But the book is useful, particularly when, at the end, he makes a comparison between sheelahs and other figures. It is also useful for its bibliography.

Anderson, Richard L. *Art in Small-Scale Societies*. Englewood Cliffs, NJ: Prentice-Hall, second edition, 1989.

Andrews, E. A. *Copious and Critical Latin-English Lexicon*. New York: Harper and Bros. Publishers, 1856.

Andronicos, Manolis (et al.) *The Greek Museums*. New Rochelle: Caratzas Bros. Publ., 1974.

Anonymous. *Ancient sex worship. A curious and remarkable work. Traces of ancient myths in the religions of today*. New York: The Commonwealth Co. (nd.). [Same as "Masculine Cross" by Rocco; same publisher.]

Appel, Willa. *The Evil Eye and Peasant Identity in Southern Italy*. Phd. dissertation. Ithaca, NY: Cornell University, 1975.

Aubigné. Théodore-Agrippa D' (1552-1630). *Confession catholique du sieur de Sancy, et déclaration des causes tant d'estat que de religion*—in *Recueil de diverses pièces servant à l'histoire de Henry III, roy de France et de Pologne*, edited by Pierre de L'Estoile, published first in 1660, not including the Confession, which appeared in succeeding editions. The edition consulted here is the Nouvelle Edition revue et augmentée, Tome II. A Cologne: chez Pierre Marteau, 1699. See under L'Estoile, below. According to Larousse, d'Aubigné was an "ardent" Calvinist, companion-at-arms of Henry IV. The sieur de Sancy was Nicolas de Harlay de Sancy (1546-1629) a contemporary of d'Aubigné, who has also a: *L'Enfer; Satire dans le goût de Sancy* etc. Whoever edited the "confession" (Dulaure says it is Le Duchat) says in a Preface: "C'est une satyre fine et délicate." But he also says that it distorts the facts to the disadvantage of Sancy, whom Agrippa meant to ridicule. Trying to put things into an objective perspective, the editor, then produced the "Remarques." The fact is, however, that Duchat's edition seems to have been important because Duchat himself is referred to, not only in relation to this work but also in relation to Henri Estienne's *Apologie pour Hérodote*.

Audierne, Abbé François Georges. "Notice sur les églises du Departement de la Dordogne." *Bulletin monumental*, Paris 1835, V. 1, No. 5, p. 208: "obscene" sculpture over church door at Besse.

Azaïs, R. P. et Roger Chambard. *Cinq années de recherches archéologiques en Ethiopie*. Paris: Librairie Orientaliste, Paul Geuthner, 1931.

B

Backman, E. Louis. *Religious Dances in the Christian Church and in Popular Medicine*. George Unwin, 1952.

Ballou, Robert. *The Nature of Religion*. New York: Basic Books, 1968.

Banks, M. M. "Primitive Fertility Figures." *Man* XXXV, 1935, No. 65. [On the origins of the name and of the carvings.]

Barstow, Anne L. "The Prehistoric Goddess." *The Book of the Goddess*, edited by Carl Olson. [She says that there were no indications that the figurines in Çatal Hüyük were goddesses but a "rather a celebration of fertility."]

Barton, Francis Rickman. "*Zanzibar doors*." *Man*, London, 1924, Vol. XXIV, article 63, pp. 81-82.

Bayley, Harold. *The Lost Language of Symbolism*, 1912. Secaucus, NJ: the Citadel Press, reprint 1988.

Bedier, Joseph. *Les Fabliaux. Etudes de littérature populaire et d'histoire littéraire du Moyen Age*. 6th edition, Latkine, Genève, 1982.

Benkard, Ernst. *Giovanni Lorenzo Bernini*. Frankfurt-am-Mein, Iris-Verlag, 1926. [Photo of one face of the pedestal of the Bernini Baldacchino.]

Berry, Veronica. "Neapolitan Charms Against the Evil Eye." *Folklore* (London), 79, 1968.

Berger, Pamela. *The Goddess Obscured. Transformation of The Grain Protectress from Goddess to Saint*. Beacon Press, 1985.

Best, Elsdon. "Maori belief concerning the human organs of generation." *Man*, Vol. XIV, article 66, 1914, [pp. 132-4, touching penis as apotropaic.]

Bible. King James.

Bible. See Bronstein, H. N.

Bible. *The Triglot Bible*. London: Richard D. Dickinson, 1890. [Triglot = Hebrew, Greek and Latin.]

Blackman, Winifred S. *The Fellahin of Upper Egypt*. London: George Harrap and Co., 1927. Chapter XIII is on the Evil Eye.

Blau, Ludwig. "Evil Eye." *Jewish Encyclopedia*, Vol. V, p. 280.

Blum, Richard and Eva. *The Dangerous Hour. The Lore of Crisis and Mystery in Ritual Greece*. London: Chatto & Windus, 1970.

Blunt, John James. *Vestiges of Ancient manners and customs, discoverable in Modern Italy and Sicily*. London: John Murray, 1823. [Compares rites and rituals to ancient "Pagan" rituals especially that of Isis and Serapis.]

Boardman, John and Eugenio La Rocca. *Eros in Greece*. Text by John Boardman and Eugenio La Rocca, Photographs by Antonia Mulas. New York: The Erotic Art Book Society 1975.

Bohannon, Paul. "Extra-processual Events in Tiv Political Institutions." *American Anthropologist* 60, 1958, pp. 1-12. Reprinted in Ottenberg's *Cultures and Societies of Africa*, Random House, 1960, pp. 328-341.

Bohannon, Paul. *Social Organization*. New York: Holt, Rinehart and Winston, 1963.

Bonner, Campbell. *Studies in Magical amulets, chiefly Graeco-Egyptian*. Ann Arbor: University of Michigan Press, 1950.

Boue-de-Villiers, Amaury-Louis R. *La Normandie superstitieuse. Le pèlerinage de la fontaine Sainte Clotilde-aux-Andelys. Les Saints grotesques*. Paris, A. Le Chevalier, editeur. Rouen, Lanctin, 1870, [p. 43, barren women rub their belly against a statue of St. Ildefonse at Pacy-sur-Eure.]

Bourdier, Franck. *Préhistoire de France*. Flammarion, 1967.

Bourke, John Gregory. *Scatologic Rites of All Nations*. Washington DC: W. H. Lowdermilk & C., 1891. Chapter III is on The Feast of Fools.

Brandes, Stanley. *Metaphors of Masculinity. Sex and Status in Andalusian Folklore*. University of Pennsylvania Press, 1980.

Brandt, Paul Hans (Hans Licht). *Sexual Life in Ancient Greece*. Barnes & Noble, 1963.

Brassaï, (Gyula Halasz dit). *Brassaï*: The Museum of Modern Art. NY, 1968.

Brault, Gérard J. "Chrétien de Troyes' Lancelot: The Eye and the Heart." *Bibliographical Bulletin of the International Arthurian Society*, 23, (1972), 142-53.

Brault, Gerard J. "Isolt and Guenevere: Two Twelfth Century Views of Women." *The Role of Women in the Middle Ages*. Edited by

Rosemarie Morewedge Thee. State University of New York Press, 1975, pp. 41-64.

Brav, Aaron. "The Evil Eye among the Hebrews." In *The Evil Eye*. Ed. Alan Dundes. New York: Garland Publishing, 1981, pp. 44-54. Reprinted from *Ophthalmology* 5, (1908), 427-435.

Bravmann, René A. *West African Sculpture*. Seattle: University of Washington Press, 1970.

Breul, K., ed. *The Cambridge Songs: A Goliard's Song Book of the XIth Century*. Cambridge, 1915.

Briquet, Charles Moise. *Les Filigranes. Dictionnaire historique des marques du papier dès leur apparition vers 1282 jusqu'en 1600*. 2nd edition. Leipzig, 1923. Reprinted by Hacker Art Books, New York, 1966. First published, Geneva 1907.

Bronstein, H. N. and A. H. Friedlander, eds. *The Five Scrolls*. Published by the Central Conference of American Rabbis, NY, 1984.

Brown, Sanger II. *Sex Worship and Symbolism*. Boston: Richard G. Badger, The Gorham Press, 1922. [Brown was born in 1884. His book contains all the same illustrations as Knight's *Discourse on the Worship of Priapus*, published in 1786. Yet does not credit Knight except for a passing reference to Knight's "two essays on the worship of Priapus," n.d.]

Budge, E. A. Wallis. *Amulets and Talismans*. New Hyde Park, NY: University Books, 1961. First Published in London, 1930. [ch. XX is on *The Evil Eye*. Reissued under the title of *Amulets and Superstitions*. Dover Publ. 1978.

Buonanno, Michael. "Becoming White: Notes on an Italian-American Explanation of Evil Eye." *Magic, Witchcraft and Religion*, edited by Arthur C. Lehmann et al., second edition, Mayfield publishers, 1989, pp. 239-246.

C

Cadbury, Henry J. "The Single Eye." *Harvard Theological Review* 47:69-74, 1954. [See his statement to the effect that the opposite equivalent of *evil* eye is not the *good* eye.] Part of a debate. cf. Smith and Cadoux.

Callet, Albert (1845-1925). "Derniers vestiges du paganisme dans l'Ain." *Revue des Traditions Populaires*. Paris 1903, vol. XVIII, p. 499. [Plouarzel custom: belly rubbing at the 'Lite au Roi near Cressin-en-Bugey. Sts. Avit, Phall, Foutin. Abdominal rubbing near St. Laurent-les-Macons.

Campbell, Robert Allen. *Phallic Worship*. 1887. [According to A. F. Niemoeller, who translated Dulaure, this work is plagiarized from Dulaure.]

Carroll, Michael P. "On the Psychological Origins of the Evil Eye: A Kleinian View." *Journal of Psychoanalytic Anthropology*, 7/2, Spring 1984. [Psychoanalytical interpretation based on the conditioning of children by the "fact" that the tip of the breast of the mother, "looks like an eye."]

Charrière, Georges. *La Signification des représentations érotiques dans les arts sauvages et Préhistoriques*. G.-P. Maisonneuve et Larose, Paris, 1970, (Collection l'érotisme populaire).

Chicago Tribune, Sunday, October 5, 1986 and Tuesday, November 16, 1993.

Cirlot, Juan Eduardo. *A Dictionary of Symbols*. 2nd edition, Routledge and Kegan Paul, 1962. Cirlot was a Spanish poet and artist who philosophized art and in so doing, he came across the problem of the meaning of symbols. His book is not terribly interesting in that he gives a kind of decadent Latin interpretation of symbols.

Claiborne, Robert. "Who were the indo-Europeans?" In *Mysteries of the Past*. Ed. Joseph J. Thorndike. Simon and Shuster, 1977.

Clément-Janin, Michel-Hilaire. *Sobriquets des villes et des Villages de la Côte-d'Or*. Dijon, Imprimerie I. Marchand 1876-8. [4 pts. 8 vo. pp. 46-8 = St. Phal and other French phallic saints and their cult. See Bidault and Bulliot. See Callet also for St Phall.]

Cles-Reden, Sibylle von. *The Realm of The Great Goddess. The Story of the Megalith Builders*. Prentice-Hall, 1962. Translated from *Die Spur der Zyclopen*.

Clottes, Jean et Michel Carrière. "La statue Féminine de Capdenac-le-haut (lot)." *Congrès Préhistorique de France*, xxe session, Provence, 1974 (1976).

Cohen, Chapman. *Religion and Sex, Studies in the Pathology of Religious Development*. London, 1919. [Continuance of older sex worship].

Colson, Elizabeth. "Ancestral Spirits and Social Structure among the Plateau Tonga." *International Archives of Ethnography*, 1954, 47, pp. 21-68, reprinted in Ottenberg, eds. *Cultures and Societies of Africa*. New York: Random House, 1960, pp. 372-387, as: "Ancestral Spirits among the Plateau Tonga."

Contenau, Dr. Georges. *La Déesse Nue babylonienne. Etude d'iconographie comparée*. Paris, Paul Geuthner, 1914. [Deals largely with the phallic character of naked goddesses.]

Cooke, Thomas D. and Benjamin L. Honeycutt, eds. *The Humor of the Fabliaux*. Columbia: University of Missouri Press 1974. [Sexual & ribald theme of the fabliaux.]

Crawley, Alfred Ernest. "Obscenity." In *Encyclopaedia of Religion and Ethics*. Ed. James Hastings. Vol. 9, pp. 441-2.

Crooke, William. In Hastings' *Encyclopaedia of Religion and Ethics* XI: 100-104.

Crooke, William. "The Evil Eye and the Scaring of Ghosts." Chapter II of Volume II: *The Popular Religion and Folk-Lore of Northern India*.

D

Dames, Michael. *The Avebury Cycle*. Thames and Hudson, London, 1977.

Dauzat, Albert, and Charles Rostaing. *Dictionnaire etymologique des noms de lieux en France*. Paris: Librairie Larousse, 1963. Very limited. Not only is it poorly researched, it is also without imagination.

Daveluy, Charles. "Légendes et Superstitions Préhistoriques CXXVIII La friction à nu." *Revue des traditions populaires*. Paris Vol xvii no. 7-8 1902 p. 406. [Barren women rub themselves naked against church pillar at Orcival (Puy de Dôme).

Delumeau, Jean, ed. *La Mort des Pays de Cocagne*. Paris: Publication de la Sorbone, 1976. [Still in the 15th C.: *Feast of Fools*. Parodies, irreverences. Church reacts. Same for farces, sotties, sermons joyeux divertissements, including dance. Cocagne: origin of the word is unknown.]

Deonna, Waldemar. *Le Symbolisme de l'Oeil*. Paris, Edit E. de Boccard, 1965.

Desaivre, Léo. Pèlerins et pèlerinages. "Les Yeux de Saint-Roch." *Revue des Traditions Populaires*. Vol. 17, 1902, p. 386.

Deubner, Ludwig August. "Charms and Amulets (Greek)." *Encyclopedia of Religion and Ethics*. vol. iii [pp. 435-6 Baring of Pudenda.]

Devereux, Georges. *Baubo, la vulve mythique*. Jean-Cyrille Godefroy, Paris, 1983.

Dictionaries:

1-*Dictionnaire d'ancien français*, Larousse.
2-Supplément au Robert en 6 volumes. *Le Robert, dictionnaire alphabétique et analogique de la langue française*, (p. 228).
3-Littré, É. *Dictionnaire de la Langue Française*. Paris: Librairie Hachette et Cie., 1883.
4-Ménage, Gilles. *Dictionnaire étymologique de la langue française (1750)*. Slotkin Reprints, Genève (suisse), 1973.
5-Huguet, Edmond. *Dictionnaire de la langue française du seizième siècle*. Librairie M. Didier, Paris, 1973. (Volume 4.)
6-Barnhart *Dictionary of Etymology*. The H. W. Wilson Co., 1988.
7-Littré, É. *Dictionnaire de la Langue Française*. Paris: Librairie Hachette et Cie., 1883.
8-Random House Dictionary.
9-Webster II New Riverside University Dictionary. Riverside Publ. Co., Boston: 1984.
10-DuCange, Charles Du Fresne, Sieur. *Glossarium ad scriptores mediae et infimae graecitatis etc.* . . . [dictionary of medieval and modern Latin published in the 17th century].
11-Esnault, Gaston. *Dictionnaire Historique des Argots Français*. Larousse, 1965.

Distasi, Lawrence. *Mal Occhio. The Underside of Vision*. North Point Press, San Francisco, 1981.

Douglas, Mary. "Heathen Darkness." Chapter V in *Implicit Meanings*. Routledge and Kegan Paul, 1975.

Driberg, J. H. "The Meaning of the Cowrie" #208, *Man*, Nov. 1940, p. 175.

DuCange, Charles Du Fresne, Sieur. Glossarium ad scriptores mediae et infimae graecitatis etc. . . . [dictionary of medieval and modern Latin].

Duerr, Hans Peter. *Dreamtime. Concerning the Boundaries Between Wilderness and Civilization*. Basil Blackwell, 1985.

Duine, F. "Le folk-Lore dans les écrits ecclésiastiques dans le catéchisme de Bossuet." *Revue des Traditions Populaires*, Vol. 16, 1901, p. 73. [For role of church in fighting "pagan" rituals. Also: feu de la St. Jean.]

Dulaure, Jacques-Antoine. *The Gods of Generation. A history of Phallic Cults among Ancients and Moderns*. The Panurge Press, NY, 1934. [Originally published in French in 1805 under the title of *Des Divinités Génératrices, ou du culte du phallus chez les anciens et les modernes*, translated by Adolf Frederik Niemoeller, who says that Robert Campbell plagiarized Dulaure.

Dumitrescu, Vladimir. *Arta Preistorica in Romania*. Editura Meridiane, Bucharest, 1974.

Dundes, Alan, ed. *The Evil Eye. A Folklore Casebook* edited by Alan Dundes. New York: Garland Publishing Co., 1981.

Dundes, Alan. "Wet and Dry, The Evil Eye: an Essay in Indo-European and Semitic Worldview." In *The Evil Eye*. Ed. Alan Dundes. New York: Garland Publishing 1981, pp. 257-312.

Durban and Bradley. "Women's Work." The Progressive, March 1986.

Durham, M. E. "Cowries in the Balkans." *Man*, May 1940, item 101.

Durham, M. E. "The meaning of the Cowrie: Stylized Cowrie-Pendants." *Man*, Jan-Feb., 1941, item 13.

E

Edey, Maitland, ed. *Lost World of The Aegean*. Time-Life Books, 1975.

Edwardes, Allen. "Sexual Hospitality." Chapter 5 in *Erotica Judaica*, 1967.

Elwin, Verrier. "The Use of Cowries in Bastar State, India." *Man*, Nov.-Dec. 1942, item 72.

Elworthy, Frederick Thomas. *The Evil Eye. The Origins and Practices of Superstition*. The Julian Press, Inc. NY, 1958. [originally published by John Murray, London: 1895. Recent facsimile of the 1895 Edition published by University Books/Citadel Press, Secaucus, NJ., n.d. The subject is so vast that, in order to explain anything at all, Elworthy feels compelled to go into a great number of associated customs, including fertility symbolism.]

Encyclopaedia Britannica, 1963 edition. "Gorgon."

Estoile, Pierre Taisan de L'. (1546-1611). See under L'Estoile.

F

Fagiolo dell'Arco, Maurizio e Marcello. *Bernini, Una Introduzione al Gran Teatro del Barocco*. Roma, Mario Bulzoni editore, 1967. [Photo of *one* face of one of the pedestal of the Bernini Baldacchino.]

Farmer, John S. and W. E. Henley, eds. "Monosyllable." *Slang and its Analogues*. Vol. III. Routledge and Kegan Paul, 1893, pp. 336-345. [On the various names for the female pudenda.]

Ferenczi, Sandor. "On Eye Symbolism." *Sex and Psychoanalysis*, pp. 228-33, New York: Dover, 1956.

Fingesten, Peter. *The Eclipse of Symbolism*. Columbia: University of South Carolina Press, 1970.

Forbes, Allan Jr. and Thomas R. Crowder. "The Problem of Franco-Cantabrian abstract signs: Agenda for a New Approach." *World Archaeology*, Vol. 10, No. 3, 1979, pp. 350-366.

Forge, Anthony, ed. *Primitive Art and Society*. Oxford University Press, 1973.

Forlong, James George Roche. "Eye" in *Faiths of Man: Encyclopedia of Religions*, Vol. 2. New Hyde Park, NY: University Books, 1964. (Orig. publ. 1906).

France, Ministère de la Culture. *L'Art des Cyclades dans la Collection N. P. Goulandris*. Editions de la Réunion des Musées Nationaux, Paris, 1983.

Fraser, Douglas. "The Heraldic Woman" in *The Many Faces of Primitive Art*, 1966, pp. 36-99.

Friedenwald, Harry. "The Evil Eye" (Ayin Hara-ah). *Medical Leaves* (44-48), 1939. [See Lilienthal and Kirshenblatt-Gumblett.]

Frommann, Johann Christian. *Tractatus de Fascinatione nevus et singularis, in quo fascinatio vulgaris profligatur, naturalis confirmatus, (et) magica examinatur; hoc est, nec visu, nec Voce fieri posse fascinationem probatur* . . . Nurimburg, Sumtibus Wolfgangi Mauritii Endteri, 1675. [Elworthy spells it Frommand. Another spelling is: Frohman.]

G

Galeries Nationales du Grand Palais, Paris. *L'Art des Cyclades dans la Collection N. P. Goulandris*. Editions de la Réunion des Musées Nationaux, 1983.

Galt, Anthony H. "The Evil Eye as Synthetic Image and its Meaning on the Island of Pantelleria" Italy. *American Ethnologist* 9: 664-681, 1982.

Gamble, Eliza Burt. *The God-Idea of The Ancients or Sex in Religion*. New York: G. P. Putnam's Sons, 1897.

Gamble, Eliza Burt. "Sex, The Foundation of The God Idea." In Stone, L. A., *The Story of Phallicism*, pp. 143-258. [Author has the right idea: 1-Sex (read "fertility") as a basis; 2-Double deity; 3-The separation of the male and the female principle, and 4-Triumph of the male principle. But has some weaknesses like a belief in the 19th century belief in a "matriarcal Age."]

Gantner, Joseph and Marcel Pobé. *The Glory of Romanesque Art*. New York: The Vanguard Press, 1952. [Magnificent photos by Jean Roubier.]

Garrison, Vivian and Conrad Arensberg. "The Evil Eye: Envy or Risk of Seizure? Paranoia or Patronal Dependency?" *The Evil Eye* edited by Clarence Maloney, 1976, pp. 286-328.

Giedion, Sigfried. *The Eternal Present. A Contribution on Constancy and Change*. Two Vols. Pantheon Books, 1962. (There is a 1957 ed.).

Gimbutas, Marija (Alseikaite). *Goddesses and Gods of Old Europe, 7000-3500 B.C. Myths and Cult Images*. University of California Press, 1982.

Gimbutas, Marija. *Ancient Symbolism in Lithuanian Folk Art*. American Folklore Society, 1958.

Gimbutas, Marija. *The Language of the Goddess*. San Francisco: Harper & Row, 1989.

Gimbutas, Marija. *The Civilization of the Goddess. The World of Old Europe*. San Francisco: Harper, 1991.

Gischia, Leon et Lucien Mazenod. *Les Arts Primitifs Français. Art Mérovingien. Art Caroligien. Art Roman*. Texte de Jean Verrier. Paris: Art et Métiers Graphiques, 1953.

Gladkih, Mikhail I and Ninelj L. Kornietz and Olga Soffer. "Mammoth-Bone Dwellings on the Russian Plain," *Scientific American*.

Goff, Beatrice Laura. *Symbols of Prehistoric Mesopotamia*. New Haven: Yale University Press, 1963.

Goldberg, Ben Zion. *The Sacred Fire. The story of sex in Religion*. New York: Horace Liveright, 1930. (Re-issued by Norton under the title of *Sex in Religion*.)

Goldman, Bernard. "Typology of the Mother-Goddess figurines." IPEX, 20: 8-15, pls. 1963. *Jahrbuch fur prähistorische und Ethnographische Kunst*. Berlin.

Goldsmith, Elizabeth Edwards. *Ancient Pagan Symbols*. London, 1929.

Gomez-Tabanera, J. M. "Les Statuettes Féminines Paléolithiques dites 'Venus.'" *Rencontres Internationales pour l'études des civilisations Préhistoriques*. Asturias-Perigord, 1978.

Goodland, Roger. *A Bibliography of Sex Rites and Customs*. London: Routledge, 1931.

Goody, Jack. *Production and Reproduction*. Cambridge University Press 1976.

Goulandris, N. P. See France, Ministère de la Culture.

Grant, Michael. *Erotic Art in Pompeii. The Secret Collections of the National Museum of Naples*, by Michael Grant. Photographs by Antonia Mulas. London: Octopus Books, 1975.

Gray, Henry. *Anatomy, Descriptive and Surgical*, edited by T. Pickering Pick and Robert Howden. A revised American Edition from the 15th English Edition. New York: Crown Publishers, Bounty Books, 1977.

Graziosi, Paolo. *L'Arte preistorica in Italia*. Firenze: Sansoni, 1973.

Graziosi, Paolo. *Palaeolithic Art*. McGraw Hill, 1960.

Grigson, W. V. "Cowrie Shells in the Central Provinces of India." *Man*, Oct. 1940, item 187.

Gubbins, J. K. "Some Observations on the Evil Eye in Modern Greece." *Folklore*. 57. [1946-1947): 195-198.

H

Hadingham, Evan. *Secrets of the Ice Age. The World of the Cave Artists*. New York: Walker, 1979.

Hammond, Nicholas G. L. *Migrations and Invasions in Greece and Adjacent Areas*. Noyes Press, 1976. [anchor amulets.]

Hansen, Donald P. and George F. Dales. "The Temple of Inanna, Queen of Heaven, at Nippur." *Archaeology*, V. 15, No. 2, June 1962, pp. 75-84.

Harou, Alfred Victor Gaetan. Pèlerins et Pèlerinages, CLXXXIX "Le saint à la petite broche." *Revue des Traditions Populaires*. Vol. XXII, No. 12, Dec. 1907. [p. 457: Aux environs de Nivelle (Brabant-Wallon), les femmes stériles vont invoquer dans une petite chapelle, munies d'une *broquette* (petite broche) en bois simulant le phallus, Saint Pierre *al'broquette* (à la petite broche.)

Harris, P. G. "Cowrie." *Man*, Nov-Dec. 1943, item 120.

Harrison, Jane. *Prolegomena to the Study of Greek Religion*. New York: Meridian Books, 1955. [Originally published by Cambridge University Press in 1903.]

Hartland, Edwin Sidney. *Primitive paternity. The myth of supernatural birth in relation to the history of the family*. London: David Nutt, 1909.

Hasluck, Margaret M. "The Evil Eye in Some Greek Villages of The Upper Haliakmon Valley in West Macedonia." *J.R.A.I.*, 53 (1923) 160-172. Also reprinted in Allan Dundes, ed. *The Evil Eye*. New York: Garland Publishing, 1981, pp. 107-123 . . . under the name of Margaret M. Hardie (Mrs. F. W. Hasluck).

Henderson, G. *Survival in Belief Among the Celts*. Glascow, 1911, pp. 27-28. Quoted by Eugene S. McCartney in Dundes, p. 25.

Herzfeld, Michael. "Meaning and Morality: A Semiotic approach to Evil Eye Accusations in a Greek Village." *American Ethnologist*, 8, 560-573, 1981.

Hildburgh, Walter Leo. "Lunar Crescents as amulets in Spain" (original article) #42 *Man*, July August 1942 pp. 73-84 (Plus a plate between 72 & 73).

Hildburgh, Walter Leo. Notes on some contemporary Portuguese amulets. *Folk-lore*, London Vol. XIX, No. 2, June 1908.

Hocart, A. M. "The Mechanism of the Evil Eye." *Folklore* 49, (1938) pp. 156-157.

Hornblower, G. D. "Cowrie and Evil-Eye." *Man*, Sept.-Oct. 1941, item 81.

Hubbs, Joanna. "The Worship of Mother Earth in Russian Culture." In *Mother Worship*. Ed. James J. Preston. Chapel Hill: University of North Carolina Press 1982, pp. 123-144.

Huet, Michel et Keita Fodeba. *Les Hommes de la Danse*. La Guilde du Livre, Lausanne, 1954.

Huguet, Edmond. *Dictionnaire de la Langue Française du Seizième Siècle*. Librairie M. Didier, Paris, 1973. (v.4).

Huntingford, G. W. B. *The Galla of Ethiopia. The Kingdoms of Kafa and Janjero*. London: International African Institute, 1955.

Hutton, J. H. "Cowries in the Naga Hills." *Man*, May 1940, item 102.

I

Inman, Thomas. *Ancient Pagan and Modern Christian Symbolism*. Fourth revised and enlarged edition by Peter Eikler Publ. Co., NY, 1922. The original edition was 1869. A second edition was issued in 1876.

Izzi, Giuseppe, ed. *Scrittori de la Jettatura*, a cura di Giuseppe Izzi. Roma: Salerno editrice, 1980.

J

Jahn, Otto. "Ueber den Aberglauben des bösen Blicks bei den Alten." *Berichte Des Gesellschaft Der Wissenschaften zu Leipzig*, 1855. [Source: Elworthy: The Evil Eye 1958, p. 9. Other source gives this as *Berichte über die Verhandlungen der Königlich sächsischen Gessellschaft der Wissenschaften*.]

Jeffreys, M. O. W. "The Cowrie-Shell in British Cameroons." *Man*, April 1940, item 79.

Jeffreys, M. O. W. "Cowry, Vulva, Eye." *Man*, Sept.-Oct. 1942, item 71.

Jeffreys, M. O. W. "Cowry and Vulva Again." *Man*, Nov.-Dec. 1943, item 121.

Johns, Catherine. *Sex or Symbol: Erotic Images of Greece and Rome*. Univ. of Texas Press.

K

Kern-Ulmer, Brigitte. "The Power of the Evil Eye and the Good Eye in Midrashic Literature." *Judaism*, Issue No. 159, vol. 40, No. 3, Summer 1991, pp. 344-53.

Keuls, Eva C. *The Reign of the Phallus*, New York: Harper & Row, 1985.

Kidder, Jonathan Edward. *Early Japanese Art*. Princeton: D. van Nostrand Co., 1964.

Kirchhoff, H. "The Woman's Posture during Childbirth, from Prehistoric Times to the Present." *Organorama*, 14, 1977, pp. 14/19.

Kirshenblatt-Gimblett, Barbara and Harris Lenowitz. "The Evil Eye (The Good Eye) Einehore." *Alcheringa* 5: 71-77, 1973. [See Friedenwald and Lilienthal who have "Ayin-Hara-ah" and "Eyin-ho-re" respectively.]

Knight, Richard Payne. *A Discourse on the Worship of Priapus, and its Connection with the Mystic Theology of the Ancients*. This was first published in 1786. It was soon withdrawn from circulation by the author because of the scandal that it created. It was re-issued in 1865, with an added *Essay on the Worship of the Generative Powers during the Middle Ages of Western Europe*. It is generally recognized now that the author of this second essay was Thomas Wright, assisted by John Camden Hotten, the publisher of the 1865 Edition. Re-issue of this edition was reproduced by Secaucus, NJ: University Books, 1974. Julian Press Inc. published a version under the title of *Sexual Symbolism. A History of Phallic Worship*, 1957.

Krahe, Hans. *Sprache und Vorzeit. Europäische Vorgeschichte nach dem Zeugnis der Sprache*. Heidelberg: Quelle & Meyer, 1954.

Krauss, Rosalind and Jane Livingstone. *L'Amour Fou. Photography and Surrealism*. The Corcoran Gallery of Art, Washington D.C. New York: Abbeville Press, 1985.

L

La Barre, Weston. *Muelos: A Stone Age Superstition about Sexuality*. New York: Columbia University Press, 1985.

Laboratoire de Préhistoire du Musée de l'Homme et Musée des antiquitées Nationales de St. Germain-en-Laye. *Art et Civilisations des Chasseurs de la préhistoire. 34,000-8,000 av. J.C.* Paris, 1984.

Lamberg-Karlowsky, ed. "Old-World Archaeology." *Readings from the Scientific American.*

Lamberg-Karlowsky, Martha and C. C. "An Early City in Iran." *American Scientist*, 1971. Reproduced in *Avenues to Antiquity*, pp. 202-211. (Fig. 9 on p. 204.)

Lawrence, Robert Means. *The Magic of The Horse-shoe*. Houghton-Mifflin, 1898.

Layton, Robert. "The Use of Ethnographic Parallels in Interpreting Upper Palaeolithic Rock Art."

Leroi-Gourhan, André. "La Fonction des signes dans les sanctuaires paléolitiques." *Bulletin de la Société Préhistorique Française*, Paris, 1958, Tome LV, pp. 307-321.

L'Estoile, Pierre de. *Recueil de diverses pièces servant à l'histoire de Henry III, Roy de France et de Pologne*. Nouvelle Edition revue et augmentée, Tome II. A Cologne: chez Pierre Marteau, 1699. Includes the work by Agrippa d'Aubigné, *Confession catholique du Sieur de Sancy et déclaration des causes tant d'estat que de religion, qui l'ont meut à se remettre au giron de l'Eglise Romaine*. (Pp. 43 et seq.) Pertinent passages are in the Livre second, Chapitre II, pp. 353-54 and in Remarques sur le Chapitre II (pp. 361-62. Published first in 1660 the Recueil included the Confession only in subsequent editions.

Lethbridge, T. C. "The Meaning of the Cowrie: Fiji, Egypt and Saxon England." *Man*, Mar-Apr, 1941, item 37.

Leuzinger, Elsy. *The Art of Black Africa*, NY Graphic Society, 1972.

LeVine, Robert A. and Barbara B. *Nyansongo: a Gusii Community in Kenya*. New York: John Wiley & Sons, 1966.

Lewinsohn, Richard. *Histoire entière du coeur*. Paris: Plon, 1959.

Lilienthal, Regina. "Eyin ho-re." *Yidishe filologye* 1: 245-271, 1924. [See Friedenwald, Kirshenblatt-Grimblett, Levy, I. J., Jewish Encycl.]

Loesberg, John, ed. *Folksongs and Ballads Popular in Ireland.* Cork: Ossian Publ., 1980.

Longworth, T. Clifton. *The Gods of Love. The Creative Process in Early Religion.* Westport, CT: Associated Booksellers, 1960.

Louradour-Ponteil, Alphonse François. "A travers le Poitou." *Revue des Traditions Populaires*, Paris Vol. XIII, 1898, pp. 266-7. [Barren women rub tummies on statues of monks.]

M

McCartney, Eugene S. "Praise and Dispraise in Folklore" reprinted in *The Evil Eye.* Ed. Alan Dundes. New York: Garland Publishing, 1981, pp. 9-38. [original publ. in Papers of the Michigan Academy of Sc., Arts and Letters, Vol. 28 (1943) 567-593].

MacKenzie, Donald A. *The Migration of Symbols and their relation to Beliefs and Customs.* Alfred Knopf, 1926.

McLean, W. *Contribution à l'étude de l'iconographie populaire de l'érotisme.* G.-P. Maisonneuve et Larose, Paris, 1970.

Mallowan, M. E. L. and J. Cruikshank Rose. "Excavations at Tall Arpachiyah, 1933." *Iraq*, 2 (1935). 1-178 (see Goff.)

Maloney, Clarence, ed. *The Evil Eye.* New York: Columbia University Press, 1976.

Marcadé, Jean. *Roma Amor.* Geneva: Nagel Publishers, 1961.

Mark, Mary Ellen. *Falkland Road. Prostitutes of Bombay.* Photographs and text by Mary Ellen Mark. New York: Knopf, 1981. [Photograph of a woman exposing her pudenda to the fire vs. Evil Eye.]

Marle, Raimond van. *Iconographie de l'art Profane au Moyen Age et à la Renaissance*. First printed in La Haye (The Hague) by Martinus Nijhoff, 1931. Reprinted by Hacker Art Books in New York in 1971. Volume I: *La Vie Quotidienne*. Volume II: *Allégories et Symboles*.

Marshack, Alexander. *The roots of civilization. The cognitive beginnings of man's first art, symbol and notation*. Revised and Expanded. NY, Mayer Bell Ltd., 1991. Chapter XIII is on "Sex and the Goddess," pp. 281-340.

Mauss, Marcel. *The Gift*. New York: W. W. Norton and Company, Inc., 1967.

Meccia, Cornelius Rocco. M.A. Star Paper. DeKalb: Department of Anthropology, Northern Illinois University.

Meek, C. K. "The Meaning of the Cowrie-Shell in Nigeria." *Man*, April 1940, item 78.

Meek, C. K. "The Meaning of the Cowrie: The Evil Eye in Nigeria." *Man*, March-April 1941, item 36.

Mellaart, James. "The Beginning of Mural Painting" *Archaeology*, 1962, V. 15, No. 2, pp. 2-12. [He makes reference to the EE in Çatal Hüyük, ie ca 6000 B.C.]

Mellaart, James. *The Neolithic of the Near East*. London: Thames & Hudson, 1975.

Ménage, Gilles. *Dictionnaire étymologique de la langue française (1750)*. Slotkin Reprints, Genève (suisse), 1973.

Milinaire, Catherine. *Birth*. Revised and updated. New York: Harmony Books, 1987. The 1974 edition contains a good photo of a woman giving birth in the position represented in the Parturient Woman symbol.

Ministère de la Culture (France). [See "France."]

Mitter, Partha. *Much Maligned Monsters. History of European Reactions to Indian Art*. Oxford: Clarendon Press, 1977.

Montaigne, Michel Eyquem de. *Autobiography*, edited and translated by Marvin Lowenthal. New York: Vintage Books, 1956.

Mookerjee, Ajit and Madhu Khanna. *The Tantric Way*. Boston: New York Graphic Society, 1977.

Mookerjee, Ajit. *Ritual Art of India*. Thames & Hudson, 1985.

Müller, F. Max. *Lectures on the Origin and Growth of Religion as Illustrated by the Religions of India*. Delivered in the Chapter House, Westminster Abbey in April May and June 1878. New York: Charles Scribner's sons, 1899.

Murray, Margaret A. "Fertility Figures." *Man*, August 1929, item 99, pp. 132-34.

Murray, Margaret A. "The Meaning of the Cowrie." et al. *Man*, Oct. 1939, item 165; Jan 1940, item 20; Oct. 1940, item 188; Nov. 1940, item 209; and Nov.-Dec. 1942, item 94.

Musaeum Hermeticum Reformatum et Amplificatum. Johann Daniel Mylius, ed. Frankfurt: L. Jennis 1625, 1678. Originally published in Francfort by Hermann a Sande. This reproduction was published in 1970 by Adademische-Druck, in Graz, Austria.

N

Needham, Rodney. *Primordial Characters*. Charlottesville: University Press of Virginia, 1978. [Ch. on *Synthetic Images*].

Neumann, Erich. *The Great Mother. An Analysis of the Archetype*. Princeton: Princeton University Press, 1955. [Dedicated to C. G. Jung.]

Nilsson, Lennart. *A Child is Born*. [A photographic essay.] Text by Lars Hamberger. A Merloyd Lawrence Book, Delta/Seymour Lawrence 1990. Copyright 1990 by Bantam Doubleday Dell Publishing Group, Inc.

O

Ochshorn, Judith. *The Female Experience and the Nature of the Divine*. Indiana University Press, 1981. [Part of her book is devoted to show how "in no sense was divinity itself conceived as solely female or male," (p. 33)].

Odent, Michel. *Birth Reborn*. New York: Pantheon Books, 1984.

Olson, Carl, ed. *The Book of The Goddess*. New York: Crossroad Publ. Co., 1988. Orig. publ. 1983.

Oursel, Raymond. *Floraison de la sculpture romane*. Zodiaque, 1973.

Oyler, D. S., the Rev. "The Shilluk's belief in the Evil Eye." In *The Evil Eye*. Ed. Alan Dundes. New York: Garland Publishing, 1981, pp. 78-85. Reprinted from *Sudan Notes and Records*, 2 (1919), 122-28.

P

Pagels, Elaine. *Adam, Eve and the Serpent*. Vintage Books (Random House paperback), 1988. "Examines doctrines of the Church, which began as a defiant sect of freedom and, paradoxically, was transformed through centuries into an institution of orthodoxy and repression," ex. blurb. Shows manipulation of the mighty and of the Church. Has something on the origins of present-day sexual attitudes.

Parrinder, Geoffrey. *Sex in the World's Religions*. Oxford University Press, 1980.

Patai, Raphael. *On Jewish Folklore*. Detroit: Wayne State University Press, 1983.

Patai, Raphael. "T'Khelet - Blue." Chapter 6 in *On Jewish Folklore*. Detroit: Wayne State University Press, 1983. [The color blue as protection against the Evil Eye.]

Patai, Raphael. "The Goddess Cult in Hebrew-Jewish Religion" Ch. 4 in *On Jewish Folklore*. Detroit: Wayne State University Press, 1983. See also Steve Davies in Olson's *The Book of the Goddess*.

Pérot, Francis 1839-1918. Légendes et Superstitions préhistoriques CXIII. "Quelques croyances superstitieuses pour rendre fécondes les femmes stériles, receuillies dans le centre de la France." *Revue des Traditions Populaires*, Paris Vol. XXVI, No. 2 Fev. Avril 1911, pp. 96-101. [Much info on fecundity-giving saints and on various phallic finds in Central France.]

Potts, Albert M. *The World's Eye*. Lexington: University of Kentucky Press, 1982. Chapter 2 is on "The Evil Eye." Potts is an ophthalmologist. Predicates his thesis on psychological theory and individual gaze.

Preston, James L., ed. *Mother Worship*. University of Carol. Press, 1982.

R

Rawson, Philip. *The Art of Tantra*. New York: New York Graphic Society. 1973.

Rawson, Philip. *Primitive Erotic Art*. New York: G. P. Putnam's Sons, 1973.

Rawson, Philip. *Tantra. The Indian Cult of Ecstasy*. London, 1973.

Rawson, Philip. *Ceramics*. OUP, 1971. [pottery in form of penis for defloration].

Reade, Rolf S., ed. *Registrum Librorum Eroticorum*, Compiled by Rolf S. Reade. London: Privately Printed, 1936. In two volumes.

Readers' Digest. *Folklore Myths and Legends of Britain*. Second edition. Pleasantville, NY: Readers' Digest Association Inc., 1977.

Redman, Charles L. *Rise of Civilization. Early Farmers to Urban Society in the Ancient Near East*. W. H. Freeman & Co., 1978.

Reither, Rudolf. "Zur Augensymbolic." In *Internationale Zeitschrift für Artzliche Psychoanalyse*. 1:159-61, 1913, quoted by Dundes.

Renfrew, Colin. *The Emergence of Civilization. Cyclades and Aegean*. London: Methuen & Co. Ltd., 1972.

Rocco, Sha (pseud. for Abisha S. Hudson). *The Masculine Cross and Ancient Sex Worship*, New York Commonwealth, 1904. Same as: *Anonymous Ancient Sex Worship. A curious and remarkable work*. This book is entered in Goodland's bibliography as: Anonymous: *The Masculine Cross; or a History of Ancient and modern crosses and their connection with the mysteries of sex worship*. London: Privately Printed, 1891.

Rochefort, César De. *Dictionnaire général et curieux*. Genève: Slatkine Reprints, 1972. [Réimpression de l'édition de Lyon 1685 Chez Pierre Guillimin.].

Ross, Anne. "The Divine Hag of the Pagan Celts." In Venetia Newell, ed. *The Witch Figure*. London: Routledge and Paul Kegan, 1973, pp. 139-164.

S

Sachs, Lisbeth. *Evil Eye or Bacteria. Turkish Migrant Woman and Swedish Health Care*. Stockholm Studies in Social Anthropology, 1983.

Saintyves, P. *Les Saints Successeurs des Dieux*. Paris, Emile Nourry, 1907. Very interesting. Certainly much more reliable than Dauzat on the origins of proper names. Saintyves seems to be Emile Dominique Nourry who is also the publisher of this book. (This, according to a note in the book).

Salvini, Roberto. *Medieval Sculpture*. Greenwich, CT: New York Graphics Society, 1969.

Schmidt, Peter R. *The Tree of Iron*. A film about iron smelting in East Africa, by Peter O'Neil, Frank Muhly Jr. and Winnie Lambrecht. Project director: Peter R. Schmidt. Funded by N.E.H. (1988). Distributed by The Foundation for African Studies, 470 Grinter Hall, Gainesville: University of Florida, 32611.

Seligmann, Siegfried. *Die Zauberkraft des Auges und das Berufen*. Hamburg: Friederichsen, 1922. [According to Dundes 1981, p. 261, this is a second version of the 1910 original.]

Sheppard, T. "The Meaning of the Cowrie-Shell." *Man*, Dec. 1939, item 200.

Siebers, Tobin. *The Mirror of Medusa*. University of California Press, 1983. (On Evil Eye).

Simmons, Leo, ed. *Sun Chief: The Autobiography of a Hopi Indian*, published for the department of Sociology by Yale University Press, New Haven, 1942.

Smith, E. W. and A. M. Dale. *The Ila-speaking Peoples of Northern Rhodesia*, 1920, II, p. 35.

Smith, Homer W. *Man and His Gods*. Boston: Little, Brown, 1955.

Smith, Kirby Flower. "Pupula Duplex" in *Studies in Honor of Basil L. Gildersleeve*. Baltimore: Johns Hopkins Press, 1902, pp. 287-300.

Srejovic, Dragoslav. *Europe's First Monumental Sculpture: New Discoveries at Lepenski Vir*. New York: Stein and Day, 1972.

Stähelin, Felix. "Aus des Religion des römischen Helvetien." *Anzeiger fur Schweizerische Altertumskunde* (1921).

Steichen, Edward. *The Family of Man*. New York: The Museum of Modern Art, 1955.

St. Leger-Gordon, Ruth E. *The Witchcraft and Folklore of Dartmoor*. New York: Bell Publishing Co., 1972.

Stone, Lee Alexander. *The Story of Phallicism*, [and other essays] (2 Vols.) Chicago: Pascal Covici Publisher, 1927.

Stover, Leon E. and Bruce Kraig. *Stonehenge: The Indo-European Heritage*. Nelson-Hall Books, 1978.

Sukenik, Eleazar L. *The Ancient Synagogue of Beth Alpha*. Jerusalem: at the University Press. London: Oxford University Press, 1932.

Symonds, John Addington, ed. *Wine, Women and Songs. Mediaeval Latin Students' Songs*. Thomas Bird Mesler, 1918, p. 117, song No. 34.

T

Talbot, P. Amaury. *Some Nigerian Fertility Cults*. Barnes & Noble, 1967. (First edition 1927).

Tappolet, Ernest. "La survivance de 'Diana' dans les patois romands." *Schweizerische Gesselschaft fur Volkskunder*, 1919, pp. 225-231.

Taylor, Jane, ed. *Le Roman de Perceforest*. Genève: Librairie Droz, 1979.

Thomas, Paul. *Kama Kalpa or The Hindu Ritual of Love*. D. B. Taraporevala Sons and Co., Bombay, 13th Edition 1963. Ch. XVII is on popular rituals eventually banned, probably because of European opinion against vulgarity.

U

Ucko, Peter J. *Anthropomorphic Figurines of Predynastic Egypt and Neolothic Crete with comparative Material from the Prehistoric Near East and Mainland Greece*. London: Andre Szmidla, 1968.

Unwin, J. D. *Sex and Culture*. Oxford University Press, 1934.

V

Van Marle, Raimond. [See under Marle.]

Vuorela, Toivo. *Der Böse Blick im Lichte der Finnischen Überlieferung*. Folklore Fellows Communication 201. Helsinki: Academia Scientiarum Fennica 1967.

W

Walker, Barbara G. *The Woman's Encyclopedia of Myths and Secrets*, Harper & Row, 1983.

Wasson, R. Gordon, Albert Hofmann, and Carl A. P. Ruck. *The Road to Eleusis. Unveiling the Secret of the Mysteries*. Harcourt Brace Jovanovich, 1978. [Ingestion of Ergot of Barley. Makes a good case, although this is not everybody's opinion.]

Waterman, Philip F. "The Evil Eye." Chapter XIII in *The Story of Superstition*.

Waterman, Philip F. *The Story of Superstition*. New York: Alfred Knopf, 1929.

Wax, Rosalie and Murray. "The Magical Worldview." In *Journal for the Scientific Study of Religion*, 1: 179-188, 1962.

Weir, Anthony and James Jerman. *Images of Lust. Sexual Carvings on Medieval Churches*. B. T. Batsford Ltd., London, 1986. [He concludes, unconvincingly, that these "images" were carved by monks to impress the horror of sex upon the faithful.]

Wernick, Robert, ed. *The Monument Builders*. Time-Life Books, 1973.

Westropp, Hodder M. *Primitive Symbolism as Illustrated in Phallic Worship or The Reproductive Principle*. First published in 1885. Reprinted 1970: New Delhi (India): Kumar Brothers. The book is devoted to the idea that the principles are both male and female.

White, Randall. *Dark Caves, Bright Visions. Life in Ice-Age Europe*. New York: W. W. Norton Co., 1986.

Whittick, Arnold. *Symbols, Signs and Their Meaning*. Newton, MA: Charles Brantford Co., 1960, London, 1960.

Williams, Paul. *Primitive Religion and Healing. A Study of Folk Medicine in N. E. Brazil*. Brewer, Rowman and Littlefield 1979.

Williamson, Marjorie. "Les Yeux Arrachés." *Philological Quarterly* 11: 149-62, 1932.

Wilson, G. "An African Morality." In *Cultures and Societies of Africa*. Ed. Simon and Phoebe Ottenberg. New York: Random House, 1960, p. 353.

Winthuis, J. *Das Zweigeschlecterwesen bei den zentralaustraliern und anderen Völkern*. Leipzig, 1928.

Witkowski, Joseph-Alphonse, dit Gustave-Joseph. *L'Art Profane à l'Eglise, ses licenses symboliques, satiriques et fantaisistes*. Vol. I: France. Vol. II, *ETRANGER*. Paris: Jean Schemit, 1908.

Wright, Thomas. See under Knight, Richard Payne.

Y

Yarden, L. *The Tree of Light. A Study of The Menorah*. Ithaca, NY: Cornell University Press, 1971.

Z

Zahan, Dominique. *Sociétés d'initiative Bambara, le N'Domo, le Kore*. Paris, 1960.

Zarnecki, George. *Art of The Medieval World*. Prentice Hall 1975.

Zervos, Christian. *L'Art des Cyclades du début à la fin de l'âge de Bronze 2500-1100 avant notre ère*. Editions "Cahiers d'Art," Paris 1957. (Includes Doumas and Renfrew.)

Illustrations

Fig. 1.1 Life sign on a field "kelli."

Fig. 1.2 Rose design on Kythnos street pavement.

Fig. 1.3 Street geometric design, Kythnos.

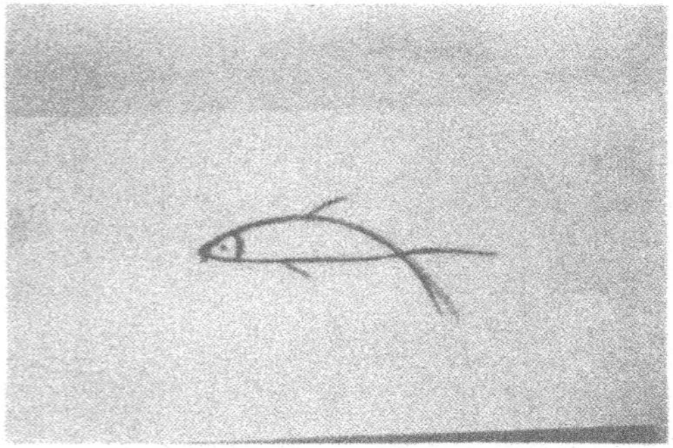

Fig. 2.1 Protective fish emblem, Kythnos.

Fig. 2.2 Protective fish emblem, Varanasi, India.

Fig. 2.3 Protective horseshoe—Vermont, U.S.A.

Fig. 4.1 Apotropaics at the entrances of shops, Varanasi, India.

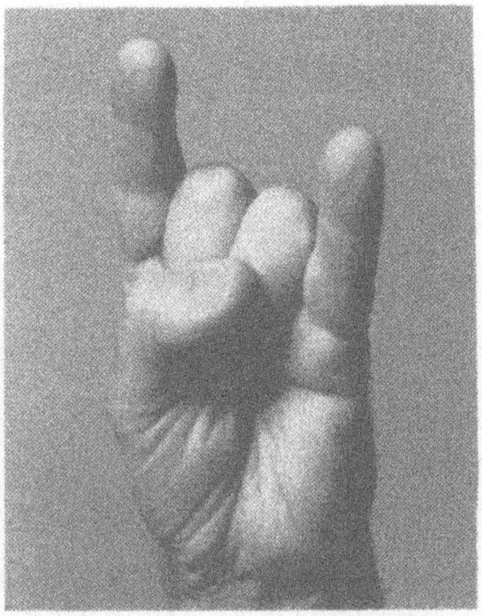

Fig. 3.1 Mano cornuta.

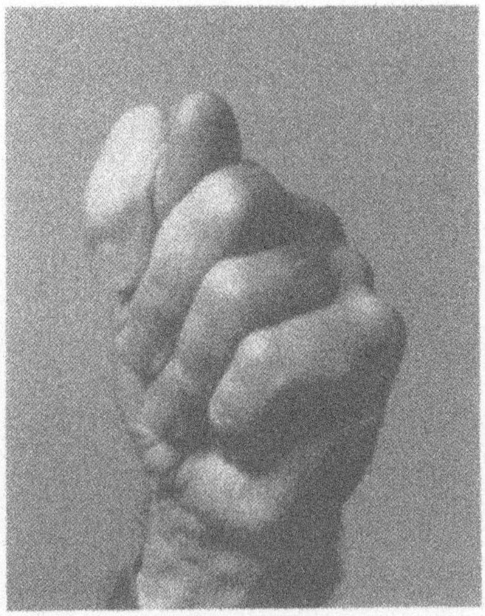

Fig. 3.2 Mano fica

Fig. 3.3 Digitus impudicus

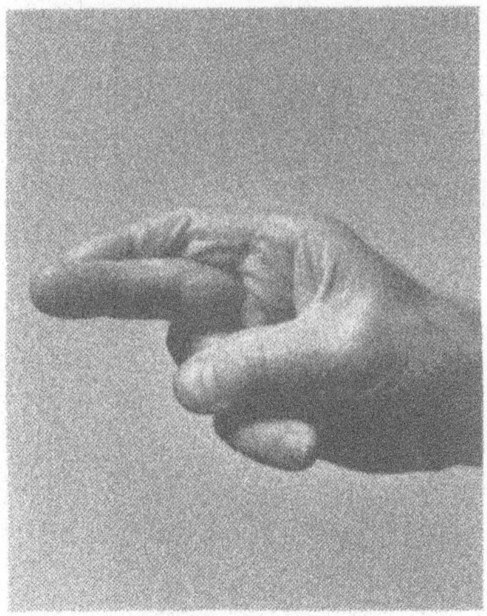

Fig. 3.4 Cross-fingers

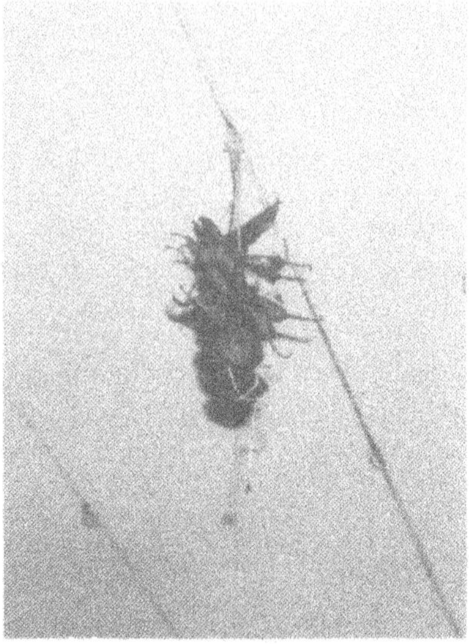

Fig. 4.2 Close-up of pepper-with-lime apotropaic, India.

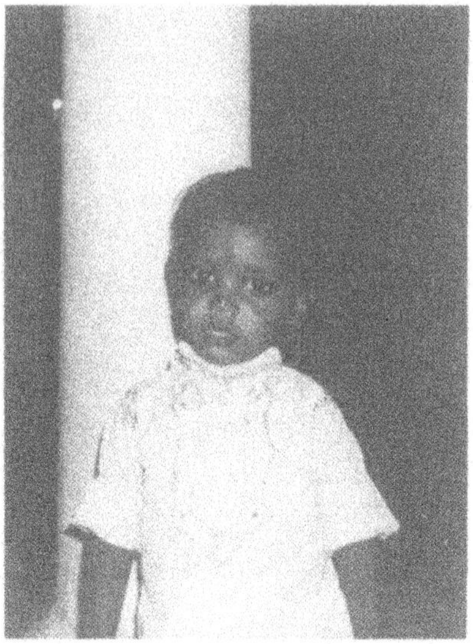

Fig. 5.1 Indian child with lampblack Evil Eye protection.

Fig. 6.1 The "Jewel in the Lotus," India.

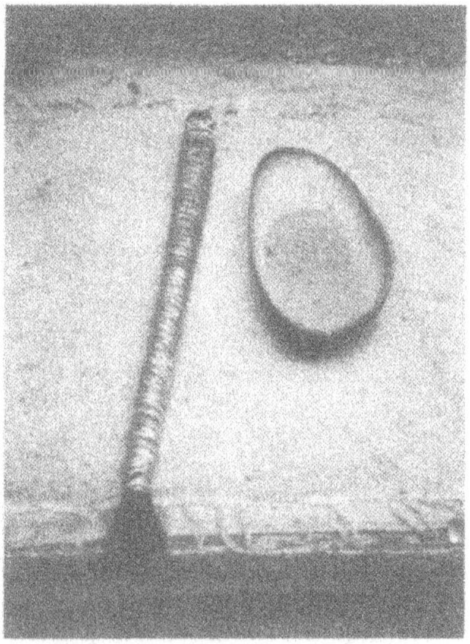

Fig. 7.1 Ritual peacock feather object, Varanasi, India.

Fig. 8.1 Protective Roman Bas-relief, Roman Lybia.

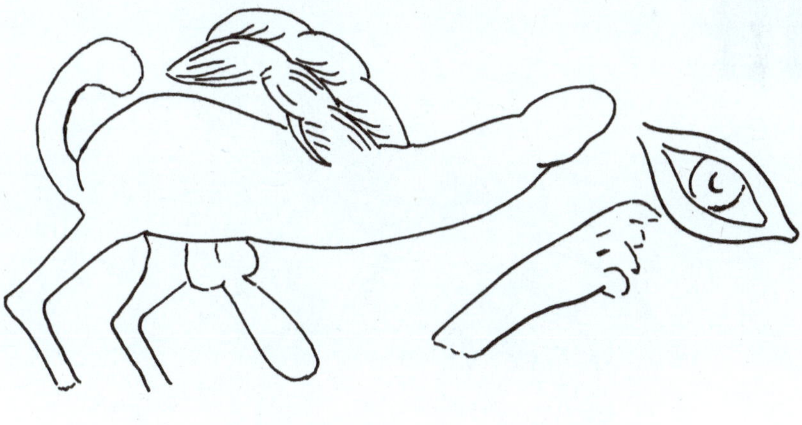

Fig. 8.2 Protective Roman Bas-relief, Roman Lybia.

Fig. 8.3 The Woburn Marbles.

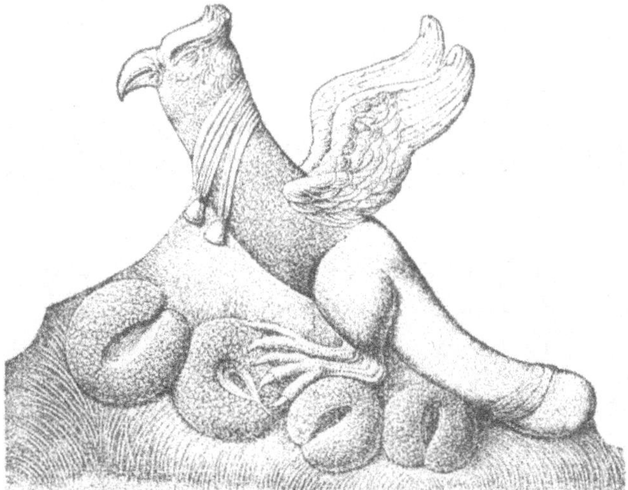

Fig. 8.4 Phallic Bird, Ancient Rome.

Fig. 8.6 Protective medals, Ancient Rome.

. Fig. 9.2 Bells from Africa, Mali.

Fig. 9.1 Bells from India.

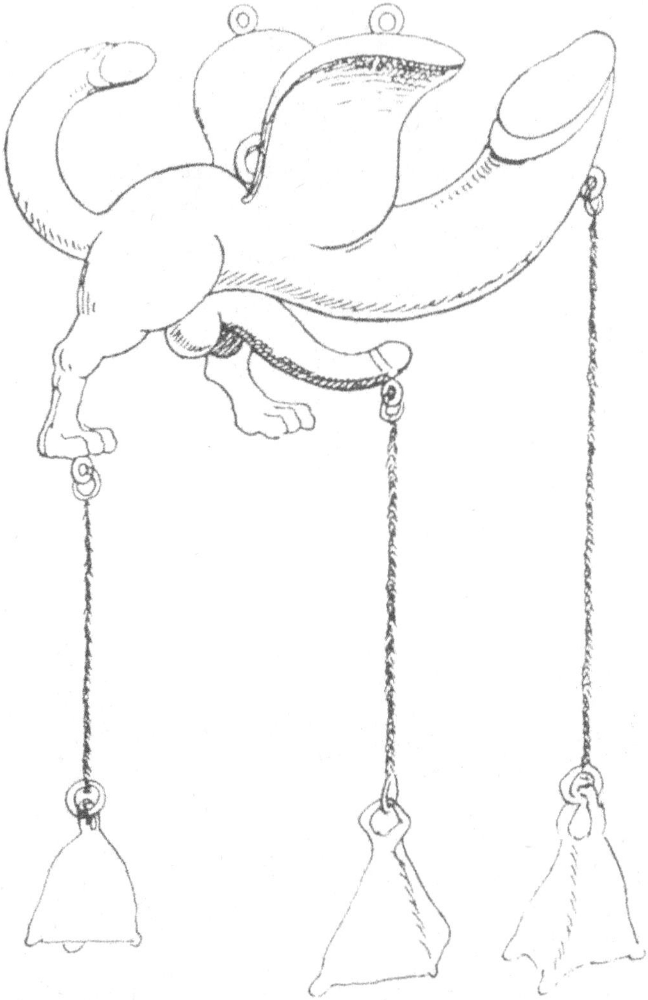

Fig. 9.3 Multiple phallic symbols, hung with kteic bells, Herculaneum.

Fig. 10.1 Ritual symbol, Prehistoric Malta.

Fig. 10.2 Ritual symbol, Prehistoric Sicily.

Fig. 11.1 Doña Sancha sarcophagus, Spain.

Fig. 11.2 "Le Triomphe de Venus," Italian XVth Century.

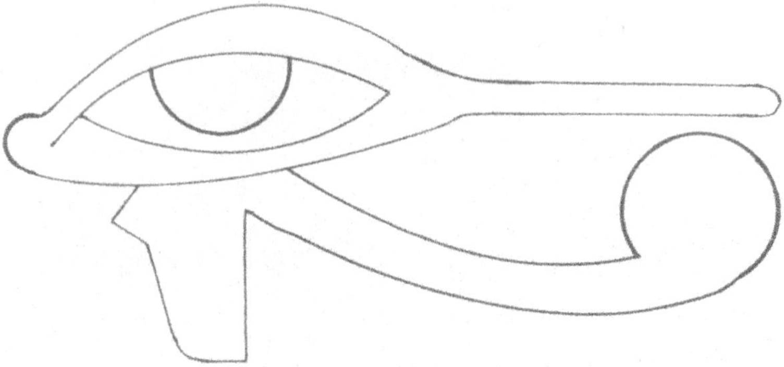

Fig. 12.3 "Eye of Horus."

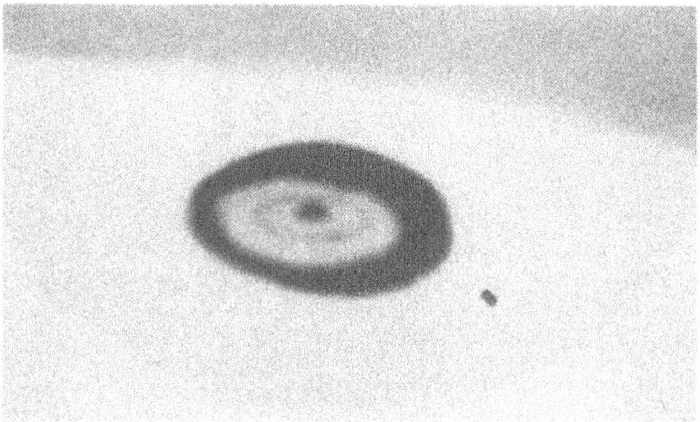

Fig. 12.2 "Eye of God," Kythnos.

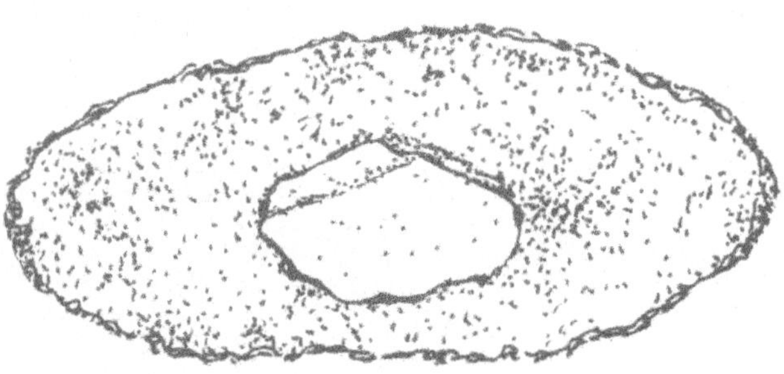

Fig. 12.1 "Eye of God" from England.

Fig. 13.1 Prehistoric effigy, Lepenski Vir, Yugoslavia.

Fig. 13.2 Prehistoric effigy, Lepenski Vir, Yugoslavia.

Fig. 14.1 The stoup in the Romanesque church, Farges, France.

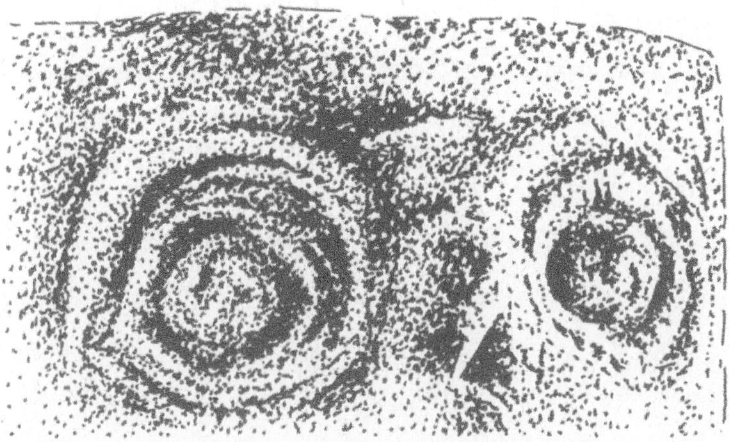

Fig. 14.2 Detail, in line-drawing, of 14.1.

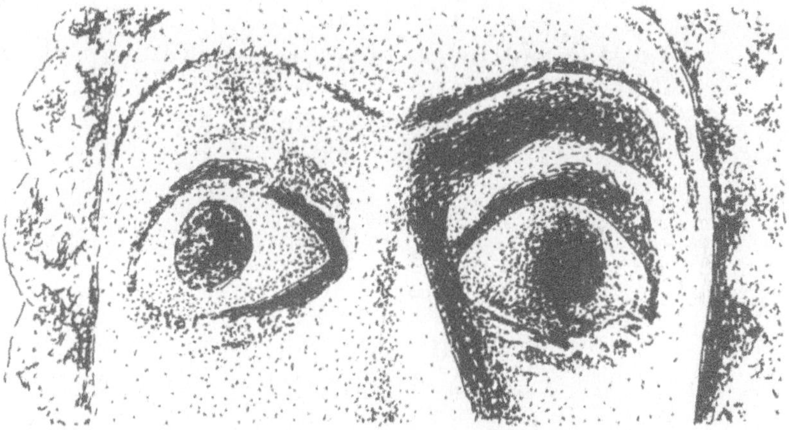

Fig. 14.4 Gypsum Eye goddess from Tell Amar.

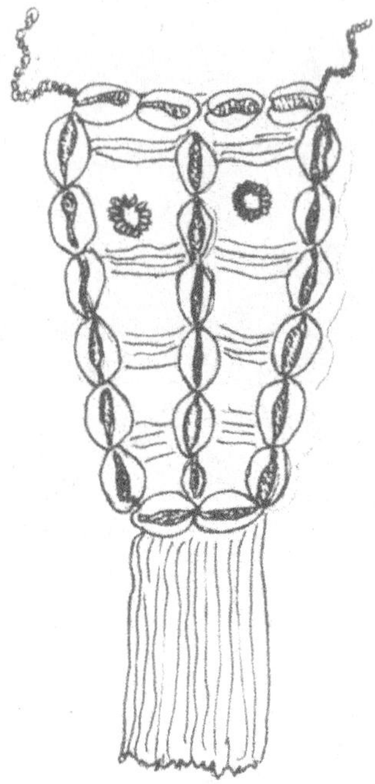

Fig. 15.1 Female initiate's belt, Chagga (Tanzania).

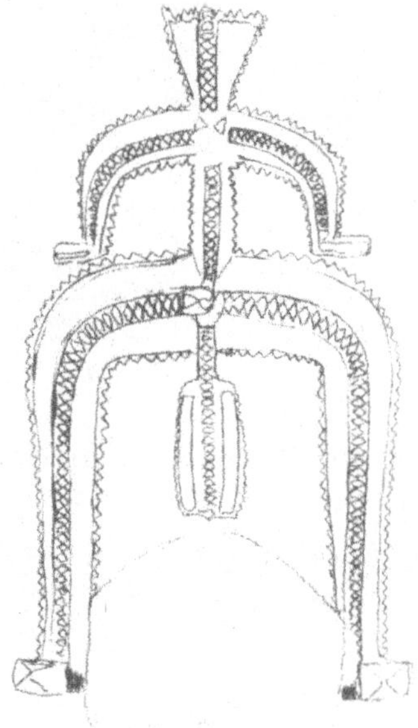

Fig. 20.3 African mask in the form of the Parturient Woman design.

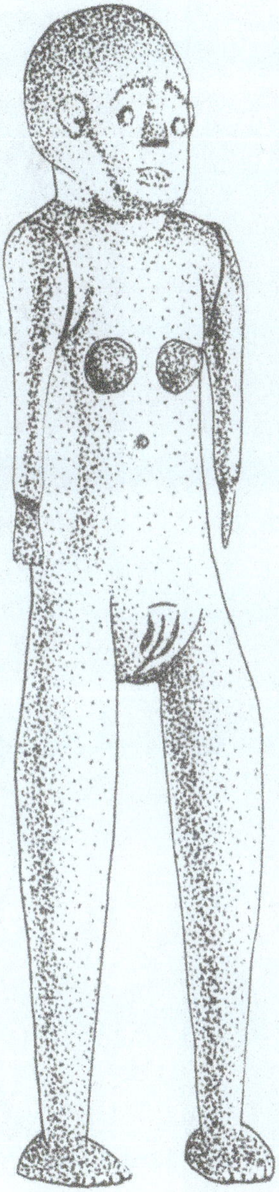

Fig. 15.2 Tsonga fertility statues from Malawi.

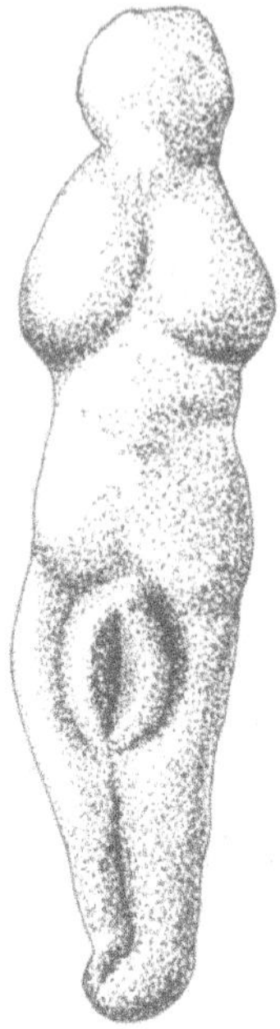

Fig. 16.2 The Prehistoric Montpazier "Venus," France.

Fig. 16.3 Corbel, Romanesque church, Villanueva de Cangas, Spain.

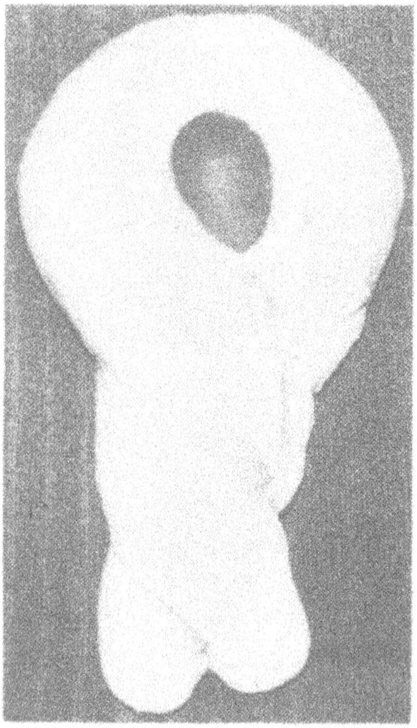

Fig. 14.5 Egg-in-bread ritual object, Kythnos.

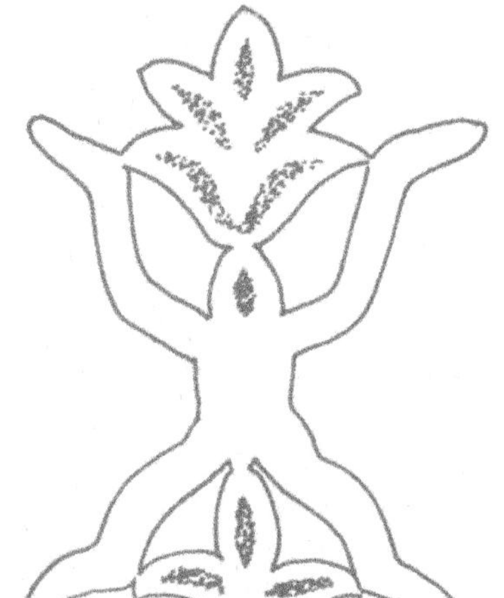

Fig. 19.6 The Parturient Woman design on a Zanzibar door.

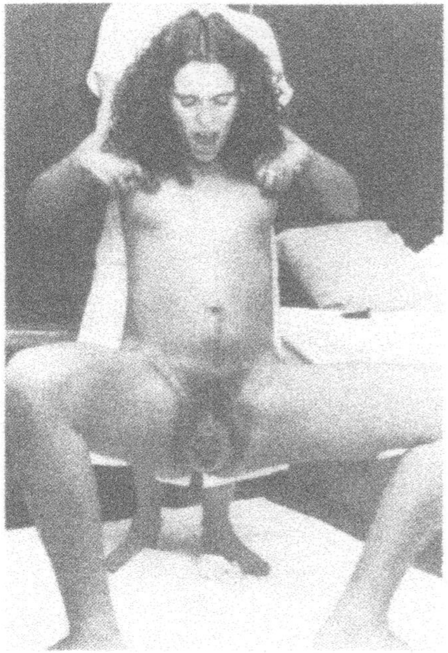

Fig. 24.1 Photograph of the moment of Crowning.

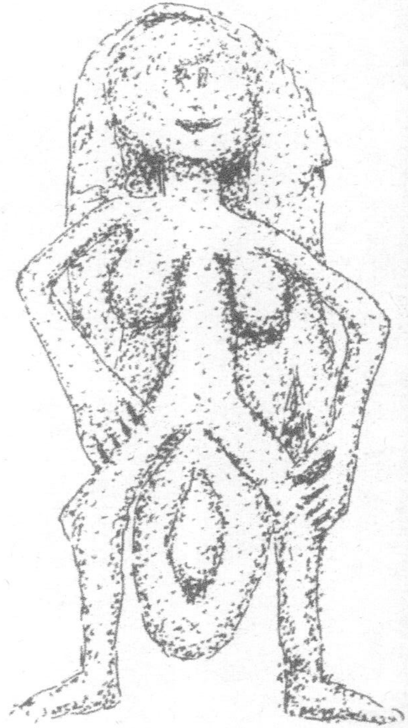

Fig. 16.1 Sheela-na-gig from Oaksey.

Fig. 17.7 Sheela from Cavan.

Fig. 17.1 The Gorgon from Etruria.

Fig. 17.3 Sheela-na-gig from the church in Kilpeck, England.

Fig. 17.4 Carving from Kathmandu, Nepal.

Fig. 17.5 Carving from Capdenac-le-haut, Lot, France.

Fig. 17.6 Carving from Lepenski Vir (Yugoslavia).

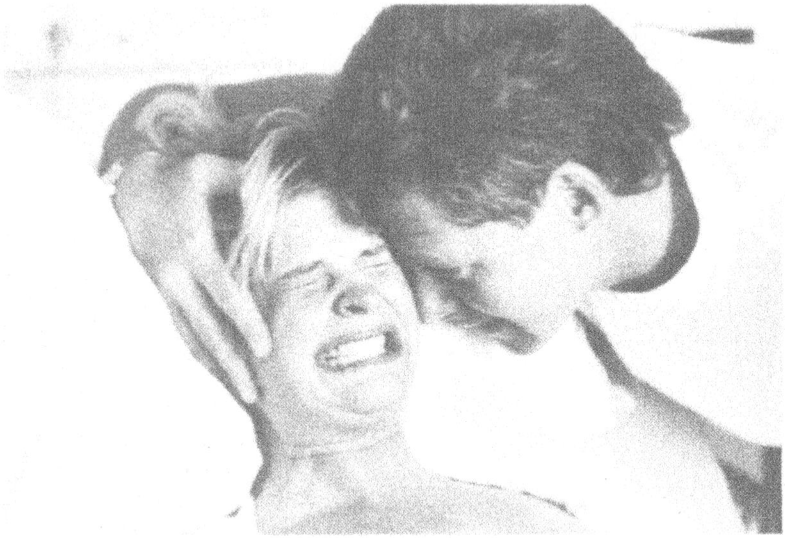

Fig. 17.8 Birthing grimace.

Fig. 17.6 Carving from Lepenski Vir (Yugoslavia).

Fig. 17.7 Sheela from Cavan.

Fig. 18.1 Double tailed mermaid, Saint-Dié, France.

Fig. 18.2 Carving from a temple in Nepal.

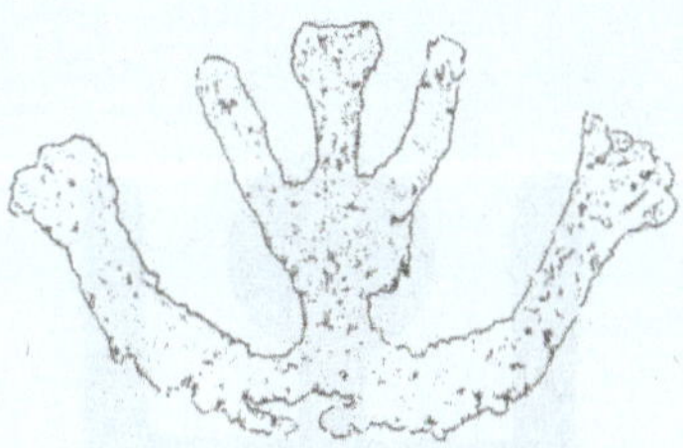

Fig. 18.3 Prehistoric Parturient Woman symbol, Japan.

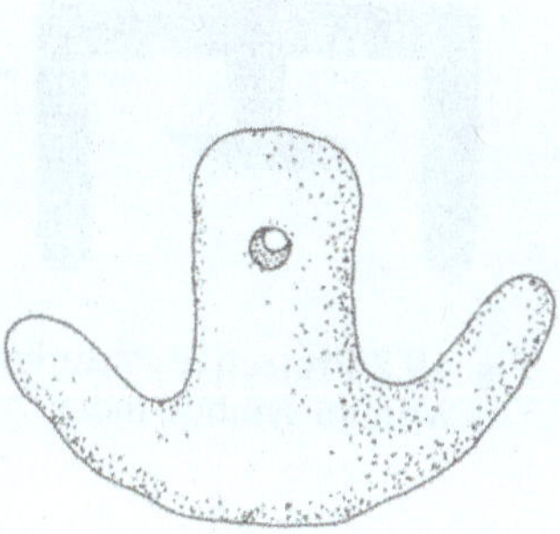

Fig. 18.4 Prehistoric "Anchor" amulet, Greece.

Fig. 18.5 The anchor as Parturient Woman symbol.

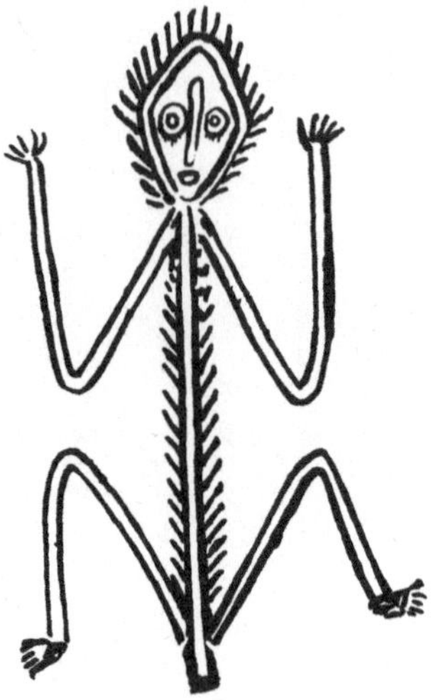

Fig. 19.3 Parturient Woman symbol, Australian aborigine.

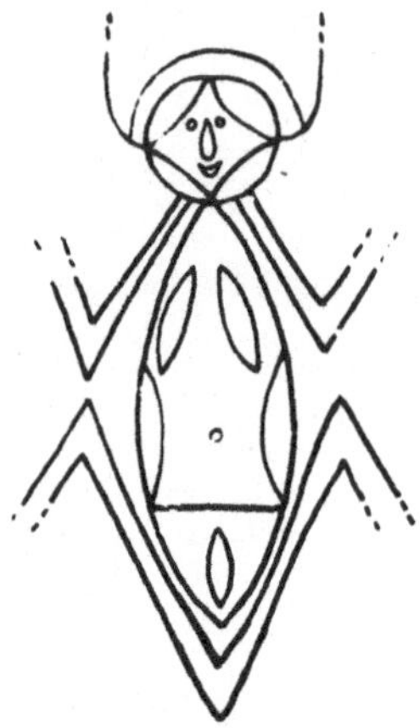

Fig. 19.4 Parturient Woman, symbol, New Guinea.

Fig. 19.1 Prehistoric Parturient Woman symbol, Italy.

Fig. 19.2 Protective Parturient Woman symbol, India.

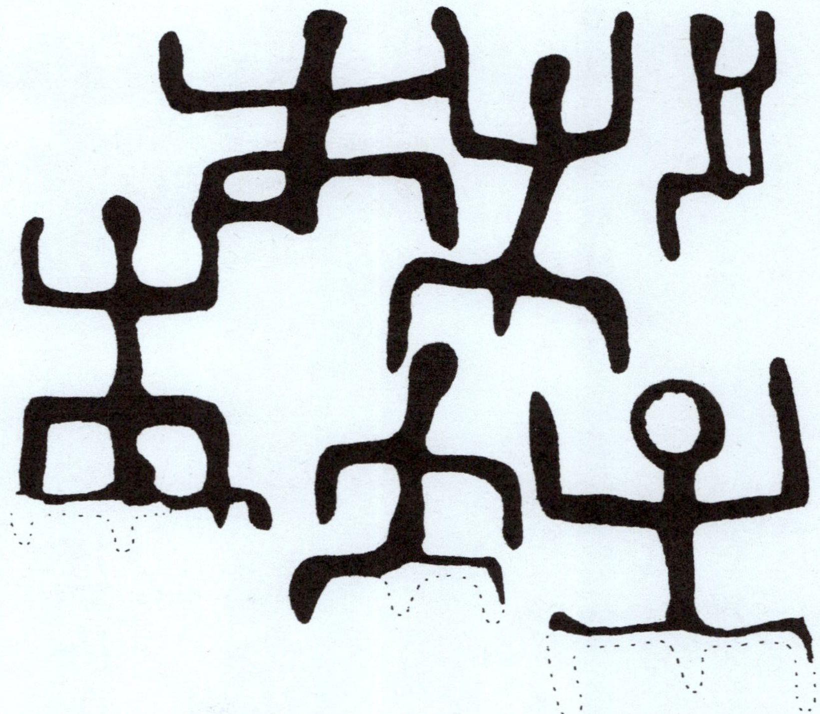

Fig. 19.7 Prehistoric Parturient Woman designs, Sardinia.

Fig. 20.1 Prehistoric Parturient Woman design, Kalesovice (Bohemia).

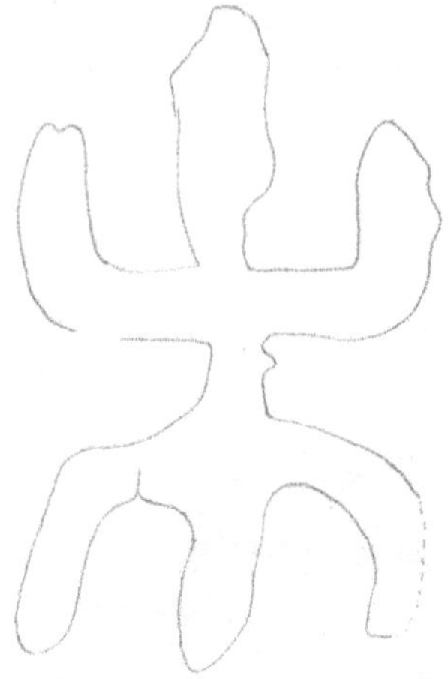

Fig. 20.2 Prehistoric Parturient Woman design, Truşesti.

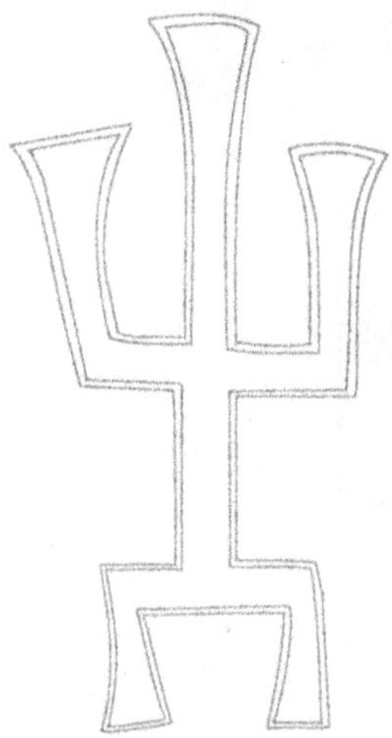

Fig. 20.4 Prehistoric Parturient Woman symbol, NE Hungary.

Fig. 19.5 Pangolin effigy from Africa.

Fig. 20.5 "Good-luck" amulet Naples, Italy.

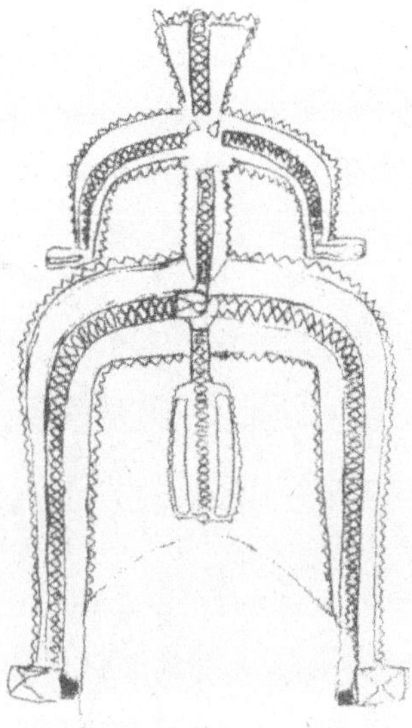

Fig. 20.3 African mask in the form of the Parturient Woman design.

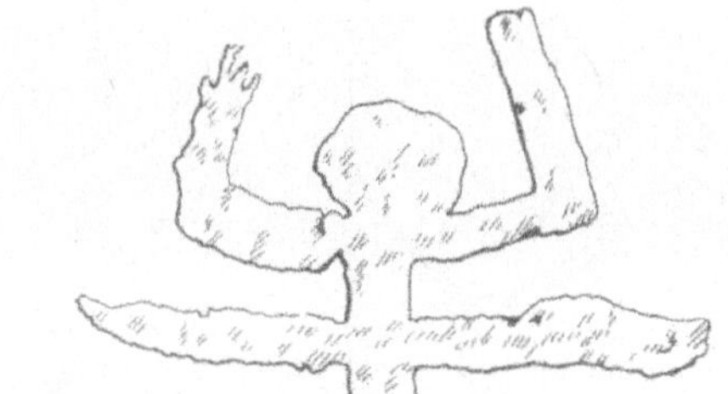

Fig. 23.2 Design on a peasant's house mud wall, Northern India.

Fig. 20.7 Dogon, Mali, Africa. Mask in the shape of the Parturient Woman symbol.

Fig. 23.3 Parturient Woman symbol on a wood door panel. Pindi: Africa.

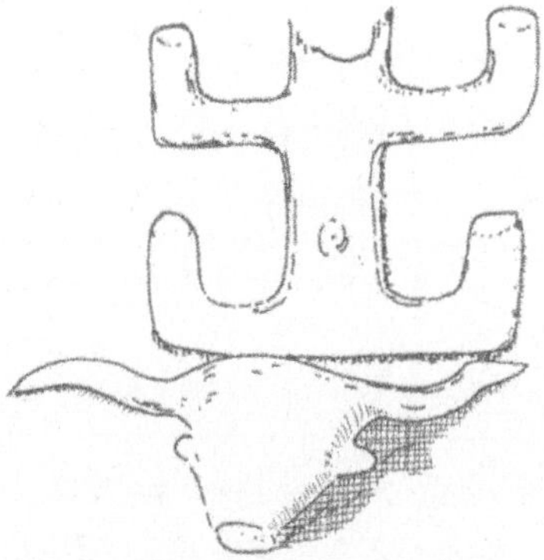

Fig. 20.8 Prehistoric Parturient Woman symbol, Turkey.

Fig. 23.4 Protective Parturient Woman, Finland.

Fig. 20.6 Prehistoric Parturient Woman design, Czechoslovakia.

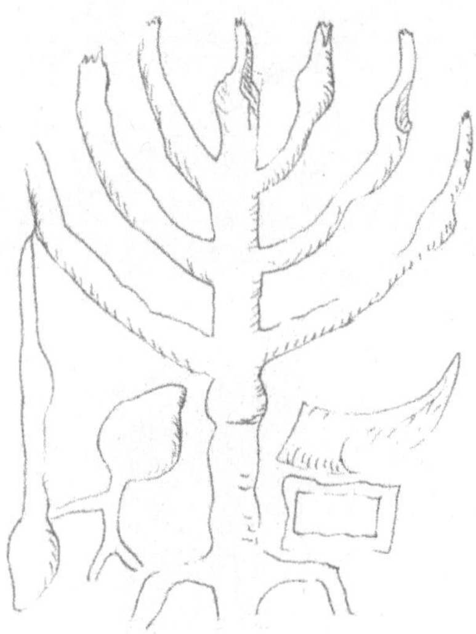

Fig. 23.1 Early Menorah.

Fig. 21.2 Plane tree leaf (*platanus*). A fertility symbol among the ancient Romans.

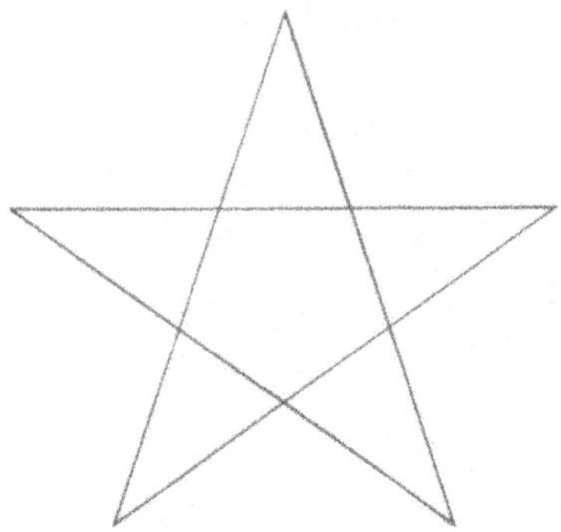

Fig. 21.1 Pentagram. A symbol for the Parturient Woman.

Fig. 19.8 Parturient Woman design, Kythnos.

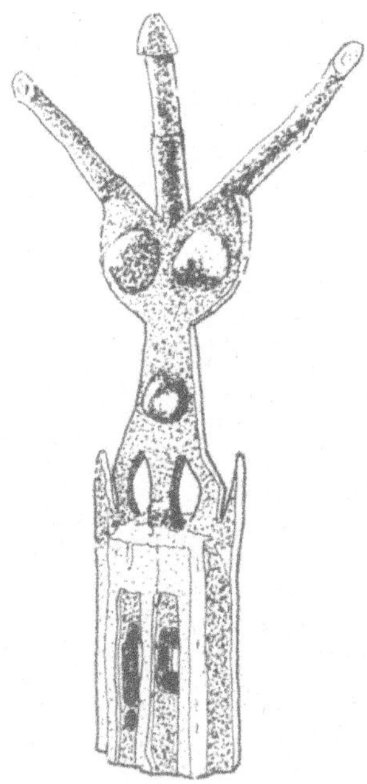

Fig. 20.9 Dogon, Mali, Africa. Wood carving.

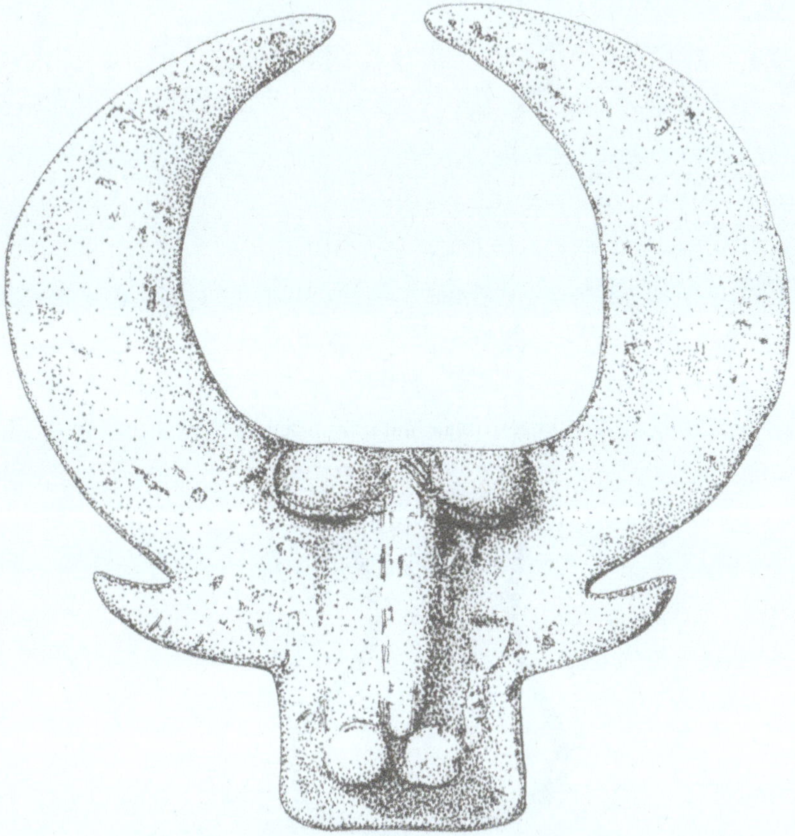

Fig. 22.1 Buffalo head from West Africa.

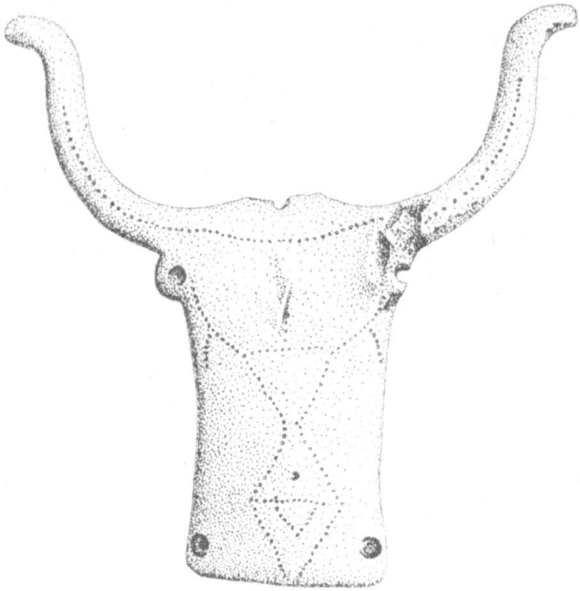

Fig. 22.3 Prehistoric bucranium from NW Bulgaria.

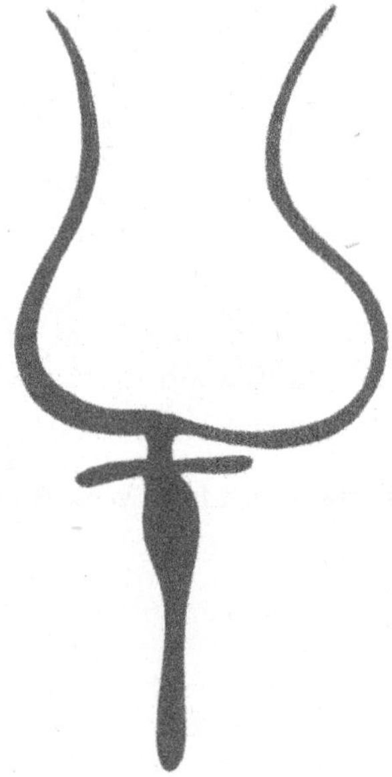

Fig. 22.2 Bucranium design on Halaf Ware.

Fig. 25.1 The Celtic Cross at Kilkieran.

Fig. 8.5 Polyphallic tintinnabulum, Herculaneum.

Fig. 27.1 The Buddhist Circle of Life.

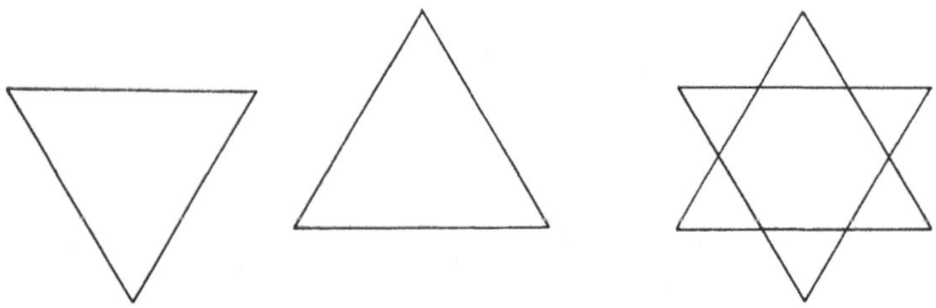

Fig. 27.2 The Shield of David, Star of David.

Fig. 27.3 The Ankh, the Mirror of Venus and the Orb.

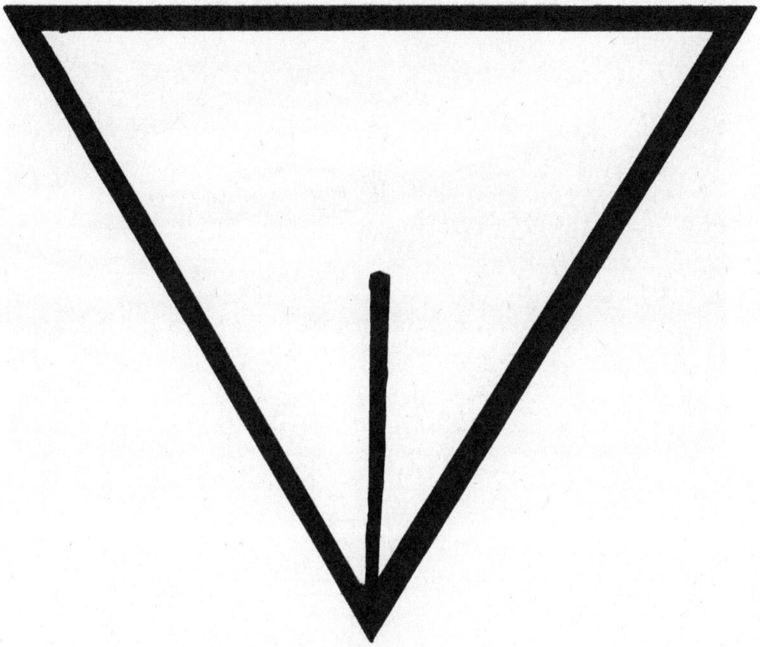

Fig. 28.1 Ideogram for woman in the pre-cuneiform writing of ancient Sumer.

Fig. 29.1 Calla Lily.

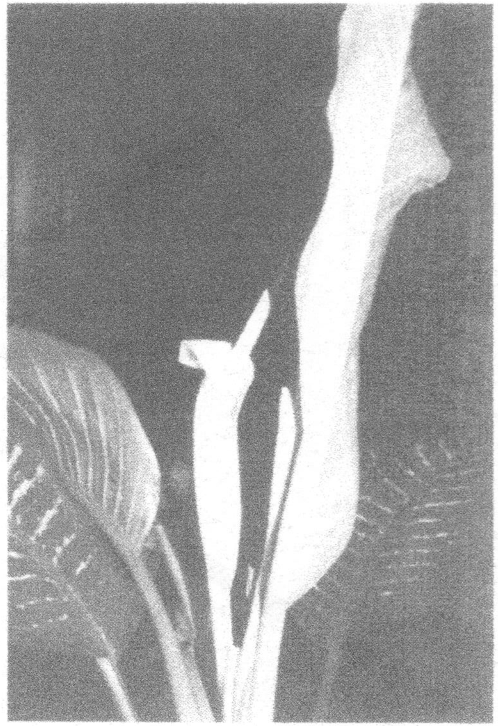

Fig. 29.2 Arum Lily (Diffenbachia).

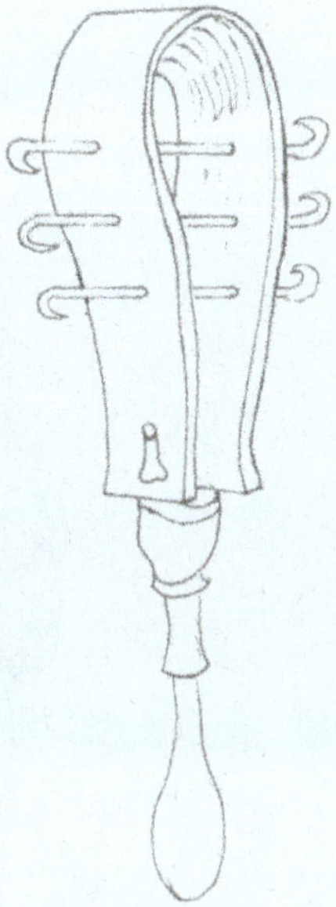

Fig. 30.1 Egyptian sistrum.

Fig. 40.1 A contemporary mantle bauble.

Fig. 32.1 Prehistoric "stick" effigy, Dolni Vestonice, Czechoslovakia.

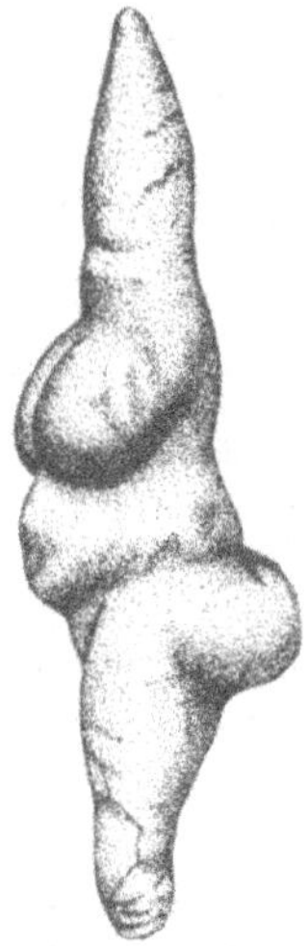

Fig. 31.2 "Venus of Savignano," Northern Italy.

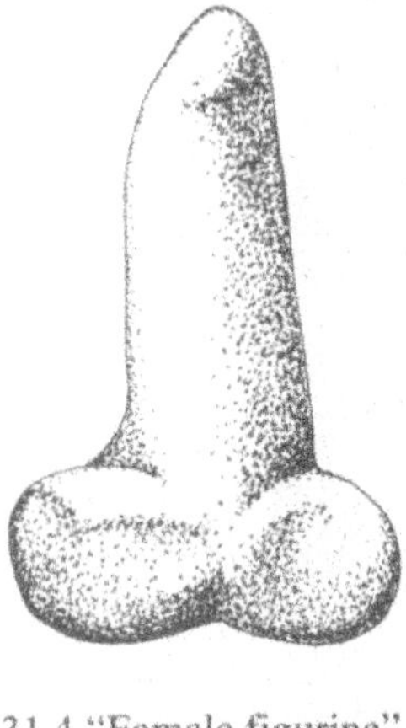

Fig. 31.4 "Female figurine" from the site of Arpachiya, (Iraq).

Fig. 31.3 Necklace bead, Dolni Vestonice, Czechoslovakia.

Fig. 31.1 Prehistoric fertility statuette, Cernavoda, Romania.

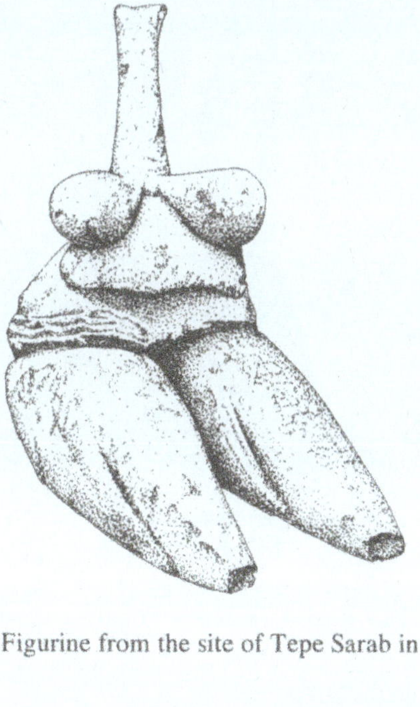

Fig. 31.5 Figurine from the site of Tepe Sarab in Turkey.

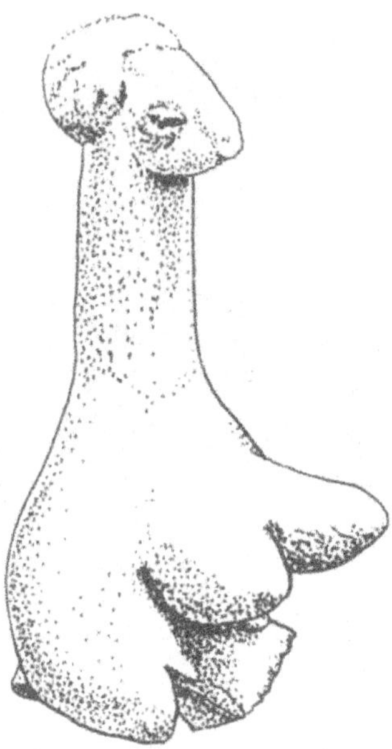

Fig. 31.6 Prehistoric statuette, Thessaly, Greece.

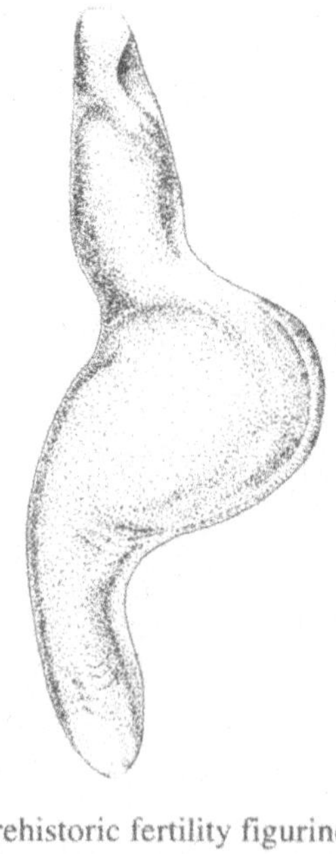

Fig. 32.7 Prehistoric fertility figurine, Petersfels.

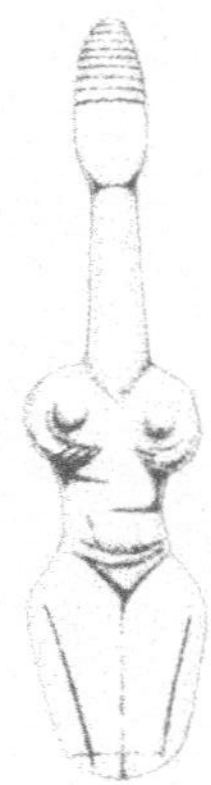

Fig. 32.2 Prehistoricic Aegean fertility statuette,

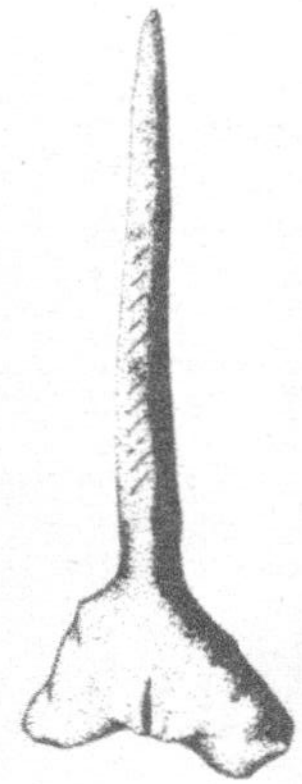

Fig. 32.3 Prehistoric "baton," Le Placard (France).

Fig. 32.4 Phallic female figurine, Siberia.

Fig. 32.5 Prehistoric statuette, Dolni Vestonice (Czechoslovakia).

Fig. 32.6 Savignano, (same as 31.2).

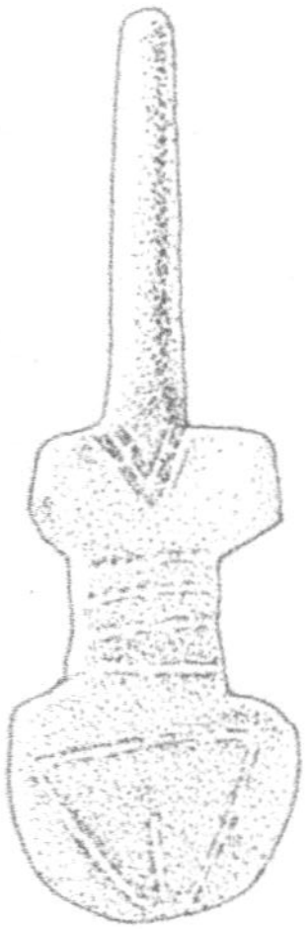

Fig. 33.1 Prehistoric "Violin" shaped "idol," Aegean.

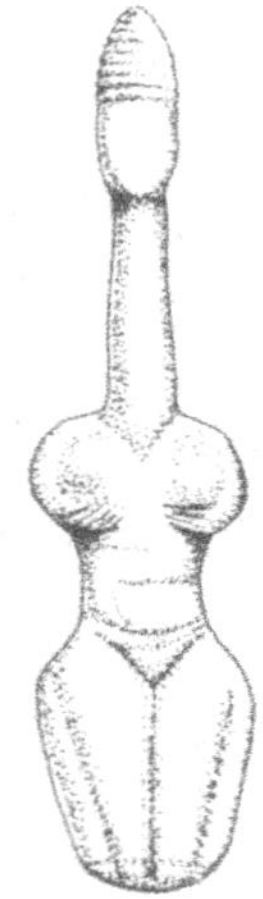

Fig. 33.2 Same as fig. 32.2.

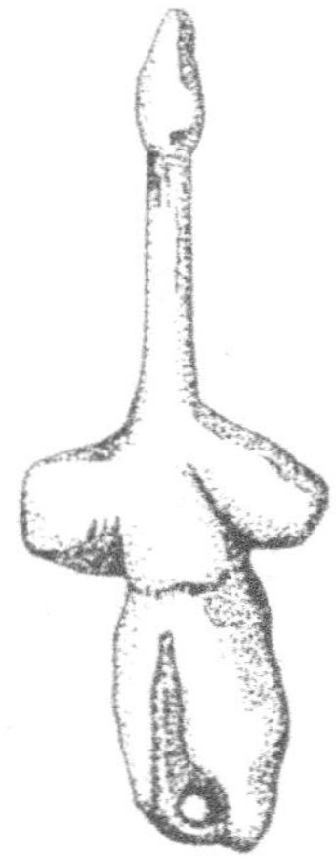

Fig. 33.3 Prehistoric fertility figure, Ma'alta, Siberia.

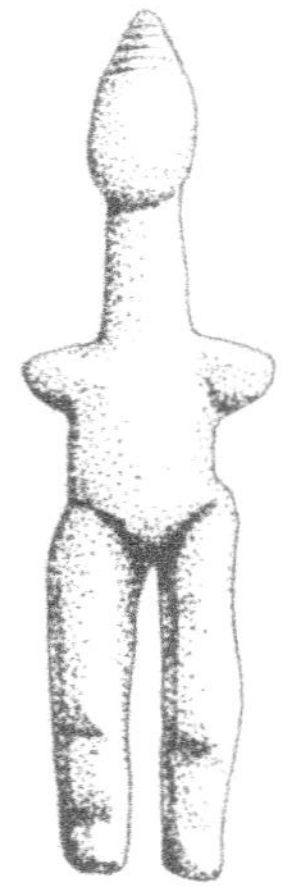

Fig. 33.4 Prehistoric female figurine from the Island of Naxos (Greece).

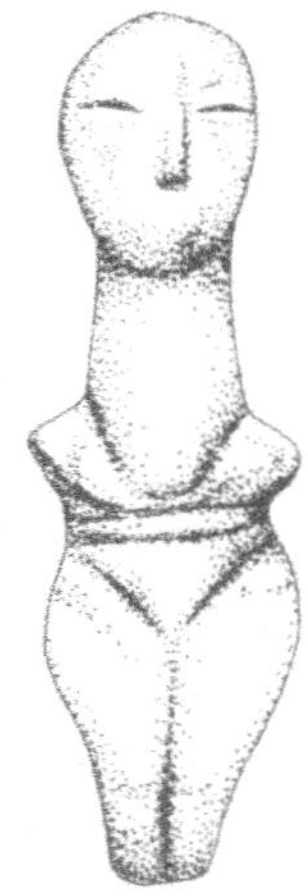

Fig. 33.5 Prehistoric female figurine from the Island of Syphnos (Greece).

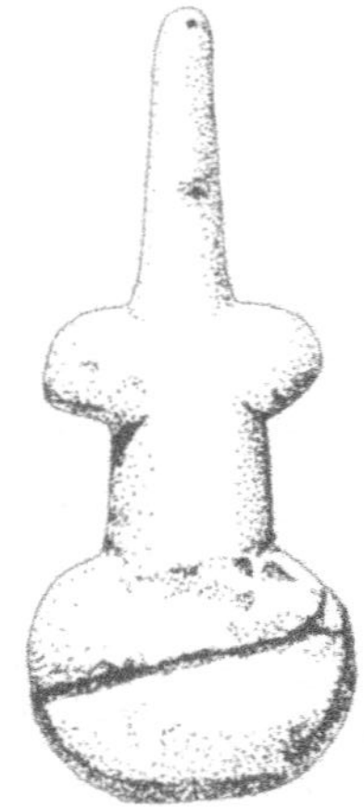

Fig. 33.6 Prehistoric female figurine from the Island of Despotikos (Greece).

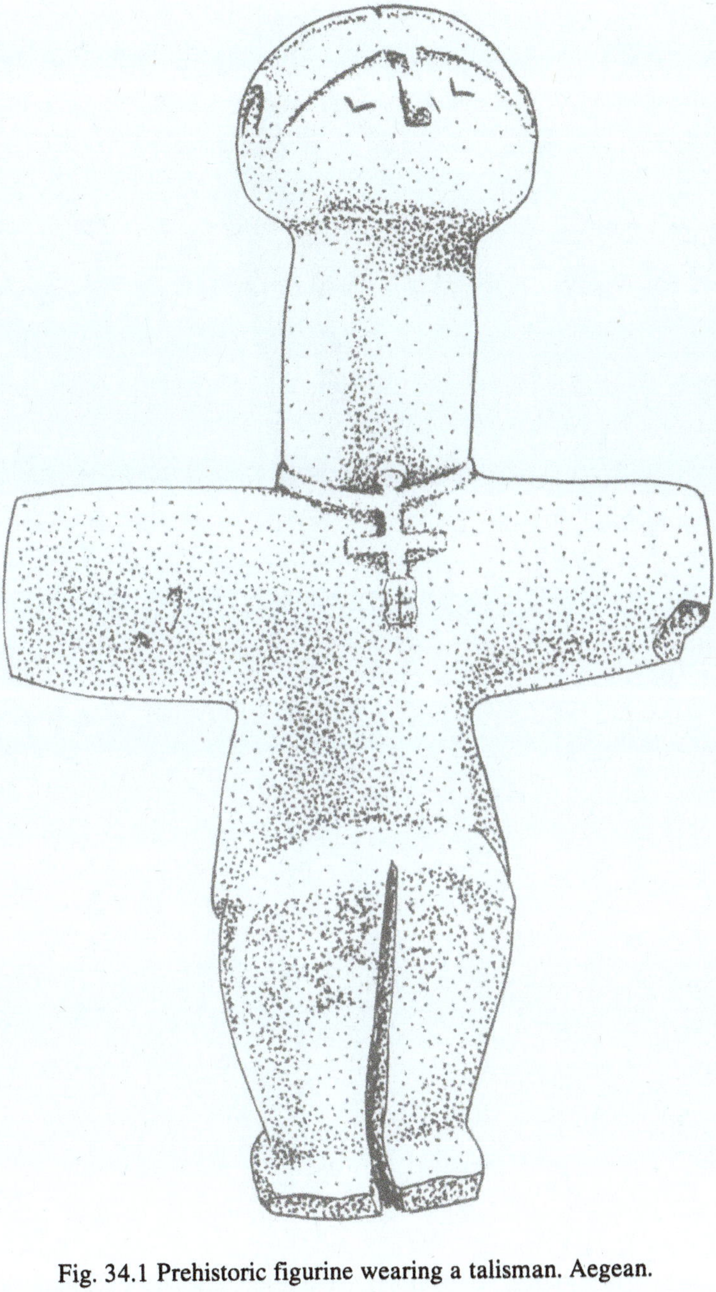

Fig. 34.1 Prehistoric figurine wearing a talisman. Aegean.

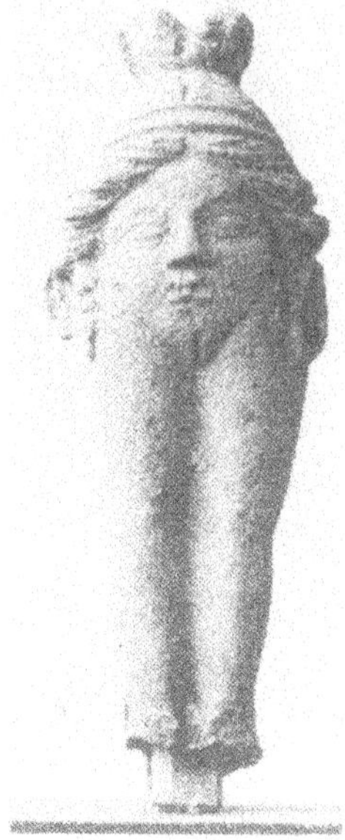

Fig. 35.1 Prehistoric figurine from Priene (Turkey).

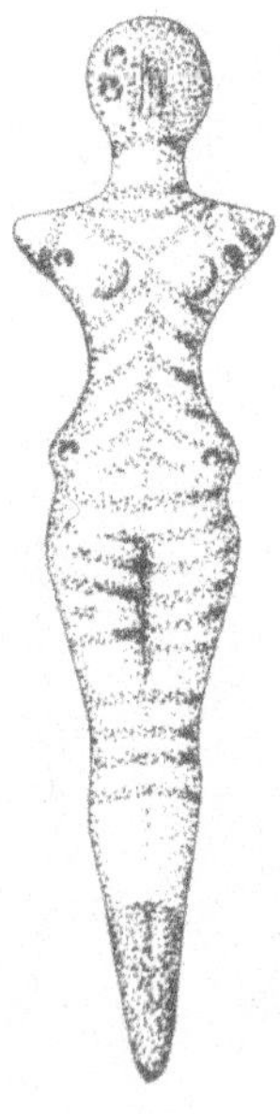

Fig. 35.2 Prehistoric figurine from the site of Ghelaesti (Romania).

Fig. 36.1 Medieval paper watermarks.

Fig. 36.2 Negative image of a graffito by Brassaï, Paris.

Fig. 37.1 Protective offerings, Ethiopia.

Fig. 38.1 Phallic Alpha and kteic Omega, VIIIth century France.

Fig. 39.1 Ancient Roman mosaic floor, Susa, Tunisia.

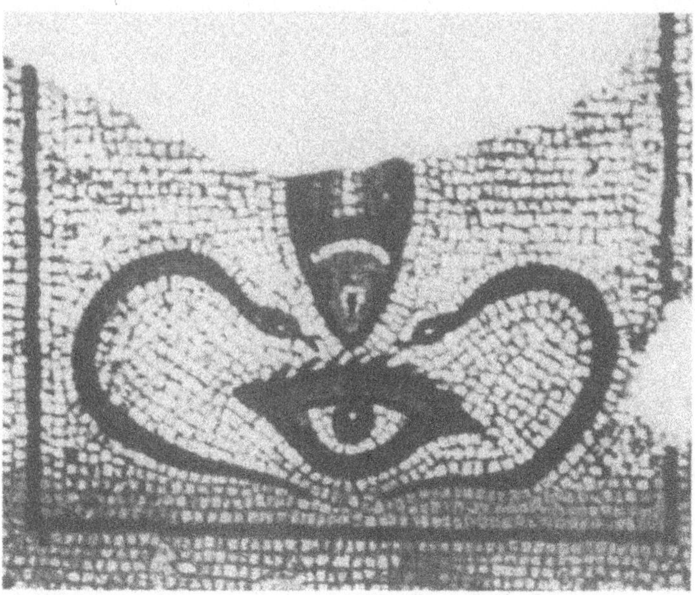

Fig. 39.2 Ancient Roman mosaic floor, Moknine, Tunisia.